D0629548

The Last Book
Of The Bible

'Tis late to aske abundance of thy grace
When wee are there; here on this lowly ground,
Teach mee how to repent. . . .

JOHN DONNE (from Holy Sonnet VII)
1573-1631

Also by Hanns Lilje in English translation:

The Valley of the Shadow (1950)

Luther Now (1952)

THE LAST BOOK OF THE BIBLE

THE MEANING OF THE REVELATION OF ST. JOHN

By HANNS LILJE

Translated by OLIVE WYON

MUHLENBERG PRESS
Philadelphia

Translated from *Das letzte Buch der Bibel*
by Hanns Lilje
(Fourth Edition, 1955)

Furche-Verlag, Hamburg

Library of Congress Catalogue
Card Number 57-9591

Printed in U.S.A. *UB797*

Preface

The last book of the Bible has always been regarded from peculiarly contradictory points of view. *Within* Christendom, even from very early days, it has often been fiercely attacked, and even rejected. This attitude has persisted down to the Reformation, and even on into our own day. On the other hand, many movements—not by any means only the sectarian ones—have found more spiritual "nourishment" in this book than in any other in the Bible. The theological work of centuries exactly reflects this situation. Even *outside* Christendom there are traces of this contradictory attitude. While many people have regarded this book as so abstruse that they have left it severely alone, others (above all, artists) have been deeply attracted by it, and have made repeated efforts to find a clue to its meaning. So this book has either been despised, or greatly valued and loved, but it has never been treated in a moderate, objective way.

A Christian who reads his Bible and finds it to be what Johann Albrecht Bengel describes as "the treasury of the church of God, from the beginning to the end of the world," must come to terms with this book, and be able to define his position.

The situation of the modern reader of the Bible is not the same as that of the biblical scholar. The scholar must examine every detail of the text with meticulous care and honesty. He has before him a difficult original text which, owing to the way in which documents have been handed down, is very complicated. The text also contains many references to various features in the history of religion in general. In consequence, sometimes the methods of scholars lead to interpretations which differ so widely from one another that the simple Bible-reader can hardly believe that they are speaking about the same book.

Anyone, however, who wants to find a clue to the meaning of the Apocalypse, must first of all learn to look at it as a whole. He must not be content to dwell on particular sayings or passages, but must try to enter into the author's mind, and understand his spacious symbols and conceptions. He must do so, not in order to appreciate the massive greatness of the book as a whole, but to gain a real understanding of the book's message. For no matter how many human characteristics and historical references this book may contain, it still confronts him as the Word of God. He will understand that, even after the most stringent efforts have been made to disentangle the different "form elements" in this book and to trace their derivation to various sources, this work is still something more than a particularly interesting example of apocalyptic literature.

A book that speaks of the return of Christ is full of a knowledge that is more than human. To use the language of this book, it must be "shown" (Rev. 1:1) to the reader. The commentator, too, must avoid giving free rein to his own speculative views, and must try to expound this Scripture in a spirit of humble listening, and believing obedience. It is no accident that Bengel's warning, "It would better serve the purposes of edification if those who teach were to say less about their own ideas, and were to study the Bible itself more intensively," occurs in the first chapter of his commentary on the Apocalypse.

So far as the language of the following text is concerned, there are two points which need to be explained beforehand.

For the sake of clarity this book of the "Revelation of St. John" will generally be called by its Greek name, the Apocalypse. When the word "revelation" is used it will refer only to the meaning of the word in the general Christian sense, i.e., the way in which God has "revealed" himself to man.

The word "apocalyptic" applies to a particular type of literature as well as to this book in particular.

The use of the word "vision" must be rightly understood. As used here, it never means a subjective "inspiration," or fantasy, or the hallucination of a diseased mind. "Vision" means the same as the German word *Schau* ("show" or "something shown"). "Show" cannot easily be used in this connection, especially because it cannot be used in the plural. Luther used the word *Gesicht* (vision, apparition) in this comprehensive active sense, but this use of the word is no longer possible in modern German. Part I of this volume deals with other preliminary questions.

This book was planned more than ten years ago. The first edition had been written when the first shattering experiences of the Second World War were beginning to pour in upon us. The necessary revision of this work was made while I was in prison, in the hands of the Gestapo. Since then world history has passed through another sanguinary stage. The task of the Christian church—to order all its life by the Word of God—has thus become more urgent than ever.

Hannover
January 1955

HANNS LILJE

Translator's Note

English-speaking readers all over the world will be grateful for this vivid and illuminating exposition of a difficult book. In his own test, Bishop Lilje gives his own version of the Apocalypse in modern German. As it is not advisable to translate a translation, the text of the Revised Standard Version has been used throughout this English translation.

For a modern English version, the new reading of the Book of Revelation by the Reverend J. B. Phillips* might well be read alongside the present volume.

One technical point alone calls for special mention. Four times in this work (German text, pp. 52, 84, 11 and 219) the word *programmatisch* (literally, "programmatic") occurs. In each instance it is used in connection with the conflict between the Christian Church and the pagan cult of Emperor Worship. That is, the "programme" or "purpose" of the Book of Revelation is to show that there is a great conflict between the Kingdom of Christ and the Kingdom of Caesar or Satan, and that "God will conquer!" "Jesus is Victor." Since no one word in English will convey this meaning, I have been obliged to paraphrase rather freely at these points. But I feel it necessary to emphasize the central importance of this word here, rather than in a footnote—lest its significance should be overlooked.

It only remains to express my grateful thanks to the author himself.

OLIVE WYON

Hinxton, England
March 1957

* *The Book of Revelation* translated into modern English (New York: Macmillan Co., 1957).

Table of Contents

PART I

Chapter 1

On Reading the Apocalypse

The difficult questions which immediately confront every reader of the Apocalypse are these: How are we to read this book? Is there a clue to the mystery which envelops it? What should be our attitude to the many visions it records?

The last book of the Bible raises many questions, and many solutions are offered for our consideration. Obviously the views of biblical scholars during the last fifty years differ so widely from one another that sometimes they do not seem to be speaking of the same book. Numerous popular expositions contain a mass of wild and arbitrary speculation which often goes beyond all bounds. Of course we cannot ignore the learning and insight of those earlier expositors, since no one can approach this book without a thoughtful, questioning spirit, striving to understand what it means, yet we feel we must find a firm position above the confusion of these many voices. Indeed, unless we can do this, we would be forced to abandon the attempt to understand the Apocalypse at all. To abandon the attempt, however, would mean that we deny that the last book of the Bible contains the Word of God.

Can we find the Word of God in the pages of the Apocalypse? Or are its chapters full of speculations and fantasies which simply belong to the environment in which the New Testament came into existence, and have here assumed a different form? If we feel obliged to accept the latter view, then—as Christians who read their Bible—all we can say is that we are indifferent to the process by which these extraneous phenomena of the religious world of those days have been collected and compiled in this particular way, and that so far as scholarship is concerned we really have no interest in all the amazing amount of toil and trouble which scholars have taken over the exposition of the book. For we are not concerned with making interesting discoveries in the sphere of comparative religion; what we want to know is precisely this: In this book, is *God* speaking to us in his Word?

But if God *is* speaking to us in this book, the question with which we are concerned must be asked in this way: Does this book contain the eschatological witness of the New Testament? Does it indeed contain that witness to the End, which forms part of the whole Christian message of the New Testament as a whole?

This question needs to be put very clearly and precisely. So we must first look at the actual historical and literary form in which the book comes to us. Even this investigation contains a number of possible interpretations. It is worth-while to make a brief survey of the main types of exposition.

The method of literary criticism has been important in the history of biblical criticism. The literary form of the Apocalypse has been examined in the light of literary criticism in the same way that the other books of the New Testament have been investigated. Characteristic of these efforts are the attempts to dissect and analyze any such New Testament book into its various literary sources and component parts. In principle, it does not matter whether an expositor carries this process to extremes, dividing the Apocalypse into a great many more or less coherent sections and subsections, or whether he proceeds more cautiously. The principle is the same. The misgivings which are aroused by this process of research are of two kinds.

First of all, as in all literary criticism, we may note a tendency to move away from the extreme position previously adopted by many scholars. We are not quite so sure as we were that everything which seems—to us—to be logically disconnected, ought also to be severed by literary criticism. The very fact that one of the most outstanding biblical scholars at the beginning of this century, R. H. Charles, took whole chapters of this book and dissected them almost into fragments, shows how easy it is to exaggerate the application of a certain method of research.

On the other hand, it has continually been recognized that such a procedure does not do justice to the actual point with which the last book of the Bible is concerned. It is not an adequate explanation to say that the book is the work of one or of several editors who have gathered their material from very varied literary sources and out of this material have made an *opus*. The best comment on this situation is by the French scholar, Sabatier, who more than two generations ago made the following apt statement: "The Christian 'editor' of the Apocalypse is not simply a 'literary' man . . . this 'John' who is writing to the seven churches of Asia, has an apostolic, or at least a directly pastoral purpose in mind; hence it is difficult to admit that an apostle or a pastor would have limited his aim to that of the simple role of an editor or commentator." [1]

Closely connected with the method of literary criticism is the method of exposition which has developed out of it: *Formgeschichte*. This method is not concerned with the somewhat primitive question of the various literary materials and their authors, but rather with the larger elements of literary tradition. This is a new and fruitful stage in New Testament criticism. Its method may be briefly summed up thus: Has this book grown out of the account of several individual visions or out of a series of visions? Was the particular vision the determining factor for the growth of the book? or was it that of the seven seals? or the seven trumpets? or the seven bowls? Although no conscientious scholar would ignore this question, it does not help us to understand the book as a

[1] Auguste Sabatier, *Les origines littéraires et la composition de l'apocalypse de St. Jean* (Paris, 1888).

whole. The subject with which the Apocalypse is concerned cannot be studied solely along the lines of *Formgeschichte.* A fundamental objection to both these views may be expressed in the two following observations.

The Apocalypse is characterized by a comprehensive method of composition which is itself a work of art. The particular characteristics of this artistic structure will have to be demonstrated in detail later on. But the very fact that the magnificent pictorial language does not degenerate into unbridled fantastic speculation proves that it is not sufficient to analyze the various elements of the work into their "forms."

The other point is that the peculiar language of the Apocalypse—the "form elements" of late Greek, the *koine,* the general language of the people of the later Hellenistic Period —is made to serve the spirit of the Hebrew language, even to the extent of doing violence to grammatical rules. This produces a quite individual, elevated, astringent style; this last book of the Bible is clothed in a unique linguistic garment. But this language dominates the whole book in a uniform way and, whatever may be said about particular form elements, it is clear that its final form is unified.

The third attempt to interpret the Apocalypse was made by using the method of the history of religion. When, about the turn of the century, the religio-historical method of research made such magnificent strides, Hermann Gunkel, one of its earliest and greatest champions, applied the theory of this school to the twelfth chapter of the Apocalypse. Wilhelm Bousset's great and masterly commentary followed the same line.[2] It must be admitted that the insight and learning of this school of thought has given us much for which we can only be grateful. These scholars opened up for us hitherto unperceived connections between the New Testament and its environment, and no honest student of the Apocalypse can

[2] *Die Offenbarung Johannis.* Cf. I. T. Beckwith, *The Apocalypse of John* (New York: Macmillan & Co.), pp. 236 ff. (Translator's note.)

ignore their researches.

Here, however, some critical observations are necessary. In the allusions to Babylon and the writings of the Mandaeans[3] we must not overlook the connection with the Old Testament. Further, we need to remind ourselves continually that a parallel is not the same thing as an explanation. It is quite possible that the apocalyptic writer may have drawn much of his material from the history of religion, and yet his message—although given in this form—may still be his own distinctive and original contribution. Even when we have discovered motifs and parallels, we have not necessarily recovered the message itself.

The historical interpretation is of special importance. Again and again we note how clearly the Apocalypse presupposes contemporary conditions. It is at this point that the stream of new knowledge has gathered the greatest volume. What concerns us most here are the following points: the connection of the book with the very early period of church history, the controversy with Judaism, and, still more, the conflict with the political cult of the day. No interpretation of the Apocalypse can be accurate which does not take note of its numerous allusions to contemporary history.

Indeed, for a careful and accurate exposition, its view of contemporary history is almost the most important of all. For anyone who undertakes to expound the Apocalypse without taking the references to contemporary history into account falls headlong into the slough of fantasy and speculation. And where the Word of God is concerned even pious speculation is unfitting.

By itself, however, even this historical interpretation is inadequate. The more one steeps oneself in the Apocalypse, the clearer it becomes that it does not merely reflect an early Christian attempt to deal with contemporary historical prob-

[3] The Mandaeans were a small group of Babylonian Gnostics whose important writings, composed in a peculiar Syriac dialect, were collected in the seventh and eighth centuries, A.D.

lems. It means much more than this. Its intention is to present, in prophetic form, the mysteries of eschatology. Eschatology points forward all the time to something beyond the frontiers of history. The peculiar message of the Apocalypse cannot be completely understood if we try to be satisfied—by itself—with any one of the methods I have named. For these methods only apply, as I have said, to the garment, or the external appearance of the Apocalypse. But its essential content, the matter which is its heart, is the testimony to the "End."

We must not confuse this message with any kind of mythology. Timelessness is not the same as eschatology. Just as the Apocalypse does not contain an eschatological calendar which fixes chronologically the moment when time will end, so also the understanding of the book is obscured if we overlook the fact that we are concerned here with real events. However colorful, varied, and even confusing this picture may be in detail, the only decisive clue to its understanding is the question: To what extent does this last book of the Bible contain that witness to the end of history which is also found in the Gospels and the apostolic writings?

It is not sufficient to emphasize the fact that the seer often uses the language of the traditional apocalyptic of late Judaism, unless we also admit that, from every point of view, he is pointing beyond the borderline of all earthly history. Hence the interpreter of the Apocalypse must show that he has felt the breath of the supernatural world which breathes through the visions and prophecies of this book.

In spite of all the difficulties of interpretation in detail, we must be able to feel that the seer, who speaks in this last book of the Bible, has gone to the very extreme borderline of human existence, to that frontier of which man is so rarely aware because the art of human life consists in hiding this frontier from our gaze. Occasionally, in sudden events, it reveals itself in solemn and terrible ways, perhaps at the death of a person who is dear to us, or in great historical catastrophes. Thus the interpretation of the Apocalypse does require more than scientific honesty or reliable orthodoxy.

What this means in detail the exposition itself must show. It will at once become clear that this question of the eschatology of this Apocalypse alone can justify the other methods. From this standpoint we gain freedom, and at the same time the obligation to lay emphasis on the amount of truth which other methods contain.

Chapter 2

Biblical Doctrine of the End

PERIODS OF TWILIGHT IN WORLD HISTORY

The approach to the enigmas of history varies from age to age. There are epochs which expand in the glow of noon-tide. All that happens lies open to the light; human existence has no background and no enigmas. At the zenith of Greek culture it was possible to receive the impression that the mysteries of the world were kindly veiled by the shimmering radiance of poetry and myth. Similarly, the Renaissance and —to a lesser extent—the second half of the nineteenth century were "peak" periods in history. The atmosphere of such epochs became so transparent and so thin that gradually the very question of history itself faded out. For history no longer had any enigmas; everything was concentrated on the present.

Such epochs, however, alternate with periods of historical twilight. Every great break in historical development shocks men into wakefulness, because they suddenly become aware that history has a background, and depths are disclosed which in time of peace had been invisible. Historical naïveté is the privilege of undisturbed periods, because then alone can we fall into the error of thinking that history presents no problems. The historical consciousness, however, is born out of catastrophes, out of the struggles and sufferings, the hopes and trials of history. For these catastrophes alone show man that history has its limits. They destroy the naïve interpretations which try to understand the course of history from within itself; and these events shatter men's sense of security—because, suddenly, they see the possibility of the end. When a generation, with its own eyes, sees an historical epoch come to an end and disappear forever, it becomes aware of the riddle of history, and can never evade it again.

We might even say that humanity only begins to ask questions about the nature of history when it has grasped the fact that history has an end.

There are only two ways in which mankind can experience this end of history: either as an end within history which takes place when a period of history comes to an end which had provided the contemporary world with axioms of thought and principles by which it lived; or, in a deeper way, when behind the breakdown of the world they have known, men see—though perhaps dimly—the end of all history coming into their line of vision. It is very clear that such periods of change are in a certain sense the most fruitful periods in the growth of thought and life. The oldest European philosophy of history, the source of all later similar systems of thought, that of Augustine, was born out of the gradual disintegration of the Roman Empire, one of the greatest historical phenomena that the world has ever seen.

Such considerations make it plain why our generation, more than many which have preceded it, is more prepared to consider the question of the end of history. In two world wars, our generation has seen the beginning of the disintegration of that old Christian Europe, of that "Christendom," whose creative thinking had influenced world history for more than a thousand years. Our generation is now moving into a period of fresh revolutionary development, ushered in with great force, whose laws of life are fundamentally different from any we have previously known. Such a generation is indeed forced to be aware of the riddle of history.

The mystery of historical crises consists in the fact that the onlooker never knows whether such a crisis heralds the dawn of a new day or the shades of approaching night. It is a rather superficial reflection to say that optimists always regard a crisis as a new morning, while the pessimists always tend to regard it as the coming of night. Those who cannot face such questions will never reach a profound understanding of history; to evade these questions means to live below the level of the dignity of human capacity, both in thought and in history.

Although biblical literature does not contain either the word or the concept of history, its thought on this subject constitutes one of the earliest contributions to this problem. For the men of the Old Testament reflected on the course of history long before the Fathers of the West began to do so. The reason for this it quite simple: they knew that the world has a Creator, and therefore that it also has a Lord; and because they worshiped this Creator and Lord, they began to be able to see his activity in the world. They saw his working in the unceasing daily wonders of creation in the world around them, as the praises of the Psalms bear witness, but they also saw the mighty hand of the Lord in the complicated historical events in the world of nations by which they were surrounded. They were the first truly universal thinkers. The reason for this is their belief in the living God. He was not only the national God of Israel or simply the religious intensification of their own national myth. He was the Lord of the nations. They proclaimed that this Lord, who had started history on its way in creation, would also bring it to an end. Hence they looked for the "Day of the Lord" which would bring the course of historical development to its conclusion—with power.

It is in this sense that the Bible bears witness to faith in the Lord of history. The Christians believed in the Lord of history all the more because they, more clearly than the prophets of the Old Testament, had before their eyes a divine fact—the Incarnation of Jesus Christ. From this fact the path of history leads towards another fact: the return of Christ.

This way of thought is not "historical" thought in the usual sense of the word because it is aware of the evening of the world,[1] but behind the approaching night of earthly history it already sees the dawning of the day of Jesus Christ. The hour of twilight in world history is therefore always twofold: an earthly decline and a divine beginning. Christian faith, however, substantiates itself in the fact that it is always open to this judgment on earthly history. "The time is near"—that is true of every moment.

The essential fundamental feature of the church history of the present day is the fact that almost all its problems are universal. None of the really decisive questions which are addressed to the church today have a merely local and limited significance; almost all are of world significance. The questions which are asked, the accusations and attacks which are made, and the decisions which are agreed upon almost everywhere affect the Christian church as a whole throughout the world. Today the arena of church history is no longer one country, or one continent, but the whole earth.

The second main feature of the church history of the present day is an outbreak of resistance to the Christian message, of anti-Christian movements, and even of persecutions, to an extent which has hitherto been unknown. Asia has been the scene of many persecutions and Asia is the mother-country of religions. It seems probable that in the last two generations more Christians have been martyred than in all the persecutions under the Roman Empire.

It is in such a setting that the question of the last book in the Bible again becomes a live one. Since it is very far from being a mediocre book, it is obvious that it has no appeal to mediocre times. As we read the great book we begin to see what we always ought to know about the Word of God, and what the church always ought to know, namely: that it does not lie in *our* power to "renew" the "understanding" of a book

[1] Cf. the phrase of the astronomer Tycho de Brahe, "*advesperascenti mundo*" on the evening of the world (Werner Elert: *Morphologie des Luthertums,* I, p. 408).

in the Bible by our own well-meant didactic efforts. Contact with this book has its own time and hour, willed by God. This springs from the fact that the church of the martyrs has always immediately understood this book, which itself grew out of the first period of martyrdom in the church.

Also we cannot forget that from the Apocalypse, Augustine drew the leading ideas for his book, *The City of God*. He did this at a moment when the ancient world and its greatest historical institution, the Roman Empire, were falling into ruins. We should also note that Augustine was the first to tread the path which deduces a philosophy of history, or a theological conception of history, out of the eschatological teaching of the Apocalypse. In so doing, he almost imperceptibly greatly altered its message.

When the course of history becomes more and more stormy, when volcanic upheavals lay bare the depths of existence, Christendom may be more inclined to listen to the message of the last book of the Bible. As the Prophets perceived the coming of the supreme Lord in all the fluctuations of contemporary history, and as Augustine in the midst of the devastation caused by the fall of Rome and the appearance of new historical institutions again inquired into God's plan for the world, so amid the upheavals of the present time we too seek to discover the lines which God has laid down for us to follow in his plan. But the church of Jesus Christ must know that she can never distil such a plan out of her own speculations on the philosophy of history; one thing only she does possess: the world of prophecy. The prophet knows the secret of history because he knows its end. From the point of view of the end the plan of God for history becomes intelligible, but in this way alone, and in no other. This prophetic word has been given to the Christian church in the last book of the Bible. What does this prophecy in the last book of the Bible mean? and what more importantly, does this prophecy mean for us in our faith today?

PROPHECY OF THE END

Since the question of the end of history does not belong to the category of questions which man can deal with arbitrarily, it reappears again and again, not as a question which men have thought out for themselves, but as one which is put to them by God himself. It penetrates into the widest spheres of man's intellectual life, even to the point where directly religious impulses cannot be discerned. Witnesses to this are the broad and colorful streams of apocalyptic, which are found not only in religious forms but also in the secular sphere.

In the history of religion, apocalyptic literature has an honored place. As apocalyptic in the narrower sense of the word, it is even older than the Biblical expectation of the End. In the religion of the ancient Persians (which flourished from the eighth century, B.C.) the Parsees spoke of a final conflict between light and darkness, which would one day break out, and would finally end with the victory of light. Teutonic Germanic mythology also had its eschatological expectation in Ragnarok, the gloomy "end of the world" of the gods. Where the Bible speaks of the beast from the abyss, the Fenriswolf appears as the monster of the period of the end of the world.

Indeed, the seriousness of the question of the end of history is so urgent that it arises even where religious presuppositions have otherwise been completely forgotten. For instance, what is the Marxist doctrine of the "future state" if it is not a secularized eschatology? Down to the smallest details it is a secularized picture of the Kingdom of One Thousand Years. And even at the present time it is not the only form of a secular hope for the future propagated with eschatological fervor, even though its forms of expression are wholly secular.

The view that "eschatological thought belongs to a Christian epoch which has already disappeared," is not correct.

Our generation is impregnated, up to the hilt, with eschatological ideas of all kinds.

The biblical prophecy of the End is very different from the various forms of apocalyptic statements in other religions. Its main concern becomes clear when we take into account two fundamental facts.

First: *If history has no end it has no meaning.* For the more deeply we delve into history the more do we perceive the contradictory character of all that happens. Indeed, we only begin to reflect upon the meaning of history when we perceive this dualism.

This contradiction is twofold in character. First of all, there is the fact that all historical life is indissolubly bound up with the finite nature of all that happens. Thus finitude and death are present in every historical event; in the very fact that something happens it also passes away. Real history impresses the terrible riddle of time painfully upon our consciousness. The oppressive shadows of finitude gather all the more darkly about our path as the historical period in which human life is mounting to a climax becomes more enlightened. Death is the dark side of all life.

The second fact is the constant failure of history. In the long run none of the great historical problems has ever found a lasting solution within history. The great creative movements of history and its great revolutions make this evident; hardly any of them has reached the goal at which it aimed. It seems as though history were condemned to continual failure, and every historical failure is in some way or another coupled with guilt.

Secular thought has given two different answers to these questions.

The first is the doctrine of progress in history. This doctrine is the secularized form of an original Christian hope. In the long run it provides us neither with historical hope, nor with joy in the present; at bottom it is a hopeless and comfortless view of history. For it means that each particular contemporary generation, at any particular period, is always being "comforted" by the consoling idea that in some unknown future the meaning of history will become clear. Thus ultimately it can offer man no other consolation than that he must die in order that the last of all the historical generations may once for all attain the aim of all life. It boasts, it is true, of the continual progress of history, but we might also say that it continually has in view the passing away of history.

Yet there is no absolute reason why the present generation should be put off so drastically with the promise of happiness at some future time.[2] This doctrine makes both the present and the past equally void of significance. So long as the meaning of history is sought within itself, it has no meaning.

Greater, deeper, and at the same time more tragic, is the other attempt to answer this question which comes from Asia, and finally exerted a sinister influence upon Nietzsche; i.e., the terrible theory of everlasting recurrence. At bottom this theory is only a grandiose way of saying that history has no future. It is probably not accidental that where this doctrine is held seriously (that is, not against the background of our western inheritance where it is blended with many echoes of the joyful hope of the Christian faith, but as the Hindu believes it), it leads only to the ardent desire that this existence may be blotted out. For this kind of eternity is terrifying. The infinitely sorrowful longing for Nirvana is the most logical result of this view of history.

Thus a third possibility alone remains: the twofold riddle of history cannot be solved within history. The solution can only lie in a region beyond history. The answer to this riddle

[2] Cf. the sarcastic remarks of Jakob Burckhardt in his *Weltgeschichtlichen Betrachtungen* (Ausgabe Kröner, p. 256): "For a time the 'present' was literally equated with 'progress,' and this was coupled with the most ridiculous conceit, as though man were on the point of perfecting the human mind, or even ethics." "Neither the soul nor the brain of man has made any appreciable progress since history began; in any case, his capacities were 'complete' long ago." "If in ancient days a man would lay down his life for another, no one has gone further than that since then."

can only be given in the hope that the tragedy of world history will not go on for ever. This presupposes that history has an end. "History only has a positive meaning if it has an end."[3] Apart from the prospect of the end, for anyone who wants to understand it, history is merely horrible tomfoolery. But when we know that history has an end, all the struggles and conflicts of history—the sense of finitude and of continual failure—are seen to have a profoundly fruitful meaning. They are now seen to be pointers to an ultimate solution of these problems in the fulfilment of the purpose of history, in a suprahistorical realm.

There is no better illustration of this situation than that of Christendom itself. For if any historical community knows the contradictory character and failure of history, it is the Christian community. In the history of the Christian community, it is true, there are great successes and mighty deeds which even secular historians have to recognize. But was not the heroism of the martyrs itself a very clear proof that they were serving a cause which, from the very outset, was a "lost cause" from the ordinary human point of view?

This question also confronts us with an "either-or": either we try to understand the historical task of Christendom in the light of the standards which only apply within history, and, if we do this we cannot avoid the view that the course of Christian history has been marked by quite ridiculous non-success; or we realize that the task of Christendom is not to be understood from within history at all, i.e., it is not simply a segment in the course of history. Then its "lack of success" is simply necessary; by its very nature it cannot reach its goal from within time in this world.

If then the idea of the end of history springs from a profound necessity, the other fundamental fact must also be faced: the Christian expectation of the end is in every respect

[3] N. Berdyaev, *The Beginning and the End.* Trans. by R. M. French (London: Geoffrey Bles, 1952).

an essential element in Christian faith in God.

The Christian faith confesses that God is LORD, without any limitations of time or space. In saying this, at the same time it affirms that God's action cannot be involved in the non-success of the course of history; if he is LORD, then for him the limitations of history cannot be any hindrance. If his work does not come to full fruition within the course of human history then it will burst the frontiers of history. As God once established the beginning of history, so also as its majestic Lord will he determine its end.

PICTURE OF GOD IN THE APOCALYPSE

First of all, let us look at the picture of God in the Apocalypse. The words the writer uses in his descriptions of God show us what he means to convey. He, whom no name can describe, is here almost always called "he that sitteth upon the throne." In sublime majesty, undisturbed by the turmoil of earth, he sits enthroned above all earthly events. Above all earthly conflict he is always present; but he does not himself intervene in the conflict. The drama of the end of history is played out according to his fixed divine plan, and he sends forth his warriors into this conflict as he chooses. When the angels step forth, as his messengers, to proclaim a fresh chapter in the final conflict, we do not even see a movement of his hand, giving them the word of command; the command comes by a voice alone—but God himself remains hidden, in untouched holy majesty.[4] The conflict rages far beneath him. This profound consciousness of his divine majesty is derived from the subject itself. Hence the writer of the Apocalypse gives God the name which (with one exception) does not occur elsewhere in the New Testament: The *Pantocrator,* ("the Almighty") the Eternal One who bears sway over all things.

[4] Cf. the proverb of French absolutism, *Le roi régne, mais il ne gouverne pas.*

The Christian faith, however, is aware that just as God's plan for the world must have a conclusion, so also the saving work of Jesus Christ must come to an end. For, according to the views of the primitive church, the reconciliation of the world to God through Christ is a world-embracing and a world-transforming act.

The Apocalypse expresses the significance of the saving work of Jesus Christ in a quite original way, yet in full agreement with the *kerygma* of the early church—when it speaks of Christ as "the Lamb." In so doing it emphasizes the heart of the missionary message of the early church, namely, the proclamation of the Servant of the Lord who died, defenseless and innocent, in order to redeem the world.

At the same time the Apocalypse unites the historical lifework of Jesus with his exaltation. The paradox—"The Lamb is the Conqueror"—sums up the faith of the first Christians.[5] It is therefore not correct to say that the Apocalypse knows nothing of the Jesus of history. Its whole message presupposes his work. In a certain sense, indeed, the appearance of Jesus Christ upon earth, and in history, is the turning point of history. The morning star (Rev. 22:16) has risen; when it appeared the new day in history had dawned. But the Apocalypse does not confine itself to speaking of Jesus only as the "Jesus of history." It sees him also in the glory of his exaltation.

This vision of Christ, which sums up the historical work and the eternal exaltation of Jesus Christ, is expressed in the Apocalypse by the vision of the Lamb standing before the throne of God. This simply means that the crucified Saviour is now the exalted Lord. This truth is shown to us in a series of glorious visions. In line with this view is the conviction that God has entrusted to the Lamb the judgment of the

[5] Weyland, in his commentary on the Apocalypse (1896), thinks he can distinguish two Christologies in the Apocalypse. Bousset, *op. cit.*, who supports this view, says that this discovery, "even from the psychological point of view, is uncommonly interesting."

world. That is the final conclusion of the work of Jesus, which began with his appearance upon earth, just as the conclusion of the action of God is for and with this world. The saying from the Fourth Gospel, "the Father has given all judgment to the Son," (John 5:22), is fulfilled in the Apocalypse. All that the last book of the Bible proclaims in its magnificent and vivid pictures is only a further expansion of the content of faith in God and in his Christ.

When we look at the *subject* with which the Apocalypse is concerned, we see clearly that it does not go beyond the limits of New Testament thought. We have just seen that its visions are simply the expansion of the glory of Christ, which is the heart of the message of the New Testament. Even in its particular eschatological message, at bottom it does not go further than the rest of the New Testament, that is, than the lines laid down in the so-called "apocalypses" of the Synoptic Gospels. Read Mark 13, for instance, at a sitting (the parallels are Matt. 24 and Luke 21). The descriptions of the "harvest of God," and the "fulfilment of the world" (Matt. 13:49) are briefer than the magnificent world pictures of the Apocalypse, but the fundamental thought, and many of the essential details are the same.

The testimony to Christ in the Apocalypse, however, is related to these eschatological statements, not only as the finished picture is related to the rough sketch, but an essential, definitely new element has been added. *The Apocalypse is the fulfilment of the Easter message of the church.* The risen Lord is not only he of whom it is said, "Thou wilt not let thy Holy One see corruption" (Acts 13:35), but he is the exalted Lord, through whose service the "End" will be achieved and completed. On this point Bousset's phrase is apt: the Apocalypse is "the Gospel of the Risen Christ."

At one point, however, the Apocalypse goes further than the Gospels: that is, in its feeling for time. Here in particular, the Revelation of John differs from earlier Jewish apocalyptic.

When it says "the time is near," this means a "certain" knowledge, for Jesus Christ has appeared. He is the Living One who has been raised from the dead. Thus the meaning of time has been disclosed. Thus the two phrases, "soon," and "in a short time," which play such an essential part in the Apocalypse, denote a compressed, urgent, explosive feeling for time. In the Apocalypse, time is no mere empty category of thought, but it is always time that is "filled"—filled with content. Time alone, because it has this particular content is real: this content is Jesus Christ. This truth is like the keystone of the arch. Were we to remove this concrete central point from the Apocalypse, it would collapse, and all that would be left would be a mass of "religio-historical" ruins. If, however, this truth is recognized, then none of the component parts of this book are of significance for the history of religion alone, but even in the smallest details, everything derives its meaning from Christ: *Tout par rapport à Jésus Christ* (Pascal).

The manifestation of Christ within time, his epiphany, was the noonday peak of history. Henceforth everything is hurrying towards the second coming of Jesus Christ, his *parousia*. The more closely time approaches this event, the more ardent it becomes; men see that, in and through time, *God* is at work. Time becomes transparent, the mystery is unveiled. The hidden threads of the past and the present become transparent, the hidden threads of the future come into sight. It is from this conviction that there emanates from the Apocalypse this vigorous sense of time which is laden with tension, an intensity which increases at a greater and greater pace until all that happens is filled with meaning, and thus "*ful*filled," and all that is temporal vanishes before the majesty of God.

The end of history is thus just as real an event as the whole of saving history (*Heilsgeschichte*) which precedes it, and is like all God's historical dealings with this world, i.e., history as a whole. Those who try to dissolve the end of history into a symbol find that everything, including the whole of the saving work of Christ, fades into nothingness. If there is no last day, then the earthly day of Jesus Christ upon earth is lost in a mist. Rudolf Otto has warned us about this danger of dissolving eschatological ideas into the realm of myth: "If we do this we hide the fact that we are no longer in contact with the ancient eschatological way of feeling, then we try to save a remnant of this truth, by means of allegory." [6] The faith and the witness of the seer move from the one to the other. He does not ask *what* is coming, but he bears witness to *Him who comes.* World history has only one theme: the manifestation of the glory of Jesus Christ. More and more world history must be unmasked; its potentialities must be exhausted, till men see what happens when they are left to themselves, and how terrible is the end of all human possibilities. Out of this process the world will be forced to see that all earthly and historical reality vanishes before the reality of the Christ-Event, and its final historical development.

[6] Rudolph Otto, *The Kingdom of God and the Son of Man,* trans. Floyd V. Filson and Bertram Lee-Woolf (London: Lutterworth, 1943).

Chapter 3

The Seer and His Vision

FORM OF THE APOCALYPSE

The form and shape of the Apocalypse are among the most impressive in the whole of the New Testament. The more carefully we read this book the more we lose the feeling that it is confused and confusing. The images used may be strange, but when we look at them with care we discover behind the whole structure an outstanding artistic composition. The wealth of pictures which it contains are welded together into an art form which is a unity; each of these pictures, by itself, transcends the power of human vision. But this was not strange even to a thinker like St. Paul; he mentions the time when he was caught up into the third heaven and heard unspeakable words, which it is not lawful for a man to utter (II Cor. 12:4).

All that takes place in the last book of the Bible is similar in character. At the end of the New Testament once more a messenger of God stands forth, at the bidding of his Lord, on the very edge of earthly time, and truth is communicated to him which is beyond the power of man to comprehend. When he tries to express the inexpressible, it is easy to understand that this effort continually threatens to burst through the frontiers of what is possible for man to behold. But at no point does he fall into unbridled fantasy; what he has to say is controlled and shaped by the unifying composition of the book as a whole. This artistic structure shapes the whole book. Its law is that of the number seven.[1] The series of

[1] Cf. *The Apocalypse of St. John* by R. J. Loenertz, O. P. (Sheed and Ward,

visions open like a seven-leaved flower, or a rocket in the night sky throwing out more and more graceful forms in showers of sparks. Thus the whole book, with its main sections, is like the pictures in a magnificent triptych;[2] they correspond to each other as regularly as the right and left side of an altar of this kind, in which the sevenfold prophecy of the central section, just as in the old altars, contains the most detailed representation. Thus out of all the colorful details, a few main lines of the design begin to appear, emphasizing with great vigor and clarity the main features of the design.[3]

Here, however, our main concern is not the wonderful artistic arrangement of the apocalyptic writer, but with the essential question which lies behind it: What is the source of these pictures?

The seer himself has given an answer, which he evidently thought would be at once understood by his readers: "I was in the Spirit" (Rev. 1:10). What kind of an experience was this?

Apocalyptic, Ecstasy and Apocalyptic Vision

From an external point of view this statement places the seer in the succession of the ecstatics who have been found in the history of all religions, even in the ancient world. Ecstasy,

1947), pp. v-vii, on the symbolism of numbers and the "septenaries" in The Apocalypse. (Translator's note.)

[2] *Ibid.*, pp. xviff.

[3] The design of this book follows Ernst Lohmeyer's *Die Offenbarung des Johannis,* although the author is aware that Lohmeyer's acute analysis of the material into sevens is not universally accepted.

The content of this interpretation of the Book of Revelation derives its formal structure from the law of seven. This is indicated by the table of contents of the original German text, as follows: (1) the introit, (2) the introductory vision, (3) the sevenfold exhortation, (4) the sevenfold prophecy, (5) the promise, (6) the final scene, and (7) the conclusion and blessing. These in turn are subdivided as in the exhortation to the seven churches, and in the sevenfold prophecy with its seven seals, seven trumpets (and seven dragon visions within the seventh trumpet vision), seven visions of the Son of Man, seven bowls of the wrath of God, seven visions of the fall of Babylon, and seven visions of fulfilment. (Editor's note.)

an overwhelming emotional religious excitement, is not at all foreign to the thought and experience of the Bible. Old Testament prophecy constantly appeals to it. Many prophetic visions of the Old Testament can obviously only be explained as ecstasy. It seems that the apocalyptic writers were in the same succession.

But this statement only concerns the *form* in which the seer's visions are expressed. The *content* of his prophecy is never based upon his own ecstasy. Its content is always simply what God has said—or, as the apocalyptic writer says in his own characteristic way—what God has "shown" him. Hence in each particular vision the Old Testament background is important: the vision develops the main line of thought further. The fact that in the Old Testament ecstasy is one way of conveying a divine message should not surprise us, since the Old Testament uses every variety of human expression. If, on the other hand, these visions are simply regarded as a literary device—often used in prophetic literature—this makes no difference to the main subject with which we are here concerned.

What matters is the content of this prophecy. This message, however, extends far beyond anything that can be attained by rational thought. Moreover the seer goes to the very frontiers of time itself, and therefore to the verge of human understanding. There is no a priori apocalyptic knowledge. Hence at this point the seer's sacred pictures, his visions, necessarily appear. Anyone who has to speak about the background of all history, of superhuman and supradimensional demonic forces, is forced to go beyond the borders of traditional imagery.

All this would only arouse misgiving if the apocalyptist's vision could not be distinguished from the ecstatic emotional outbreaks of an overstimulated religious psyche. But the difference is undeniable. First of all there is the link with the earlier biblical tradition. Our commentary will show to what a great extent the seer is linked both with the witness to God of the Old Testament, and to Christ in the New Testament proclaimed by the early church. Had the writer of the Apocalypse not felt compelled to extend the witness to Jesus Christ still further, the book would never have been written.

A further suggestion in this direction is the great clarity of the structure of the book. This becomes particularly clear in the arrangement of the material, which is strictly and artistically controlled by the number seven.

Apocalyptic Numbers and Symbols

None of the apocalyptic numbers has a merely intellectual or mathematical significance: they all have a deeper meaning. If we pause to consider the numbers mentioned in the Apocalypse, we are reminded of the saying of Pythagoras: "Numbers are next in importance to names." The first great intellectual activity of man consisted in giving names to things. In so doing he created the "notion" or "idea" of the "thing." It was an intellectual achievement of equal importance when he began to arrange the confusing succession of phenomena in order; placing them in relation with one another, and estimating their extent. Measure, relation, and number only became clear to Pythagoras in connection with the mysteries of music and of tones. For him the "music of the spheres," which the human ear could not detect, was the image which gave meaning to the laws which ruled the universe.

In the Apocalypse a deeper conception lies behind this use of numbers. Not only the universe, but the whole of history comes under this rule: nothing happens by chance, or in opposition to the rules that regulate the cosmos, but according to a fixed and holy plan which had been laid down before time began. We might describe this mystery best in the profound words of the great German mathematician Gauss: "God counts." Human efforts to record the mystery of the course of history in numbers are only a reflection and an imperfect imitation of the great eternal order which God himself has given to things and events. In the human copy they only reflect the great glory of God as Creator who has given to all things and events their essence and their extent. This is the impression that the numbers used in the Apocalypse are intended to convey. It is true of course that in so doing the writer makes use of the traditional sacred numbers. Three and seven are the ones most used; twelve refers to the twelve signs of the zodiac.[4]

But, like all the rest of the traditional material in the Apocalypse, numbers are subordinate to the book's great point of view, and thus become a witness to the glory of God. All events, even the most terrible, are under the control of a holy order; everything takes place in accordance with an eternal plan. Thus there are gleams of divine order shining through the stormy clouds of eschatological terror. The Christian who gazes at this drama of the end of history should not be disturbed by any doubt or anxiety, because he sees behind it all the hand of God ordering all things according to his will. We must judge in the same way the rest of the material which the seer has taken over and used for his purpose, remembering that all this imagery is eschatological.

Frequently the writer simply connects the images with those of Old Testament prophecy. These instances need no explanation. But it is striking how independently he uses this traditional material. Often he makes it serve his new vision, and then it reappears in an intensified form. It is precisely in his greatest imaginative passages, for instance, at the close of the vision of the heavenly city (Rev. 22:1-5), when the wealth of the vision almost exhausts his powers of expression, that he brings the richness of his own vision and his own language to a close with words of Old Testament prophecy, with which to crown the whole.

[4] Cf. Rev. 12:1, "the crown of twelve stars." (Beckwith, *op. cit.* p. 255.) (Translator's note.)

For the modern reader of the Bible the influence of Babylonian ideas is more difficult to understand. We shall see that echoes of Babylonian astrology continually recur and influence the imagery. There is a quite simple explanation for this. These Babylonian echoes are nothing more than references to the scientific view of the world at that time; for it is from the Babylonians that we have received the beginnings of systematic concern with the universe. At the time when the apocalyptist was writing, Greek astronomy was still at that high level it had reached some two centuries earlier. In these echoes therefore the seer is only using current ideas of the contemporary world; but they do not affect the fundamental character of his vision. All he has done is to dip boldly into the rich and colorful imagery of his own day, using it all to serve the glory of Christ.

Finally, a word about the imagery which the apocalyptist himself has created. It is at this point that most misunderstandings have arisen. The main reason for a mistaken interpretation of this imagery is the fact that people are in too great a hurry to *interpret*, without first of all taking great care to understand what those images are intended to convey. Still more disastrous is the tendency to "rationalize" particular passages without reference to the context as a whole.

This misuse of this book is due to a somewhat philistine misunderstanding of the pictorial imagery of the apocalyptist himself. We cannot examine his images as though they were paintings in which we could point to this or that detail in the picture and say "this means so-and-so, and that means something else." Here however the scenes pile up so dramatically one upon another, and one flows so much from another that everything is in motion. These images pass before our eyes like scenes in a magnificent film. Many-colored lights flash across the screen like lightning, developing into a still more impressive play of lights. There are echoes and sounds of heavenly voices, and in this play of color and of celestial voices the stormy movement is concealed.

If we approach the apocalyptic imagery in this spirit, we cease to regard these images as unregulated and confused, although this may be our first superficial impression. The hard "objectivity" of its descriptions is transformed into a testimony to a "felt" presence. The seer is himself closely involved. We understand that, apart from the moments when all is hushed in the silence of deepest adoration, the presentation of the theme knows no *moderato*. Only the most stormy methods of presentation are adequate; the structure of the world bursts open, and with it the traditional forms of thought and observation break down. Those who gaze at these eschatological visions cannot remain spectators. They are drawn into the current of this stormy movement.

We need to take great care, it is true, to try to understand this imagery. The main difficulty is that, first of all, we have to get behind the language of the Apocalypse in order to discover *what* this imagery is trying to describe. On no account must we confuse the actual subject with the images used to describe it, but at the same time we must not dismiss the images as a merely literary device. What is required is some accurate information about the "sources" from which the creative visions of the seer have been derived. In order to begin to understand the Apocalypse, therefore, we have to ask an essential preliminary question: Are the elements of particular visions derived from Jewish sources? or from those of other religions? Thus the reader must follow the same path as the seer. When John wrote down what he had seen in visions full of color and motion, the ecstasy had to be recorded in literary form; thus the reader of the Apocalypse has to gather the eschatological message of this book out of the wealth of all that the seer "saw" and "heard" in his experiences on Patmos.

CONTEMPORARY BACKGROUND

The contemporary background of the Apocalypse usually seems so remote as to have almost no significance. It is only occasionally that echoes of that Hellenistic world—with its flourishing culture just entering a late stage of development—reach that quiet realm in which the seer is living. The life of the seven churches in Asia Minor seems as yet to be scarcely affected by the coming struggle with Hellenism which was to become so acute in the second century. All the emphasis seems to be on the conflict with Judaism.

In spite of this, however, there are, now and again, references to contemporary history which our exposition must take into account.

There is only one point where a real collision with the world of that day becomes visible. This is the point at which the first persecutions appear in church history—those persecutions which, later on, left such terrible traces upon the history of the church. It is this fact of persecution which determines the immediate aim of the Apocalypse: it is meant for the consolation of the church at the outset of a period of danger and suffering. The first violent persecutions came from the Jews who poured into Asia Minor in great numbers after the fall of Jerusalem. Already St. Paul had found, repeatedly, how difficult it was for the growing church to sever itself from its spiritual home. For the Jewish enmity to Christ was very different from that of the pagan—and far more acute. Persecutions of a more severe nature which were caused by the conflict with the Roman Empire were still in the future.

In the early days of Christianity there was no conflict with Rome; indeed, at the outset the young church had not felt—in principle—any fundamental opposition to the Roman state. The part which Pilate played in the trial of Jesus makes it plain how little he, as Rome's representative, was regarded as guilty. St. Paul for instance, exercises his right of appeal to the emperor as though it were the most natural thing in the world; this does not suggest that he had a shadow of doubt about the right to act thus. Romans 13 itself shows that the rejection of the state, on principle, does not form part of the mental stock in trade of the New Testament. The well-established legal system of the Romans must have given very little occasion for such ideas; for some time the initial assault on the growing church was made by the Jews.

When, in spite of this, the conflict with Rome broke out on the question of emperor worship, this seems, to the historian at least, almost like a tragic misunderstanding of history. In contemporary writings we can read how Augustus, who was a really great ruler, was not ostentatious, and treated the question of his deification with reserve. But as a statesman he was far too astute to reject such a magnificent way of uniting the multiracial communities of the Roman Empire when such unification became possible in favorable circumstances of time and environment, especially in the Hellenistic East. Thus what had at first been only political *pietas* finally became an established cult. That is where the fundamental conflict began. For the cult of the old Roman gods could afford to be tolerant, but the cult of emperor worship could not. Once the doctrine had been formulated that the divinity was present in the emperor, this *numen praesens* had to receive absolute recognition. This conflict showed how profoundly Hellenistic thought tended towards political monotheism. On the other hand, the fact that the Christians were bound to their confession of the triune God, must have seemed like futile and unwarranted arrogance.

It was this spiritual contradiction which made Christian opposition to emperor worship so acute. The Neronian persecution was not based on principle; it was simply the bloody outburst of the tyrant's mood of a decadent Emperor. Later on, the Christian struggle against the institutions of a political religion became increasingly severe. For nearly two hundred and fifty years this conflict continually demanded new sacrifice of human life. The spiritual conflict only came temporarily to an end in the fifth century, at the earliest, through Augustine.

The seer of the Apocalypse, who described these possibilities of future development with prophetic clarity, learned through them that first and foremost, far beyond the sanguinary chaos of world history, Christendom owes obedience to her Lord.

This great figure in the primitive church has great qualities, one of which is the dignity with which—in addition to his impressive power of pictorial presentation—he treats this difficult question. Above all, he excels in the great personal earnestness with which he reminds every one of his fellow Christians that faith in the coming Lord must be preserved at one single point: the seriousness of the call to holiness, to the personal obedience of faith.

The church of Christ is not only "contemporary" with the Jesus of history, but with the returning Christ. We can only understand the impressive sense of time in the Apocalypse, and its great earnestness, when we note the words, "the time is short." In this book we are not urged to think of the end of history as something far off which becomes more and more vague, losing itself in mists the longer the history of the world goes on. Rather the seer insists that the exalted Christ is *here,* at our door, as the decisive, final, essential reality, at every moment standing at *our* door. Hence the only spirit in which we can study this book is that of the obedience of faith. *"Semper parati simus"*—"Let us always be ready," Luther used to say, and thus put his finger on the decisive point in all truly religious eschatology.

FIGURE OF THE SEER

The question of the personality of the seer himself still remains.

He appears in a remarkable twofold light. The almost

casual reference to his name (Rev. 1:1, 4, 9; 22:8) leaves him almost in the darkness of anonymity; "I, John"—that is all. Who is this, of whom we know no more than the actual name? Since, in contrast to other Jewish apocalypses, he does not attempt to introduce himself under the cover of some borrowed authority by giving his document the weight of the author's name, we must assume that behind the name John there was a personality of high and unquestioned authority who could count on gaining a hearing without any further mention. With one voice, the early church proclaimed the author to be the Apostle John, as we learn from Irenaeus.[5] The early church tradition could not imagine that anyone but John, the disciple of the Lord, and the Apostle, could have spoken thus, in his old age, with such wonderful vividness and with such boldness, faith, and courage, to the growing Christian church.

Later views, which do not accept the idea of this authorship are based on misgivings about the content of the book. Modern scholars have gone into the matter very thoroughly, weighing all the reasons for and against this traditional ascription to John the Apostle, and have probably reached the point at which research and argument can carry us no further. The question of the author seems to be the one mystery of this book which is insoluble. In any case, there is a fully satisfactory answer from the historical point of view since, quite evidently, this writer never intended to say any more on this matter. There is no point in indulging in speculations about the various bearers of the name "John" who have lived at Ephesus. Even so, that is not decisive from the factual point of view. We do not need to know who the seer was in order to understand that he speaks with authority. And if the last book of the Bible means something for our faith, then we

[5] The first certain and weighty evidence for the Apocalypse occurs before A.D. 150. Justin Martyr names the author as "John, one of Christ's apostles." But as the word "apostle" was used in various senses (cf. Rom 16:7), this quotation does not help us.

are summoned to obedience, not to the person of the seer, but to the message which he brings. If we understand it in this way, and take care not to make unfounded assertions, we can leave it to the statement of a modern expositor, that "we do not know any more credible name than that of the Apostle John."

PART II

Chapter 4

Introit

(Rev. 1:1-8)

1 The revelation of Jesus Christ, which God gave him to show to his servants what must soon take place; and he made it known by sending his angel to his servant John, 2 who bore witness to the word of God and to the testimony of Jesus Christ, even to all that he saw. 3 Blessed is he who reads aloud the words of the prophecy, and blessed are those who hear, and who keep what is written therein; for the time is near.

4 John to the seven churches that are in Asia:

Grace to you and peace from him who is and who was and who is to come, and from the seven spirits who are before his throne, 5 and from Jesus Christ the faithful witness, the first-born of the dead, and the ruler of kings on earth.

To him who loves us and has freed us from our sins by his blood 6 and made us a kingdom, priests to his God and Father, to him be glory and dominion for ever and ever. Amen. 7 Behold, he is coming with the clouds, and every eye will see him, every one who pierced him; and all tribes of the earth will wail on account of him. Even so. Amen.

8 "I am the Alpha and the Omega," says the Lord God, who is and who was and who is to come, the Almighty.

The introduction to this book is monumental in character. The whole opening section is impregnated with the dignified solemnity of liturgical worship, for the apocalyptic writer is the liturgiologist among the apostles. In the third verse there is a fleeting allusion to the worship of the primitive church, brief but unmistakable: to the public reader, and to those who hear the book read.

The actual opening of the epistle moves on a high plane, for it consists of condensed liturgical formulae which lift the mind up to the level of public worship on the Lord's Day, far above the turmoil of everyday life. And if we may regard the epistolary introduction as a sung introit, then both the sayings in the seventh and eighth verses may be regarded as "prophecy"—to use the language of early church worship—that is to say, the lesson from the Old Testament and the "Word of the Lord," the New Testament word of Scripture.

The superscription (verses 1-3), which is full of reverence for Him who is the real author of the book, falls into three parts.

The first statement is clear: God himself is the author of the book, but not directly. Jesus Christ is the "author" who has received this revelation from God.[1] Throughout the whole of the Apocalypse God himself remains remote from the dramatic conflicts and processes which are unfolded in the course of the story. As the "One who sitteth upon the throne" and the All-Ruler, he reigns holy and serene above all earthly events, himself untouched by conflict and the world "that is passing away." Thus here too the whole Apocalypse is given to Jesus Christ, who in turn gives it to his servant John. While John is living alone on the island to which he has been banished, on the mainland the churches of Asia Minor are gathered for Sunday worship. And the remembrance of this fact has influenced the whole style of the book, as well as these introductory verses. Even before the celestial liturgy has begun to be celebrated—that worship which embraces the whole of heaven and earth—before Christ himself appears, and heaven resounds with the songs of praise

[1] J. A. Bengel, *Gnomon of the New Testament* (New York: Revell). "The Lord Jesus is the author, and John has wielded the pen."

of those who have been "sealed"—liturgical echoes already affect the style of the book.

The mention of John is so brief that it is striking. This brevity makes it difficult to believe that the author is using some great name of the past as his *nom de plume,* as writers of apocalypses were wont to do. As a rule these writers are more verbose and artificial. The fact that the writer considers it quite sufficient to say "John" (and to leave it at that) suggests, on the one hand, that the name itself was well known and carried a great deal of weight, and on the other, that the seer dared to step forth to address the Christendom known to him in his own name, because he knew that he was so evidently overshadowed by the presence of a higher power, the authority of Christ himself. He is not proclaiming his own message, but that which God has given him. This alone makes his "prophecy" legitimate.

The second fundamental idea in the superscription is that of the "testimony of Jesus Christ." The Apocalypse is that part of Holy Scripture in which the original meaning of the word "witness" or "testimony" begins to expand before our very eyes, and to express the idea of martyrdom. The "witness" in word becomes the "witness" in blood, just as Jesus Christ is himself the "faithful witness" *par excellence* sealed with his own blood. The great biblical line which began with the proclamation of the "Servant of the Lord" by Second Isaiah, is here carried to its conclusion. The Second Isaiah created the martyr-theology of the Bible (cf. Isa. 43:9, 12), just as the Johannine writings have created the ecclesiastical conception of the "martyr."

It is well known that the theology of the "Servant of the Lord" was of great significance in the life and thought of the primitive church. From several allusions (e.g., Acts 4:25 and the eucharistic prayers in the *Didache* IX:2-3; X:2-3) we can see that this testimony to the "Servant of the Lord" was probably used more frequently to explain the saving work of

Christ than the Pauline theology of the cross, with which of course it is in complete agreement. Here, in the Apocalypse, this line of thought comes to a climax in the thought of Jesus, the arch-martyr, the true and faithful witness.

Now the fact that the "testimony of Jesus Christ" is mentioned here at the very beginning of the book suggests the twofold significance of the phrase in this book as a whole: on the one hand it gathers up the historical result of the work of the incarnate Lord; on the other hand, it makes it clear that to "follow" Christ involves "bearing witness" to the point of martyrdom. Through this twofold conception that the divine revelation concerning the end is understood only as the fulfilment of the "testimony of Jesus Christ," and that, at the same time, the personal challenge to Christian martyrdom is always emphasized, shows that even in the superscription we can see that the book itself is very far from being a work of empty and fantastic eschatological speculation.

This emphasis on "witness bearing" in the whole book is closely connected with the fact that in these first two verses the word "servant" or "slave" is used twice. This has a twofold significance. First of all, it signifies the prophet; John stands in the succession of the Old Testament witnesses to God. We shall meet this high sense of his vocation frequently in this book. But behind this prophetic meaning of the word "servant" or "slave," there is also the original meaning of the word which we must not forget. The slave obeys. Christian "witness bearing" involves obedience to Christ. Only the obedient "servant" who is prepared to follow Christ, will be able to understand this "revelation."

The first beatitude of the Apocalypse, of which there are seven in the whole book, is recorded here (verse 3) for obvious reasons. It is based upon a saying of the Lord himself (Luke 11:28). Here already, as we shall see frequently later on, it becomes evident that the seer is controlled by the historical record of Jesus and his message; but he does not simply repeat what the Lord has said; the testimony of the church goes further. That is why he gives the traditional saying in a different original form. He has expanded it in two directions.

He does not speak simply of "reading" and "hearing" the Word, but of reading aloud in public worship. This is important, because it supports the view that the Apocalypse is a message to the church as a whole. Secondly, for "hearing" he here uses the word to "keep," which is used elsewhere for the careful observance of the Law and the Prophets. This again confirms the fact that this book is of equal status with the law and prophecy of the old covenant. On this beautiful beatitude Bengel remarks that some people have such a negative attitude towards this book that they seem to think that this first beatitude means: "Blessed are those who do *not* read this book!" [2] "This" he says, "is quite unfitting, and is a gross misunderstanding." His warning was not unnecessary, owing to the fact that there are those who "confuse the search for truth in these things with toil, slothfulness of mind with sobriety, silence with wise reserve." "It is better, in seeking to understand the signs of the times—in so far as only faith, hope and love are in our hearts—to be mocked and scorned ('Behold! this dreamer cometh.' Gen. 37:19) than with the proud spirits of the world to despise these mysterious warnings, and at the end be taken by surprise by the course of things." [3]

Finally the third main feature of this superscription is the characteristic feeling of the primitive church for time. "The time is near" (verse 3)—so near, that one is tempted to translate it, *"It is here!"*.[4] Moreover we already feel a breath of that air which tells us that the divine mystery is near which is about to be unveiled. This primitive sense of

[2] Bengel, *op. cit.*
[3] *Ibid.*
[4] Otto, *op. cit.*

time in which time has become so transparent that as we look back we not only see the veins of history clearly in the past but we also see the lines along which they will come to an end, is one of the most striking phenomena in the history of the human mind. In the introduction we have already noted something of its fundamental significance. The short sentence "the time is near" is like a wave of the hand, by which the seer summons the readers and hearers of this book to come with him to the outermost ramparts of time, to the point where time will be fulfilled, where at last all the confusion of the course of history will fade away into the evening of world history, and already the light of the new morning begins to shine, which is no longer that of this world at all.

Just as it was said of the first historical coming of the Lord, that the kingdom of God is near, is "coming upon you," (or, is about to dawn), so here we can say of the close of time willed by God: it is near; the dawn is breaking. Here there is nothing but time that is fulfilled; the day of God of creation at the beginning, the earthly day of Jesus in the center of history, and finally the great, new day of God and of Jesus Christ after time has been gathered up in fulfilment. "The time of twilight" is also the hour at which the Apocalypse begins. But the seer knows that it is the "twilight" which precedes the dawn of the great day of Jesus Christ.

The greeting to the readers which follows (verses 4-6) sounds still fuller than the first threefold announcement of the superscription of the book. It has become doubly threefold, as if after the first sound of the bell the full peal were being rung.

The pattern of these verses is determined by the primitive Christian style of letter writing, based on the ancient original style of correspondence: the name of the writer, the name of the one to whom the letter is addressed, good wishes, and a thanksgiving. But the independence of the apocalyptic writer gives a new turn to this primitive tradition of letter writing.

After an emphatic but cursory allusion to the writer and the recipients of the letter,[5] which dismisses them as of secondary importance, the "letter" proceeds to the greeting of good wishes. Where St. Paul, for instance, would say: "Grace be with you, and peace from God our Father and from the Lord Jesus Christ," here this greeting is expanded in a double threefold form.

Of God, whose name is not mentioned, out of reverence, it is said ". . . who is, and who was, and who is to come." Even in this turn of phrase we see the dawn of the light of the new day; when the Jews mentioned the name of Jahweh in their services of worship they used to say: "who is, and who was, and who will be." John expresses this differently, because he is looking towards the dawn of a new day of God, and he speaks of ". . . the One who *cometh*" ("is to come").

The name of Jesus is also more exactly defined in a threefold way. The basis of this threefold expansion of the name of Jesus is the early Christian confession of belief in him as him who died, who has risen again, and is exalted to God's right hand. But the expansion of the primitive Christian *kerygma* in this passage is absolutely essential for the whole message of the Apocalypse. For the Prince of Life who is here—in the language of the primitive church called the "first-born from the dead" (cf. Col. 1:18)—is also called the "faithful witness" and "the ruler of the kings of the earth." These two titles are of fundamental significance.

The combination of the two ideas of "witness" and "king" reminds us of one of the greatest scenes in the Gospel of John, the interrogation of Jesus by Pilate (John 18:28ff). There in the words of Jesus himself, both these ideas of kingship and witness bearing are indissolubly connected. At the same time, at that moment of world history, for the first time the claim of the empire to world dominion clashed with the claim of Jesus Christ to be the King of kings. It is therefore significant

[5] "In Asia": The Roman province in the western part of Asia Minor.

that in this passage the exalted Lord is given a title which the Roman emperor officially claimed for himself: Ruler of all the kings of the earth (verse 5). Here we see a definite relation between the Gospel of John and the Apocalypse. Here we see that the great claim Jesus made when he met the representative of the Roman Empire is now being realized. It is this realization which is here proclaimed.

Of course this proclamation is not confined to that historical incident, but it is significantly expanded. The witness which Christ bore in his earthly life before the representative of the Roman power now becomes visible to the whole world as a totalitarian claim. He steps forth out of the mystery of the Incarnation, out of the incognito of lowliness, at the moment when the event which is being revealed in the Apocalypse begins to appear. This becomes the theme of the whole book: how at the end of world history this sovereign claim of Christ will emerge from obscurity and will become public, visible to the whole world, when the lightning of his coming will flash across the darkness of the night sky of human history.

In verses five and six we not only begin to hear the songs of acclamation which will resound more clearly later on, but we cannot fail to see that here we are being reminded of the historic saving work of Christ.

The seer closes the greeting with the words "for ever and ever," more completely than is usual in the epistles of the New Testament. In so doing he helps us to lift our eyes to look beyond the barriers of time and space and to view from afar the eternal fulfilment.

"Prophecy" and "the Word of the Lord"—in accordance with the order of worship in the primitive church—close the introduction to the book (verses 7-8).

First of all, the seer himself, boldly summing up in his own way the witness of the Old Testament, proclaims the prophetic promise of the Lord's return (cf. Dan. 7:13; Zech. 12:10).

In so doing he goes beyond the sphere of historical reminiscence. The "good confession" of Jesus as king and "faithful witness" includes not only his historic witness, but also his death, his resurrection, and the royal triumph of his coming in judgment. Verse seven fulfils the word of the Lord in Matt. 26:64.

The brief eighth verse again brings out very clearly the bold originality of the seer. He formulates the "thus saith the Lord," which the Old Testament prophets had used so often, in a new way, and in so doing shows the high sense of prophetic mission which fills his soul. Since the days of the prophets there has been no fresh expression of the "whisper of Jahweh"; now once more here is a prophet of the Lord, so once more we can hear the words, "thus saith the Lord."

Not only do the words "Alpha" and "Omega" sound better in the ear of the modern reader than the letters A to Z; to the Ancient world the phrase was actually more comprehensive, for at that time men were attached to the magic of numbers and letters of all kinds and loved such phrases. The rabbis too, were fond of these plays on words. To them, for instance, the Hebrew word for "faithfulness" (*emeth*) was a "seal of God"; for it was formed by the first, middle, and last letters of the Hebrew alphabet, and moreover it symbolized the phrase "God is all in all." Thus the "Alpha and Omega" is only a translation of this symbolism into Greek. As we know, Alpha and Omega are the first and last letters of the Greek alphabet. Here it seems as though the phrase were being used to suggest the all-inclusive sovereignty of God over space. He is Lord of all, just as the phrase "who was, and who is, and who is to come" glorifies him as Lord of time. Time and space, without which man cannot think, are gathered up in him; there is nothing before him, and nothing afterwards, nor is there anything outside of him. Between this beginning and this end everything is included. It is a witness to the sovereignty of God that no one and nothing can place itself outside of this series.

The last word of this introduction to the book also is original: the ruler of the kings of the earth. Paul only uses this word once, when he is giving a quotation from the Septuagint (II Cor. 6:18); in the Apocalypse this word is used nine times. It belongs to the time of "unveiling." The period has begun when all the world will know that God is supreme. As the history of the New Testament approaches its end, the messenger of the primitive church who is bringing to us the final biblical message looks far beyond the confines of this present world, and he takes the early church with him, helping them to look more firmly than ever before to that world where God reigns, where soon all men will bow in homage before the exalted Lord.

NOTES

The angel (verse 1) is probably that particular angel who always appears when John needs to have a "sign" or a "vision" interpreted. Every reader needs to be assured once again that John did not express his own ideas in colorful language, but that he gave instructions which he had received from God and passed them on.

The Apocalypse contains seven beatitudes; they stand over against fourteen woes. This too suggests the way in which this book has been composed, and helps us to see the significance of the number seven in the Apocalypse.

In verse four for the first time the number seven occurs which plays a great part in the mysterious terminology of the Apocalypse, with its use of pictures and numbers. Here we are reminded of the seven days of creation, and here, as usual, this means the complete divine number.

The Greek word for "ruler" (verse 5) is used as the translation of the Latin word *princeps,* that is, the official title of the Roman emperor.

The quotation from Zech. 12:10, 14 in verse 7 is given from the original Hebrew text, not from the Greek translation, the Septuagint, exactly as in John 19:37.

Chapter 5

Introductory Vision: Christus Imperator

(Rev. 1:9-20)

9 I John, your brother, who share with you in Jesus the tribulation and the kingdom and the patient endurance, was on the island called Patmos on account of the word of God and the testimony of Jesus. 10 I was in the Spirit on the Lord's day, and I heard behind me a loud voice like a trumpet 11 saying, "Write what you see in a book and send it to the seven churches, to Ephesus and to Smyrna and to Pergamum and to Thyatira and to Sardis and to Philadelphia and to Laodicea."

12 Then I turned to see the voice that was speaking to me, and on turning I saw seven golden lampstands, 13 and in the midst of the lampstands one like a son of man, clothed with a long robe and with a golden girdle round his breast; 14 his head and his hair were white as white wool, white as snow; his eyes were like a flame of fire, 15 his feet were like burnished bronze, refined as in a furnace, and his voice was like the sound of many waters; 16 in his right hand he held seven stars, from his mouth issued a sharp two-edged sword, and his face was like the sun shining in full strength.

17 When I saw him, I fell at his feet as though dead. But he laid his right hand upon me, saying, "Fear not, I am the first and the last, 18 and the living one; I died, and behold I am alive for evermore, and I have the keys of Death and Hades. 19 Now write what you see, what is and what is to take place hereafter. 20 As for the mystery of the seven stars which you saw in my right hand, and the seven golden lampstands, the seven stars

are the angels of the seven churches and the seven lampstands are the seven churches.

We now come to the impressive beginning of the book itself; the preceding section was merely a kind of extended introit. This is the situation which it describes:

A memorable Sunday dawns upon the tiny island of Patmos, a unique Sunday in the history of the church. The island, which is about ten miles long and about five or six miles broad, lies in the center of the Aegean Sea, some fourteen hours' journey from the mainland, in the same latitude as Miletus and Ephesus. Although we cannot force this interpretation it seems most likely that John was here in exile. For Patmos was one of the islands scattered throughout the archipelago to which the Romans banished offenders of higher secular rank. We may however assume that the persecution which sent John to Patmos was not so severe as the later ones. Probably John's exile was lighter in form than others, having been ordered by the proconsul at Ephesus to prevent actual or alleged disturbances of public order in his province, for Patmos was pleasanter and healthier than most of the islands which were used for this purpose. Thus, in Roman terms, it was not a *deportatio,* but the milder form of *relegatio* to which John had been sentenced.

However, to John, the highly respected spiritual head of the church in Asia Minor, the pain of separation on that Sunday morning was acute. Longing and concern alike prepared him for what was coming, as now at the hour of worship on "the Lord's day" he sent his thoughts and his prayers to the distant coast. This, at any rate, is the situation which is here assumed. We must assume that John is on Patmos, and that this is where he is writing. Of course we cannot actually prove that on one particular day, John received his vision, and began to write it down. All such considerations are rationalistic platitudes. "John was now prevented from serving the places where he had previously preached the gospel; but God's Word was not bound. In Patmos the glory of the Lord appeared to John, and he was able to describe what he saw in such a way that it has been spread abroad throughout the world, even to us in our own day. Blessed are the companions of the kingdom of Jesus who have surrendered themselves to his royal dominion, and have given themselves to him in obedience, trusting in his mercy, and have been delivered from the power of darkness and sin, and can know, in freedom of spirit, that they belong to God as His own property! Although tribulation tries them for a time the companions of the kingdom are preserved and kept in patience." [1]

Immediately there occurs the event to which we owe this book. John describes it himself in the words: "I was in the Spirit . . ."

In the introduction we have already dealt with the question: Are ecstasies a means of divine revelation? and how is the vision of John related to the ecstatic phenomena in the history of the church and of religion? What I have said above seems to be confirmed by further important observations. Above all, the connection with the divine revelation which was already known, the Word of Scripture, here becomes quite plain. The Old Testament example of which this first vision reminds us is the call of Ezekiel (Ezek. 3:12ff). This does not mean that the dependence is only literary, but something concrete and decisive must be said: John does not depart from the line of biblical prophecy. Thus we cannot say that John offers us fantastic individualistic speculations.

The introductory vision of the Apocalypse is indeed definitely placed at the point where, in the stories of the Old Testament prophets, we usually have the account of their call. Here however, almost without a word, it is assumed that the seer is a prophet. It is not necessary that he should have any particular "whisper of Jahweh," any concrete "word of

[1] Bengel, *op. cit.*

the Lord," at any particular moment in history. Nor does he need any spiritual disclosure of coming historical events, as in the case of Isaiah or Amos. All he has to do is to receive and impart the teaching on the fundamental spiritual laws of the period when history comes to an end.

Hence this first vision simply impresses upon him the royal majesty of Christ. In this way it is made clear that, on the one hand, he has been carried far beyond anything that any prophet of the Old Testament ever had to proclaim, and that, at the same time, he is no more than a simple member of the church, awaiting the Lord's return. And although his prophetic sense of mission happens to show itself plainly, his own figure completely disappears, and all that remains is the content of his vision.

Even the beginning of this section shows this very clearly. "I John"—only once more does John speak thus of himself (Rev. 22:8). Otherwise he retires completely into the background. The sense of possessing a special prophetic mission is here completely absorbed into the sense of solidarity so characteristic of the primitive church. Through the brotherhood in tribulation, but also in that of royal glory and expectation (verse 9), he is bound up in the bundle of life with all those to whom this book is addressed. The threefold expression, "the tribulation and the kingdom and the patient endurance," is a particularly beautiful testimony to the spirit of the primitive church.

Christ's royal sovereignty, which is still wholly hidden, whose disclosure and public proclamation however will be so majestically recorded later on, is embedded in the consciousness of *tentatio* (as the Reformers put it)—the present tribulation and testing—but at the same time it is connected with that power of resistance, of confident expectation, which awaits the coming Lord. The fact that John says nothing here about his dignity as a prophet and a seer, but only presents himself as the companion of their trials and of patient waiting for the fulfilment of the promises, shows that in order to understand the Apocalypse it is not necessary to be an ecstatic oneself, but it *is* necessary to share in the tribulations of the church. It is not possible to understand this from the point of view of interesting parallels in the history of religion, however enlightening these may be for the intellect, but only through primitive Christian solidarity with the way of the cross which the church must tread as the Lord has ordained. For in the primitive church "tribulations" are never mentioned as something merely personal which happen to an individual, but they are always also first of all understood as trials which the church has to bear. Hence such an experienced teacher of fundamental spiritual laws as Bengel says of this book: *"In tribulatione fidelibus hic liber maxime sapit"* ("in time of tribulation this book is best understood by believers").[2]

Thus in order to understand this passage it does not matter whether the seer is speaking of a persecution which is sweeping over the churches in the Roman province of Asia or not. In any case the "tribulation" was there, a precursor of the sharper conflicts which will finally come to a head in the great "tribulation" at the end of time.

The seer has a peculiarity which also appears in the visions of Ezekiel, namely, that the actual vision is prefaced by something *heard*. Before the first picture begins to unroll before his eyes, he hears an impressive sound, like the sound of the trumpet which ushered in the worship of the ancient covenant (verse 10). An angel's voice commissions him to write this

[2] Bengel, *op. cit.* Bengel adds to the above-mentioned passage the following deeply spiritual consideration for church history: "The church in Asia Minor, especially from the heyday of Constantine, has never valued this book very highly! In the writings of Christian teachers of this period the Apocalypse is rarely mentioned; when we find a quotation from it in the works of Chrysostom, this very fact shows that it is a later addition, from another hand. The African church, on the other hand, which came more fully 'under the cross,' had always a very high regard for this book!"

"Tribulation is essentially the Christian attitude to the world." (J. T. Beck, *Erklärung der Offenbarung Johannis.*)

book, and thus confirms the fact that this vision, and all that is based upon it, is not based on human effort, but upon divine power.[3] So once more the truth is emphasized that this vision must never be understood as the result of subjective speculation. Although the seer is thus placed in the line of the Old Testament prophets, with an equally important message (Rev. 10:11), yet this is not the record of a call, in the sense of Old Testament prophecy, but rather a clear commission at the beginning of the spiritual path which was shown to him on that Sunday in Patmos.

In this divine introit the names of the churches are explicitly included which later gain so much significance. They are not placed here like so many names in a row; that was already done in the superscription of the epistle. The fact that their names are here repeated has a special significance: these seven towns were the headquarters of the official cult of emperor worship in Asia Minor. Thus we are here confronted by that phenomenon which has influenced the whole message of the Apocalypse, including its language and style. It is true that in this passage this influence can scarcely be detected, and that we cannot speak of a contradiction, but simply of an opponent. But in the following verses it becomes evident that behind this tranquil and moderate description there looms already the necessity for a fundamental decision. In the later chapters of the book this theme will be expanded, and the difficulties which it involves will be faced.

"Then I turned. . . ." When such movements are described we must as it were follow the seer, if we are to understand, with him, the picture and the vision; with him everything is in motion. As soon as he looks round, the mighty vision unrolls before his eyes. If the movement in the picture is not very obvious here, (but see verse 17) it is not due to the fact that

[3] Bengel, *op. cit.* "No book in the Bible has been thus *ordered* to be written down. Thus it has a very close relation with revelation. When will we begin to use this great gift aright?"

we have a static picture presented to us, but to the solemnity which pervades the whole scene. In this clear and magnificent description which does not linger on distracting details, as well as in the reverent and adoring language which suggests more than it says, this first vision of John far transcends the Old Testament examples in Ezekiel 3 or Daniel 7.

And now each detail is full of significance.

As the seer turns round, the solemn light of the seven-branch candlestick shines upon him. These are necessary elements in the cult of emperor worship; during excavations at Ephesus giant candelabra were discovered which had been used in this cult.[4]

The shining half circle of light directs the seer's gaze naturally upwards to the point where the exalted Lord stands in sovereign majesty, whose name out of reverence the seer does not even utter. The whole scene, set within a beautiful frame, is full of a bright yet tranquil golden radiance. In the light thrown by the great candles the figure on the throne stands out—the long flowing priestly garment of bluish-purple, the girdle high under the armpits, as was prescribed for the high priest (Exod. 28:27), the head gleaming silvery white, the eyes in the midst of all this light are like flames of fire, and even the feet seem to glow with the radiance of burnished brass.

In the expressive manner peculiar to the seer, even His voice is described as "the sound of many waters" (or the roaring of many waterfalls). I remember the deep impression made upon me by the sound of Niagara Falls. When the waters of the gigantic circle of the two falls rush together, it sounds like a roaring symphony of power. The tributaries which flow more gently, and are almost idyllic in contrast, gather force as the waters widen, rising to a majestic crescendo of sound when the masses of water, almost dissolved in clouds of silvery spray, finally plunge over the great cliffs. Something

[4] E. Stauffer, *Theologie und Liturgie* (Hennig ed., 1952).

like this is suggested by the expression the "sound of many waters." We can also think of the sound of the sea (Ps. 29:3; Isa. 17:12).

Such pictures are inevitable when the impossible effort is being made to describe the transcendent voice of the exalted Lord. We must also pay great attention to the visions of the Apocalypse which are connected with sound. This rushing sound of great waterfalls, or of the roaring of the waves of the sea, is as natural a sound as that of thunder, which is also often mentioned. Anyone who reads the Twenty-ninth Psalm without preconceived ideas feels what is meant: the profoundly numinous awe of primitive man in the presence of these "voices of nature." Similar, and still more profound, is the awe felt in the presence of the exalted Lord.

Above the celestial vision there gleams again a fresh radiance—a crown of seven stars. The mouth which speaks with this majestic voice far above all human speech seems to gleam like a shining sword. And the whole is as "the sun shineth in his strength" (Judg. 5:31).

Of course for the seer this whole vision is not a matter for aesthetic admiration. "It is the Lord!" The picture also contains certain features which were doubtless directly understood by the first readers, which prevented them from interpreting the vision in any bypath of aesthetic terms. The very mention of the seven lamps and the seven stars are not images chosen at random; they are symbols taken from the cult of emperor worship. There are of course similar images in the Old Testament; the seven-branched candlestick belongs to the tabernacle; the lamp is a frequent symbol in the writings of the prophets (Zech. 4:2). But these and other Old Testament features are transferred into the sphere of emperor worship. It was characteristic of the worship of the emperor to have his portrait set up solemnly between great lights, in order to be worshiped. The crown of seven stars has been found on imperial coins. For hundreds of years this "symbol" had been used in popular astrology as a sign of imperial world domination.

Finally too the comparison of the reigning emperor with the sun—an anticipation in antiquity of the *roi soleil,* the sun king—was usual. Only in this connection do we see the special significance of the feet, which are not mentioned here to complete the vision of the figure bathed in light, but because in the worship of the emperor it was the feet which were adored. The act by which this was done is described in the Apocalypse by a word which it often uses: to prostrate oneself in worship (*proskyneō*).[5] Gold was also a widely used symbol of royal dignity and power. The long flowing garment of bluish-purple, however, was the mark of the office of high priest. So here too (as in Rev. 1:5ff) high priesthood and kingship are combined. The kingly claim of Jesus blends with the dignity of the great high priest; but in this picture of the priestly king the dominant features are those which emphasize his sovereignty: he is *Imperator.*

All this wealth of imagery and language is used quite deliberately. Almost silently we are here presented with a startling contrast. Here the seer proclaims: the exalted Lord is the heavenly *Imperator.* From the outset we see plainly who has "given" the Apocalypse to His servant, and what this claim involves. The theme has been announced, the development of which will be described in a series of dramatic visions in the coming chapters. The course of the book will show what this conflict, which is beginning to be felt, really means.

Whether this conflict, in which the Christian church begins to feel the hatred of the world, is necessary, is a question. Even within the pages of the New Testament, the presence of this stumbling block has been regarded differently at different times. But two things are quite clear: (a) at all times the Christian church, even when faced by a quite different power than that of the imperial world power, will only be

[5] Cf. Rev. 11:1; 5:14; 4:10; 7:11; 11:16; etc. (Translator's note.)

able to follow her Lord through times of trial and testing; and (b) the great conflict which dominates the period of the End will come to a head, in all its acuteness, in the clash between political monotheism and the royal claims of Christ.

Under the overwhelming impression of this first vision John breaks down (verses 17-20), just as before him other chosen spirits who have received special revelations from God have also prostrated themselves in awe and self-loathing: "Woe is me! for I am undone, for mine eyes have seen the King, the Lord of hosts" (Isa. 6:5; cf. Luke 5:8). Human self-assertion must fade when the exalted Lord begins to work. "A great mortification of nature goes before a great manifestation of spiritual and divine things." [6]

But the Lord stretches out his hand towards the seer, and the word of the Lord dispels his fear. This brief gesture is a consoling illustration of the gospel: the Lord laid his hand upon countless people. All through his life on earth healing, comforting, forgiving, inspiring! But now the exalted Lord has received a name which had hitherto been reserved for God alone. The earthly life of Jesus lies behind him ("I was dead"). Eternal life has begun, with him as with God himself, in order that he may have unlimited power over death and all its powers.

[6] Bengel, *op. cit.*

Chapter 6

The Sevenfold Exhortation

(Rev. 2:1—3:22)

THE SEVEN CHURCHES

"In spite of some awkwardness and angularity in expression these letters are some of the most weighty writings in the New Testament." [1] This is a truth which has been emphasized and confirmed by the experience of the church in its reading of the Bible. There are not many passages in the Bible which have brought more consolation to Christian hearts than these two chapters addressed to the seven churches of Asia Minor.

These so-called "epistles" are placed at the entrance to the actual apocalyptic visions, as the representatives of reality. For, apart from some special details, nothing in them is shrouded in apocalyptic mystery; rather, they refer very directly and clearly to their own ecclesiastical contemporary situation, and, apart from the Book of Acts, they do this more fully than any other book in the New Testament. From this fact, however, we can draw several conclusions.

For not only does the spiritual, cultural, and political world of that day touch the New Testament at this point more closely than anywhere else, but from these pages we may draw some important conclusions for our view of the Apocalypse as a whole.

First of all there is the question of authorship. One who can address the churches with such priestly and apostolic authority, is more than an apocalyptic compiler, whatever may be our view of the literary unity of the whole book.

[1] Bousset, *op. cit.*

A further important conclusion concerns the witness to Christ of this book. For the Christology of these "epistles" is almost the most advanced in the whole of the New Testament.[2] There is no longer any essential difference between the exalted Christ and God himself, as there is—at least in appearance—in the apocalyptic descriptions of St. Paul (I Cor. 15:24, 28).

Above all, it is of the first importance that a book dedicated so completely to the apocalyptic point of view, far beyond the frontiers of earthly time, should deal so explicitly in this passage with a quite definite section of human and church history.

We do not know why these particular seven churches were chosen. Other important churches in the same district such as Troas, Colossae, and Hierapolis are not mentioned. Probably it was a wholly external reason which led to the mention of these particular churches. Perhaps it was because they alone bore the title of "metropolis"; or it may be that they are mentioned because they were in this order on one of the ancient routes for the Imperial Post. Still more likely is the suggestion that only those churches are mentioned where John himself had done missionary work. We cannot come to any conclusions on this point. But it is significant that these churches form the crown of seven stars of the early church. For they belong to the most outstanding representatives of the Christianity of that day; and while John was addressing these seven churches in Asia Minor, he was really addressing the whole Christian world of his own day.

This is due to the following historical reasons. At that time Asia Minor was the noblest and the most cultured province in the whole of the Roman Empire; it was indeed the intellectual center of the Empire. This land was the intellectual heir of Greece. It was already fitted for this by its geopolitical position. Over the Aegean Sea it stretched out its hand to the thickly scattered islands of that part of the world,

[2] *Ibid.*

and, with the Greek mother-country, geographically and intellectually formed *one* region. It had almost become the eastern half of Greece; at a time when the classical Hellas had fallen into a rapid decline, Ionia, the "new Greece," had kept the Greek spirit alive in a vigorous and powerful way. Here from time immemorial some of the noblest flowers of Greek life had blossomed. Homer was born in Greek Asia Minor and the Homeric poems are some of the noblest in Greek lyric poetry. Greek art had enriched Ionia (Thales and Pythagoras, Heraclitus and Herodotus all came from this country) with some of its greatest creations—think only of the world-famous temple of Artemis at Ephesus in which according to tradition Herodotus placed his chief work, or of the Altar of Zeus in Pergamum which was one of the seven wonders of the world. Ionia took good care to guard this great inheritance. In the New Testament period this province contained the intellectual elite of the Roman Empire.

It has not been sufficiently realized that the first great "flowering" of the Christian church took place on the soil of this richly endowed culture of antiquity. The unfortunate division of the life-work of the Apostle Paul into different missionary journeys has prevented us from seeing the individual stations on his travels in the right proportion. According to the records in the New Testament, during his whole period of missionary activity he stayed longest at Ephesus (Acts 19 and 20). It is no accident that he spent at least three years there; it is a sign of the strategic statesmanship of this great missionary that he chose the capital of this intellectually most important province as the starting point of his activity.

The idea that Paul spent the greater part of his missionary work on the fringes of the world of culture, among the inhabitants of little country towns and among the proletariat of great cities (which is suggested by a great many commentators on the basis of I Cor. 1:26ff) certainly needs to be corrected.[3] The Christian mission could not have found a soil which was better prepared for the seed of the gospel than that of Asia Minor. The address of Paul on the Areopagus at Athens, whose practical fruit even in Acts was not rated too highly, has attracted more attention than the rich missionary history of early Christianity in Asia Minor. At this time, however, Athens, both politically and intellectually, had almost ceased to count. When Augustus made his journey through Greece in the winter of 20-21 he does not seem to have visited it.[4] It is to the credit of early Christian missions that its messengers did not stay unnecessarily long with those of whom Jesus had said "Let the dead bury their dead." It was not Athens and Corinth which were the centers of the earliest history of the church, but the seven cities of Asia Minor.

It is not certain, however, whether the effect of the lifework of St. Paul was very lasting. In the immediate sense of the word it evidently was not. For the memory of St. Paul and his influence seems to have disappeared very soon.[5] This was due in the main to a decisive event: when the primitive church lost its geographical center at Jerusalem, Ephesus took its place. We do not know, it is true, whether all the personalities of the primitive church whose names are connected with Ephesus really lived there. In addition to Paul and John, Timothy, Philip, and Mary the Mother of the Lord have all been named. But we know for certain that at that time Asia Minor was the most widely Christianized province in the Roman Empire, and that in actual fact Ephesus took the leading position which had previously been held by Jerusalem.

[3] Cf. A. Oepke, *Die Missionspredigt des Apostels Paulus,* pp. 20ff.

[4] John Buchan, *Augustus.*

[5] Karl Holl, *Gesammelte Aufsätze zur Kirchengeschichte,* II, 66ff., says decidedly that the growing church "eliminated" all Pauline elements from the church in Asia Minor, above all his conviction of the fundamental independence of each Christian community. The Pauline doctrine of apostolic authority was retained, but the increasing number of converts from paganism made an organic center necessary. Rome became this center.

In addition to the "epistles" of the Apocalypse another famous collection of letters proves the great importance of this part of Christendom. These are the letters which Bishop Ignatius of Antioch wrote to the churches of Asia Minor. Several of these churches are the same as those mentioned here. None of them is without claims to either political or cultural importance. They too witness directly to the fact that at this time Asia Minor was the intellectual center of antiquity.

Thus, in addressing these churches, John was speaking to the most outstanding and visible part of the church at that period.

Here then, more than anywhere else, the Christian mission met the religion of the educated men of that day. Here there were flourishing centers of education, the lecture system, and the practice—so much liked in antiquity—of traveling professors. Here there was a tendency to observe festivals, and to foster a culture with religious sanctions; nowhere would the archaic dignity of the language of the Apocalypse be more easily understood than here. Here too, moreover, was the intellectual vortex of those currents of oriental religions which began to penetrate into the Roman Empire about the turn of the century; indeed, at this very point, under the influences of Hellenism, they were actually being transformed. Artemis of Ephesus, to whom that celebrated temple was dedicated, is not the virgin sister of Apollo but a Hellenized fertility goddess of Asia Minor. Here too was the point at which the oriental cult of the stars was able to gain a footing, a cult which was new to the Greeks, and was destined to exert a wide influence.

Here too first arose that phenomenon which is so important for the background of the Apocalypse: political religion and emperor worship. A recently discovered inscription, which for the first time extols the reigning Emperor Augustus as "the Saviour of the world, the Saviour and Benefactor of all men, the invincible Son of God," was composed in the year

A.D. 9 in Priene in Asia Minor. In Pergamum, however, the first attempt was made to place the cult of emperor worship above all the other cults, and at the same time to develop it into its most flourishing and absolute form. Thus we come to the significant conclusion that the very province which by its very nature was the most tolerant in the Roman Empire became the arena of the first historical clash with the growing Christian church. Although here, as we know, the Roman administration was more lenient than in any other part of this great empire, probably it was here that the first blood of the martyrs was shed in the clash with the Roman cult of emperor worship.

The seven letters to the seven churches are addressed to this situation. They are the expression of a perception of the seer which was a burden on his mind and heart. The end of time is directly at hand; the Lord is on the verge of taking up his power and reigning (Rev. 2:17). The signs of the approaching end are unmistakable. The Lord himself had said that one of the sure signs of the approaching end was the appearance of false teaching, and, above all, the outbreak of persecution (Matt. 24:9ff). This twofold danger now threatened these churches. While the menace from without came through the cult of emperor worship, the strength of the churches was being undermined from within by confusing heresies.

Before the seer fixes his gaze wholly upon what is to happen in the future, and upon the Lord who will usher it in, he looks once more at the church on earth: will it be able to withstand the approaching trial? Some of these churches, like Philadelphia and Smyrna, are full of faith and firm in their Christian loyalty. But there are others such as those at Pergamum, Thyatira and Sardis whose inner strength has been sapped by a peculiar carelessness and readiness to compromise. Finally there are churches like those at Ephesus and Laodicea, whose faculty of moral discernment has already been paralyzed, or has almost disappeared.

From this point of view the seven churches really represent Christendom as a whole. Historical detail and local color may perhaps help to interpret some particular features within the epistles, but they are not really important. What *is* important is simply that the church must know where she stands clearly and surely, since before the end comes, she is bound to go through inward and outward periods of impending danger. Only as she sees her position clearly will she be able to meet these dangers in the strength of an undivided obedience.

In each case, the letters are addressed to the "angel" of the church in question. What does this mean?

One widespread interpretation says that he is the bishop of the church in question. From the linguistic point of view this is quite possible; in Greek-speaking Judaism the word "angel," in its original meaning of "messenger," was probably applied to the ruler of the synagogue. But this view scarcely does justice to the characteristic outlook of the Apocalypse. In the whole of the rest of this book "angels" are "heavenly messengers," and in a document which is full of prophetic visions from beginning to end, it does not seem very likely that in these two chapters alone the same expression would be used in an ordinary human sense. The seer, who beholds the church on earth and the church in heaven "in the Spirit," and who sees the hosts of angels around the throne of God, was certainly thinking of an angel. In his mind there would be no room for the skeptical question of modern man: Do "angels" actually exist?

Thus we are here confronted by a thought of peculiar and profound significance. In the countless hosts of the heavenly multitude there is always at any particular time one angel who directly connects a particular church with the throne of God. Each particular church on earth, in its sorrow, tribulation, struggle, and distress has its own heavenly representative. He is here addressed, and in him the whole church, as once more in the individual churches the whole church is being addressed. For it is one of the most daring ideas of the primitive church that each local church represents the whole church, as indeed the Greek word for "church" is the same for the local body in any particular place.

This is evidently the case here. The seven churches which are addressed are types, spiritual archetypes of the church as a whole. In the history of the church on earth *every* feature in the picture of these seven churches reappears. Hence every one of these epistles is directly contemporary.

The outline of the letters, in its main features, is the same for all: a solemn introductory phrase or two which introduces what is to follow like the word of a prophet or of a royal decree, then the main content of the message which is almost always composed of appreciation, blame, and summons to action of some kind, and finally, like a benediction, the promise of "overcoming," or of victory, at the close.

Like the introductory sayings, the introductory phrases of the main section are also fitted exactly to the community to which they are addressed. But the first words sound equally solemn, like the sound of a clock striking seven times: "I know thy works . . ." this means the whole of Christian conduct: "I know thy doings." There is no idea of "good works" here. The spiritual diagnosis is followed in regular rhythm by words of exhortation and promise. In spite of their stylized solemnity these sections still give an extremely living picture of the inner condition of the church. What a difference between the church at Philadelphia, which is greatly praised, and the severe rebuke to the church of Laodicea, which is almost like a sentence of rejection! In no instance is the situation of the churches particularly brilliant from the spiritual point of view; the mundane pressure of everyday life which we know from the epistles of St. Paul determines the picture. There is no idealizing. For the present-day reader this is a comfort.

For it is precisely the character of the content of these letters which constitutes the lasting significance of the Apocalypse. Since the seven churches are types of *every* Church, they show that the church of Christ at all times needs the same diagnosis, the same warning, the same exhortation, the same promises. In this deeper sense the letters apply to us today, as well as in the past. Without the purifying testimony of these two chapters, no wholesome study of the rest of the book is possible; for repentance and obedience alone preserve man from turning the following chapters into eschatological speculations which are merely a futile curiosity.

Further, this reminds us of the profound truth that knowledge of the End is not a private matter, but that it is only for the church as a whole. Outside the Christian church this book must be continually exposed to misunderstanding; its true meaning is only disclosed to the church which receives its message in faith and obedience.

This ought to impress upon us all still more deeply the meaning of the continually repeated phrase: "He that hath ears to hear, let him hear what the Spirit is saying to the churches!" Here the "Spirit" is understood in the Johannine sense of the Fourth Gospel; he is the Comforter, the Paraclete, the Advocate, who represents the exalted Lord in his church. This Spirit alone can open the way to the understanding of this book.

NOTES

The traditional description of these chapters as epistles is not accurate, since they are not apostolic letters like those of St. Paul, but are addressed to the church in the apocalyptic style which can be used to address the church as a whole.

On the arrangement of the letters: Approbation does not occur in the address to Sardis (Rev. 3:1-6) nor to that at Laodicea (Rev. 3:14-22); there is no blame in the words to the church at Smyrna (Rev. 2:8-11) nor to the church at Philadelphia (Rev. 3:7-13).

The opposition to the cult of emperor worship is not exclusively distinctive of the Apocalypse; it runs more or less plainly through the whole of the New Testament. In the Gospels, and above all in the apostolic writings, now and again there are definite expressions from this cultus, which have been deliberately taken over and transformed for Christian use.

Ephesus

(Rev. 2:1-7)

1 "To the angel of the church in Ephesus write: 'The words of him who holds the seven stars in his right hand, who walks among the seven golden lampstands.

2 " 'I know your works, your toil and your patient endurance, and how you cannot bear evil men but have tested those who call themselves apostles but are not, and found them to be false; 3 I know you are enduring patiently and bearing up for my name's sake, and you have not grown weary. 4 But I have this against you, that you have abandoned the love you had at first. 5 Remember then from what you have fallen, repent and do the works you did at first. If not, I will come to you and remove your lampstand from its place, unless you repent. 6 Yet this you have, you hate the works of the Nicolaitans, which I also hate. 7 He who has an ear, let him hear what the Spirit says to the churches. To him who conquers I will grant to eat of the tree of life, which is in the paradise of God.'

Amidst so much that made Asia Minor so distinctive, Ephesus was the crown. Not only was it the most thickly populated city—in New Testament times its population certainly numbered more than a quarter of a million—but it also controlled the spheres of politics, thought, and culture. It was the most important strategic center for world communications between the East and the West. Here was the official seat of the Roman proconsul; the moment when his vessel anchored on the shores of Ephesus with ceremonial pomp constituted his official entry upon his office. This harbor of Ephesus-Miletus, where Paul knelt in that poignant moment of farewell with the elders of the church at Ephesus, had seen many demonstrations of the political power of Rome.

The importance of Ephesus, as the official center of Asia ("*alterum lumen Asiae*" the Romans said, when they placed Ephesus alongside Pergamum) from the point of view of the

Roman government, comes out in the fact that Augustus visited this city no less than four times. Here was the world-famous Temple of Artemis which is mentioned in the book of Acts (19:24ff);[6] here too was the first sanctuary for emperor worship, the Augusteum. Here too—so far as we can gather from some rather mysterious allusions—the typical representative of the new political religion and its cult, the "high priest of Asia," was wont to open the sessions of the provincial synod with ritual ceremonies connected with emperor worship; this man was a highly respected official.[7] If Pergamum was the chief center of emperor worship, Ephesus was the place where this cult was most widely practiced.

We may therefore assume that here too the Christian church had an outstanding position, and was a kind of official center for the churches of Asia Minor.

Against such a background the beginning of this epistle at once becomes intelligible. The power of the heavenly Lord confronts the power of the earthly ruler. That is why strong, vital words are chosen to bear witness to the royal claim of Christ to supreme sovereignty: "Thus saith the Lord . . . he that holdeth the seven stars in his right hand, he that walketh in the midst of the seven golden candlesticks."

"Thus saith the Lord"—thus begin the great sayings of the prophets of the Old Testament which announce a dire admonition from God. So also began the decrees of the great kings of Persia, and until New Testament times this phrase appeared in royal proclamations. The seven stars and the seven golden candlesticks are royal symbols taken from the practices of emperor worship, as well as from Hellenistic court ceremonial. Since they are here also a

[6] Actually the goddess was not Artemis, but a Hellenized goddess of fertility, the *Magna Mater*.

[7] His official title was that of "Asiarch." Possibly it was some men who had formerly held this high office who were so helpful to St. Paul on the occasion of the riot at Ephesus (Acts 19:31).

significant token of the seven churches, the introductory saying simply means: Here the Heavenly Emperor, the One who is their true Lord, is speaking to the churches.

The picture of the church which is being addressed stands out more clearly in this letter than in any of the others which follow.

The words of praise (verses 2-3) lay stress upon great vigorous Christian virtues which evidently have been exercised under difficult conditions, and possibly even under the pressure of opposition and persecution. Ephesus stands out as a flourishing Christian church, full of strength and the power of resistance. Its conscience was tender and its Christian power of judgment strong. It is also plain under what pressure these virtues have been preserved: false prophets have threatened the life of the church.

The later letters of the New Testament already reflect the heavy burden imposed upon the growing church by the infiltration of false doctrines, which were propagated by false prophets. At a time in the history of the church when everything depended upon the guidance of the Spirit, and the security of ecclesiastical organization was scarcely visible, this must have been a very heavy burden. There is a good deal of evidence for this.[8] In the case of Ephesus we can only surmise what form the false doctrine took in actual detail, for, although the "evil men" whom this church had so firmly resisted are even mentioned by name, the situation is still not clear.[9] We do not know who these "Nicolaitans" were. The references to them in the writings of the early church are so few that they do not amount to more than attempts to throw light upon

[8] I Thess. 5:20; I John 4:1; II Peter 2; Acts 11 and 12.

[9] Bousset, *op. cit.*, takes the view that this reference to the Nicolaitans is an allusion to some special occasion, and suggests a comparison with the letter of Ignatius to the Ephesians (IX:1). In any case, we may assume that the references in the first four "epistles" are to the same heresy or at least to the same type of "false apostles" who had begun to try to spread their "teaching" in the churches of Asia Minor. In Sardis they have just appeared; Ephesus seems to have almost got rid of them.

this passage.

But although we know very little about them in detail we learn enough to be able to see how a conscience enlightened by God ought to judge in a syncretistic atmosphere like that of Ephesus. Obviously the Nicolaitans represent a group of people who did not react sufficiently vigorously against the particular temptations for the religious life in Ephesus. The intellectual atmosphere of Ephesus—a religion of culture, tolerance, liberal ideas, conformity to the world, and the humanism which is always connected with these phenomena—was one single temptation: to fail to take seriously the truth of Jesus Christ as the only source of salvation.[10] However obscure the picture of the Nicolaitans is and remains in detail, the fact remains clear that in the realm of faith God has made a clear separation between flesh and spirit.

It is quite evident that such a danger needed to be met by clear thought and acuteness of mind. For from the allusions in the text before us we must assume that these heretical tendencies did not issue from the church itself, but had obviously crept into the church through itinerant Christian preachers. Hence redoubled watchfulness and clarity of spiritual and intellectual judgment were essential.

The fact that the church at Ephesus earned such high praise is due to the fact that it was very watchful and very shrewd. However, in spite of this, at this particular point it fell into the sin with which it is reproached. Our intellectual gifts become sinful if we use them in a human way and not in continual obedience to God. It is the danger which menaces all doctrinal controversies: they may lead not only to preservation, purification, and the strengthening of faith, but also to hardening and stagnation. When the struggle against false doctrine ends in that self-assertion which is "always in the right," the heavenly flower of all Christian conduct—love—is easily

[10] Bengel, *op. cit.*, aptly comments on this passage: "There is a certain purity and tenderness about truth."

lost.[11] But if that is lost, it is a proof that the relation with Christ has been weakened, or even severed. Then, inevitably, all Christian action becomes empty and sterile. The church at Ephesus knew the sacred boundary beyond which human tolerance must not go. But to abide by this line in a self-opinionated and self-righteous manner is just as disobedient as to go too far beyond it. In both instances the obedience which ought to follow nothing but the guidance of God, has been weakened and spoiled.

But if the life of faith has been injured at this decisive point, it is already on the slippery slope which leads to spiritual death. Where there was once a love of Christ as fresh as morning dew, there is now simply conventional Christianity. That is why such strong expressions of blame are used in verse five. The three stages of decline show plainly that unless the warning is heeded, the church will cease to expand, and it will then fade out of existence. The greatness and the seriousness of the apostolic method of training the churches in "a right judgment in all things" comes out very clearly here. Such spiritual severity was needed in order to prevent a conventional Christianity from developing into pious hypocrisy, which finally leads to stagnation and spiritual death. Times of trial reveal the seriousness which lies behind all life; under pressure there is no place for mediocrity. The great decisive spiritual conflict which the following chapters describe is intimately connected with the daily life of the struggling and confessing church.

The beginning of verse seven simply means here, and in the following letters: "He who can hear . . ." That is, not everyone can "hear." He must have the kind of "ear" to which hearing is granted. "Faith is the hearing of the soul" says one of the Fathers of the early church, and this is only given as a

[11] "Orthodoxy does not prevent one from becoming morally obsolete." (Volkmann)

"All work for others, if it is to be worth anything, must spring from love. But in the midst of work we often forget love." (Bengel)

gift from above (Prov. 20:12; Matt. 11:27; John 17:25ff, etc.). He who "can hear," however, must use this gift of hearing in order that he may not lose it again.

The promise (here and in the following letters) speaks of "overcoming" (or victory), and thus introduces a very significant element in the thought of the primitive church. The early church loved images which suggested the *Militia Christi*; from the time of St. Paul onwards and on into the subapostolic age there is a long series of images and ideas which gather round this word. This "victory" is a share in the victory of Jesus Christ. Since, however, this victory lies wholly in the light of the world beyond, here too the promise of victory has no connection with ordinary human views of what constitutes "victory" or "success." "Victory is achieved by death," says Bengel, significantly. Thus all the promises about "victory" point beyond this world to another, and this first one most decidedly of all. The greatest promise, which will be the last to be fulfilled (Rev. 22:14) stands first in the letters; for the tree of life is the sign of the restoration of Paradise. Finally, the divine order will be restored; the life which is God's actual gift to the world will once more be present, and the "victor" will have a share in this life.

The whole Apocalypse is the exposition of these sentences. The coming Lord will fulfil them.

Smyrna

(*Rev. 2:8-11*)

8 "And to the angel of the church in Smyrna write: 'The words of the first and the last, who died and came to life.

9 " 'I know your tribulation and your poverty (but you are rich) and the slander of those who say that they are Jews and are not, but are a synagogue of Satan. 10 Do not fear what you are about to suffer. Behold, the devil is about to throw some of you into prison, that you may be tested, and for ten days you will have tribulation.

> Be faithful unto death, and I will give you the crown of life. 11 He who has an ear, let him hear what the Spirit says to the churches. He who conquers shall not be hurt by the second death.'

The introductory words of the letter to Smyrna point clearly to the theme which dominates the following verses: life and death. From the outset, therefore, all that follows is seen in the light of the resurrection of Jesus Christ. And his church needs the certainty which flows from the radiant light of Easter, for this "prophecy" foretells a time of trial and testing which may issue in martyrdom. "How greatly this description of Christ strengthens a believer against death." [12]

The seer continues to follow the circle of the seven churches, since he follows the ancient road to the north, and then in a great sweep turns eastward, and finally comes back in a south-easterly direction to Laodicea.

Smyrna, which at the present stage of research is regarded as Homer's birthplace, had been from time immemorial an important center for trade, with a harbor which was much frequented. Under Roman rule Smyrna had been able to preserve its old position as a metropolis, and even to extend it. The Christian church there, of which we here receive the first information, seems to have been poor, although it was set in the midst of this wealthy city, with its flourishing trade, both at home and overseas. Its spiritual condition seems to reflect this situation to which John makes a distinct reference in the words of St. Paul: outwardly poor, but rich in God (II Cor. 8:9).

This spiritual law, which has been confirmed by many Christian generations, is a symbol of a yet deeper conception.

The outer life and the spiritual destiny of the church at Smyrna were closely related to the way of life followed by Jesus himself. Over it there broods the shadow of the cross

[12] Bengel, *op. cit.*

of Christ. It too lives in poverty in the sight of the world and has to bear persecution and death. But the most striking resemblance lies in the fact that the cross laid upon the church at Smyrna was caused by the Jews. After the fall of Jerusalem a large number of Jews had settled in this district. These Jews managed to "settle," with such success that they had acquired a position of real influence in the city. As so often from the days of Paul, and later on during the whole of the first and second centuries of the life of the Christian church, so here too the most violent and venomous attacks on the young Christian church were launched by the Jews. Since even imprisonment is mentioned (verse 10), the Jews at Smyrna seem to have stirred up a public persecution, with which they co-operated. According to an old account (*Mart. Pol.* XII:2) the hatred of the Jews appears to have gone so far in the case of Smyrna that, forgetting the basic principles of their faith, they seem to have made common cause with the adherents of emperor worship and in the public riots which ensued they too shouted "Our gods are threatened!" So far did the Jews of Smyrna go in betrayal of the fundamental principles of their religion, and their special calling; all religion based upon man alone inevitably ends in the denial of God and his revelation. Finally they are unable to hear the voice of God; they can no longer recognize his step, even when, in the most marvelous way, he works his wonders before their eyes. The name of "Jew" (which was never used in contempt or derision in the New Testament) had sunk so low at Smyrna that it had become a "synagogue of Satan" (verse 9). This is a very severe expression, especially when we compare it with the phrase of the thirteenth verse about the "throne of Satan." By the very act of rejecting Christ this Jewish community which was so hostile to him was reduced to the level of the pagan world. It had lost everything which it had once possessed as heir of the covenant of the Old Testament, and it had been forced to abandon the leadership of the spiritual Israel in favor of the church of Christ. This distinction between the true and the false Israel, which Paul already saw (Rom. 9:6) is essential to the thought of the Apocalypse.

Thus the whole of this epistle is simply a preparation for martyrdom. This circumstance gives it a special aura of consecration. There is no word of blame in it. The whole letter is filled with the conviction that there is no more effective witness to the purpose of God for the world than the fact that his servants openly confess Christ by taking his cross and passion upon themselves, even unto death, and still do not cease to love. Thus Smyrna became the vehicle of the most profound message that God has to give to the world. Christians of every age may well praise their exalted Lord for the fact that he has permitted others to follow the steps of the church at Smyrna—men and women who have carried this message to the world with the same fidelity and passionate conviction.

This letter suggests that this church will only have to go through a short and sharp period of persecution and testing; we may guess that this is the meaning of the expression "ten days." Thus this church may have the comforting certainty that the days of suffering of the saints are counted, and that God controls their extent. In the following sentences it is clearly indicated that one of their number will have to suffer martyrdom. We know that this prophecy was fulfilled in a most striking way, by the Bishop of Smyrna, Polycarp, who died a martyr's death on the twenty-third of February, A.D. 155. The record of the death of this blessed witness to Jesus Christ was written immediately after it happened, and the account agrees in many striking details with the references in this section. So these few lines illuminate the history of the church with a peculiar radiance—a light which often shines out of this tenth verse on some person at a special "hour" in his life, as for instance on the day of his Confirmation.

The promise of victory already resounds at the close of the tenth verse, although the actual promise is only formulated at the end of the eleventh verse. The "crown of life" was a picture which was immediately understood by the people of Smyrna, because it reminded them of the annual games and races which took place in their city. The eternal prize which the exalted Lord offers goes further than all honors that this world can give, and so often refuses to give to the Christian church. Bengel asks, "What is this compared with the worthless honours the world can offer!" He adds, however, "The promises of Christ are great; but there must be people who are able to receive them."

The last great promise that the victor shall not be affected by the second death, goes once more, far beyond the boundaries of time and space: our real destiny will be fulfilled beyond this life. According to rabbinical views the second death was everlasting damnation on the day of the final judgment. But the victor does not need to fear this day. "As one is at death, so he remains"; for one who dies following the way of the Prince of Life martyrdom leads to eternal life. For people who were daily confronted by bitter persecution, and who were aware of the final fate of the world at the day of judgment, this promise was a great consolation.

NOTES

Verse 10 is an obvious play on the Lord's words in Matt. 10:28—one of the numerous instances where the Apocalypse mentions words of Jesus, even when they are not quoted literally.

The simile of the crown occurs also in I Cor. 9:25; James 1:12; II Tim. 2:5, 4:8; I Pet. 5:4.

Pergamum

(*Rev. 2:12-17*)

12 "And to the angel of the church in Pergamum write: 'The words of him who has the sharp two-edged sword.

13 " 'I know where you dwell, where Satan's throne

> is; you hold fast my name and you did not deny my faith even in the days of Antipas my witness, my faithful one, who was killed among you, where Satan dwells. 14 But I have a few things against you: you have some there who hold the teaching of Balaam, who taught Balak to put a stumbling block before the sons of Israel, that they might eat food sacrificed to idols and practice immorality. 15 So you also have some who hold the teaching of the Nicolaitans. 16 Repent then. If not, I will come to you soon and war against them with the sword of my mouth. 17 He who has an ear, let him hear what the Spirit says to the churches. To him who conquers I will give some of the hidden manna, and I will give him a white stone, with a new name written on the stone which no one knows except him who receives it.'

Pergamum was the most impressive of the seven cities of Asia Minor with which we are here concerned. When the last king of the Attalian dynasty left his wealth and his kingdom to the Romans in 133 B.C., he added a jewel to the Roman possessions in Asia Minor. Pliny called it *Longe Clarissimum Asiae,* and the geographer Strabo called Pergamum a famous city which for a long time had shared in the prosperity of the country under the Attalian Kings. Here, after the death of Alexander the Great, one of his generals deposited an enormous treasure in the citadel; here too was one of the most valuable libraries of antiquity. The Romans respected this tradition and carried it further. Pergamum became the seat of the proconsul of the province of Asia, not his official residence at Ephesus; here as a rule the provincial assembly took place. Since 1878 a great deal of excavation has been carried on by German archeologists which has brought to light the splendor, exceeding all expectations, of a Hellenistic city.

Above all in Pergamum there was a flourishing religious life. The city possessed countless temples, which attracted an immense number of pagan pilgrims every year from the whole of Asia. The city was beautifully situated on the slopes of a steep hill, crowned by magnificent temples, among them the gigantic altar to Zeus of shimmering white marble against the blue sky—one of the seven wonders of the world. In the Acropolis of Pergamum was the temple to Athene. Finally, in the temple consecrated to "the divine Augustus and the goddess Roma" Pergamum possessed the central place of worship for the new cult of emperor worship in Asia Minor. This was indeed the first and oldest sanctuary of this kind, having already been consecrated in the year 29 B.C. From the very outset this cult had a large body of priests. The most celebrated sanctuary, however, and the one which was most constantly visited, was the shrine of Askelepios, the god of healing, which was said to work miracles and attracted more pilgrims than any other. It might indeed be described as the Lourdes of that day. This belief in its wonder-working powers may have been partly due to the spring of healing waters which it contained which—as well as a marble swimming bath —is still being used today. Here the city life of the baths of the ancient world, and its religion, seem to have formed a unique combination. Galen, too (b. 129 B.C.), the most famous physician of the ancient world, came from Pergamum and studied there at the *Askelepion.*

Since we cannot be quite sure which cult was most widely practiced in New Testament times—that of Askelepios or that of emperor worship, there must inevitably be some uncertainty in our exposition. But the very fact that the clash between the Hellenistic world with its various cults and the Christian faith was so sharp, was because here two cults, equally dear to those who practiced them—both of which enjoyed official and popular recognition—felt that they were being attacked. In any case the young church never came into sharper conflict with Hellenistic religion than at this place.

The whole of this letter therefore is influenced by this fact, as the introductory verse (twelve) shows: Jesus Christ wields the sharp sword of the Word of God, and in so doing he makes any religious compromise impossible. The words at the opening of the main section are particularly significant: "I know where you dwell." Nowhere else in these letters is the double significance of this phrase so plain; it is the language both of judgment and of mercy. This majestic "I know!" covers the whole of Pergamum, its countless shrines and temples and all the splendor of its city life.

The Christian church in Pergamum also sees, behind the brilliant external picture, the place where the first martyr from their community met his death. For the first time the term "martyr" is used. The fact that the name of this one martyr, Antipas, is known to them all, suggests that his death occurred at a very early stage in the clash between the world and the church. Obviously there were no other martyrs at that time. No premeditated persecution, decreed by the Roman authorities had yet taken place—Antipas must have been the victim of a sudden outbreak of popular hatred and fury, possibly caused by some offence to their religious susceptibilities, whether by Antipas himself, or by the church as a body.

The worldly and yet superstitious religious world of Pergamum deserves the name which was given to this city: the "Throne of Satan." Commentators have given many different interpretations of this phrase; it certainly must mean the world of Hellenistic thought and religion which was so brilliantly displayed in Pergamum. Deissmann has suggested that this wording is due to the towering pagan sanctuaries which dominated the city. But the most probable interpretation seems to be that the expression "throne" is used to cover the whole space occupied by pagan cults. This significant expression is also derived from the political sphere. Symbols taken from the political cult to describe the appearance of *Christus Imperator* (Rev. 1:12ff), and later on the homage before the heavenly throne, in Revelation 4, suggest that the sharp clash with the earthly cult of the "ruler" has a very exact meaning here: the whole of Pergamum, as the site of famous cults, above all as the seat of emperor worship, was a "Throne of Satan."

With the closing words ". . . where Satan dwells," the verse returns harmoniously to the beginning of the section and rounds it off, as Lohmeyer expresses it, as though it were a kind of epitaph.[13]

The fourteenth verse, with which the blame begins, seems once more to confirm the fact that the opposition to the whole atmosphere of religious practice and thought is intended; it does not refer to one cult alone. For with the mention of Balaam (Num. 31:16 and 25:1ff) the tendency to pagan life and pagan piety is meant, that is, syncretism, which always leads to an accommodation to pagan ways of life. In point of fact, Pergamum presented very vividly an extraordinary picture of the variety of pagan cults. The natural desire for religion was doubtless met more easily by the varied Hellenistic cults with their elements of humanism, vitality, and a deep longing for beauty, than the great austere religion of revelation. The fascinating impression of political power, reflected in the religious sphere in emperor worship, was more satisfying to the mind of the natural man than the idea of the sovereignty of God.

The difficult problem which faced the young Christian church was this: in the civilized world of that day, how far was it possible to "exist" at all, since at such a vital point as "belief" it could not under any circumstances co-operate with it? The effort to cope with this problem must have led many Christians into a mistaken "tolerance" of paganism. People do not like to be thought "intolerant"; to an educated person it is always a temptation to be regarded as "understanding." "But when we think we are winning the people of

[13] Lohmeyer, *op. cit.*

the world, Christianity itself may be lost in the attempt."[14]

The gravity with which this letter speaks of this lax "tolerance" has a permanent impressiveness and significance. As the tendency to compromise is of the essence of false prophecy, so unhesitating obedience belongs to the truth of following Christ. There are limits to "tolerance"; especially when religious conflict is acute, these limits can only be ignored at the price of losing eternal salvation.

Hence here too (verse 16) the warning is so unusually severe. The sharp sword in the mouth of the exalted Lord, the Word of God, proves its clarifying, divisive, and judging power. Here with a slight sense of horror we realize the extent to which the earliest Christians had to oppose so sharply the culture and beauty of the ancient world in the midst of which they were set. But the person who forms his judgments on aesthetic grounds at the present day forgets that the ancient monuments of superb beauty which today still adorn our museums were then the living expression of pagan beliefs, and that no pagan venerated them primarily for their aesthetic value. Even aesthetic dreams fade before the judgment of the holy Lord.

The Christian church at Pergamum, even when surrounded by the highest earthly beauty, could not ignore the fact that here faith was opposed by faith, doctrine by doctrine, spirit by spirit, in an irreconcilable conflict. It knew that it was confronted by a decision which the aesthete never understands, for he does not perceive that the world is a battlefield in which a tremendous spiritual conflict is being waged. But for those who, by faith, understand the nature of this conflict, one thing alone is possible: to follow the Lord in his temptation, when Satan showed him all the kingdoms of the world and the glory of them (Matt. 4:8ff). And like his Lord, for the Christian there is only one way of holding on steadfastly under the temptation to false belief, or the attacks of

[14] Bengel, *op. cit.*

demonic powers, without becoming confused and with undaunted courage—the sword of the Word of God. If he does not take this and use it in his struggle, there will come a time when the Lord himself will use it against him.

The reference to victory (verse 17) brings with it a beautiful promise, freshly expressed by the seer. The Jewish tradition (II Macc. 2:4-8) expected that in the last days the celestial bread of the desert period—the manna—would again become the food of the people of God. John takes up this expectation and reshapes it in New Testament terms. The victor will receive "the bread of life"; this promise too contains an echo of the thought of the Fourth Gospel (chapter 6). It is placed alongside the other expectation, that in the last days God will refresh his people with the "water of life" (Rev. 7:17; 21:6; 22:17).

The "white stone" recalls the athletic contests of the ancient world. The custom was that the *agonothetes,* the man who was in charge of the games, distributed to the winners, as a sign of victory, smooth white stones or pebbles on which their names were incised (white is the color of victory); when they went home with these "white stones," everyone could see that they were winners in the contests. This heavenly honor the Lord bestows on him who gains the victory; his name is written down, and in glory, when all anonymity will be over, it will be openly proclaimed.

There is a quiet allusion to grace in this comparison. When the name of the victor is proclaimed the athlete is declared to have won. "The names which are created in heaven are never empty, but they are all accompanied by reality." [15] Hence this picture means no less than this: There will come a time when the victor will actually *see* what he could only *believe* while he was here. The form in which the Apocalypse proclaims the justification of the sinner is this: Only those who have depended wholly on God's grace are "justified."

[15] Bengel, *op. cit.*

This is what the "new name" means. It is an impressive image; the old nature is completely eliminated and is replaced by the "new name," that is, the name of Jesus Christ. In the end, the complete victory of Christ will be his own victory too. A vivid, impressive picture of the certainly of eternal victory in the midst of all the sorrow and suffering of the present day—consolation and stimulus at the same time!

NOTE

In verse 17 the hidden manna is mentioned, because according to ancient Jewish views the heavenly food which until then has been hidden will again become visible, just as the new name too will become known "at the end of the days."

Thyatira

(*Rev. 2:18-29*)

18 "And to the angel of the church in Thyatira write: 'The words of the Son of God, who has eyes like a flame of fire, and whose feet are like burnished bronze.

19 " 'I know your works, your love and faith and service and patient endurance, and that your latter works exceed the first. 20 But I have this against you, that you tolerate the woman Jezebel, who calls herself a prophetess and is teaching and beguiling my servants to practice immorality and to eat food sacrificed to idols. 21 I gave her time to repent, but she refuses to repent of her immorality. 22 Behold, I will throw her on a sick-bed, and those who commit adultery with her I will throw into great tribulation, unless they repent of her doings; 23 and I will strike her children dead. And all the churches shall know that I am he who searches mind and heart, and I will give to each of you as your works deserve. 24 But to the rest of you in Thyatira, who do not hold this teaching, who have not learned what some call the deep things of Satan, to you I say, I do not lay upon you any other burden; 25 only hold fast what you have, until I come. 26 He who conquers and who keeps my works until the end, I will give him power over the

> nations, 27 and he shall rule them with a rod of iron, as when earthen pots are broken in pieces, even as I myself have received power from my Father; 28 and I will give him the morning star. 29 He who has an ear, let him hear what the Spirit says to the churches.'

Thyatira receives the longest exhortation of all the seven churches, although it is the least important of them. At Pergamum the post road which connected the seven churches with one another, turned in a south-easterly direction, and then reached the Lydian commercial city of Thyatira, of which we know little (save that it was noted for its trade in dyeing, and the manufacture of woolen goods, and especially for the trade in "purple"). But on the whole it was not an important place. Possibly the expression Pliny uses, who calls it a "dishonorable commune" suggests that its reputation was not very good. Even in church history Thyatira does not play an outstanding part; apart from this passage we know nothing about the church there, either its origin or its later history. The Alogi, a sect of the second Christian century which rejected the Apocalypse, even went so far as to say that there was no Christian church there at all; this was their main argument against the prophetic gifts of the seer. But the special respect which breathes through the long address to the church there is a proof that the standards of the exalted Lord for what is important and unimportant are very different from those which the world regards as important or not.

It seems, however, that from the religious point of view the danger that menaced the church there was that it might *become* a "dishonorable" community. Lot did not live in Sodom without being affected by it, and a great deal of "openness" to the world is only the preliminary stage in a decline of faith and morals. That is why the exalted Lord here stands forth with the strongest self-designation, which we find in the letters; here alone in the Apocalypse is Jesus called by the messianic title "Son of God." This is connected with the mighty vision at the beginning of the book: flaming eyes, which nothing can escape, feet of shining brass which stride over all opposing obstacles.

On the other hand, the spirit of the gospel comes out in this passage in the fact that the city of which we know least receives the highest praise. Its real spirit of love, its fidelity to Christ, its readiness to serve the brethren, and its courage in resisting pagan influences are signs of a really flourishing condition, and testimony is borne to the genuine living growth of its Christian character. It is indeed shattering, after all this appreciation, to see that even where spiritual growth was so evident, this church was threatened by the kind of danger to which the following verses refer!

It is not easy to discover the actual nature of this danger. It seems to be connected with the figure of a woman who claimed to have prophetic gifts. Probably "Jezebel" is a merely symbolical name, chosen deliberately in order to recall the story of the queen in the Old Testament (I Kings 16:31). Similarly, the mention of "adultery" must certainly be taken in the symbolical sense familiar from the days of Hosea onward, that is, "adultery" here means falling away from God, with a tendency to yield to heathen influences. It is of course a well-known fact that many heresies have been connected with erotic influences. We may perhaps assume that through this woman and the movement which she had started the same great danger was appearing in Thyatira which had already been mentioned in the letter to Ephesus.

It is possible that this was one of the early stages of the movement—the first great heresy—which was to sweep the church in the second century: Gnosticism. From verse twenty-four we can take it that this group was already firmly entrenched; Paul also alludes to such tendencies in the first epistle to the Corinthians (2:1). There were people in the church who boasted that they had a special gift of the Spirit by means of which they could fathom the "depths of God." The seer here confronts them harshly with a sarcastic reversal of their main slogan. They think that they have had a profound insight into the Spirit of God; but actually the influence was that of Satan; at the most, all that they have done is to gain an insight into "the depths of Satan" (verse 24). In contrast to the two other churches which have been mentioned, the great danger here consists in the fact that the false doctrine had already gained a footing within the church itself.

To throw a kind of religious glamor over a life which is fundamentally disobedient, both in doctrine and in ethics, is the worst kind of error. Anyone who knows anything about psychology and the spiritual life is aware that there is always a danger that religious and erotic elements may form a dangerous liaison; the choice of the term "adultery" for this pagan outlook is no accident. A church which gives way at this point has lost its authority just as much as a man who in the interest of his supposed religious genius goes beyond the borders of discipline and sobriety.

Spiritual discipline alone can preserve a church from falling into these false ways, of which there are only too many examples in the sphere of church history. This prophetess and her adherents come under the judgment of God. Where the Lord with the flaming eyes is at work, and he strides forward on his feet of burnished brass which shine like gold, there is an end to such disobedience. The Lord "who knoweth man's heart" (Ps. 7:10) also sees the secret stirrings of such arrogant, mistaken piety. For the church it is particularly true that "God is not mocked." Certainly the phrase "I gave her time" is still a silent promise. For the "time" itself without words is often "a real sermon on repentance for the sinner." [16]

The gospel spirit in this message comes out in the fact that immediately after the stern words of judgment and the call to repentance, and announced with the same urgency, the Lord

[16] Bengel, *op. cit.*

exhorts the faithful "remnant" of the church to "hold fast what you have" (verse 25).

The words "I do not lay upon you any other burden" certainly reminds us of the words of the Lord (Matt. 11:30) about his "easy yoke" and his "light burden." If the church holds firmly to the truth of Christ, no other burden of a legalistic kind will be imposed (Acts 15:28). In the present as in the past, the grace of God is with this church. "God makes a gracious distinction." [17]

Finally, the promise of victory is equally urgent (verses 26-28). It is the only passage in the letter where the expression "victor" is more closely defined by a relative clause. This sentence is a genuine Johannine turn of speech, for it is concerned with keeping God's commandments and "doing" his work (John 8:41).

The promise itself is developed along two lines. First of all, it has a visible meaning which is related to this world and also points forward to a fulfilment in the world beyond. The authority over the heathen, originally an apocalyptic promise, has here a deeper spiritual sense. It signifies the great missionary service of the church in the world. But this promise will only be fulfilled if the temptation which now threatens Thyatira is resisted. Where discipline, sobriety, and obedience are at a low ebb, authority disappears. Not only the history of every church, but also that of every Christian disciple, proves how strictly this rule must be applied.

But this promise extends far beyond fulfilment on this side of eternity. The morning star is Venus; even among the pagans this star was the symbol of world dominion. The whole letter to Thyatira is permeated with echoes from the second Psalm, the prophecy of messianic dominion. In the preceding verses the light of this hope only appeared now and then; now it shines out in full radiance. Jesus Christ, the heavenly ruler of the world, now brings in the new day for the

[17] *Ibid.*

world of nations, and the victor will have a share in this new order, in the purer and clearer world of God. The Lord gives him "the dawn of the eternal clearness, of the exceeding brightness of eternity, as a reward for the fact that he fled from the works of darkness and the shades of night. Jesus calls himself the bright and morning star. When he sheds his light upon a soul, he is giving himself to him. For one upon whom this light shines, it is always morning and never evening."[18]

NOTE

From this point till the end of the letters the promise of victory always precedes the phrase: "He who has an ear, let him hear . . ."; probably for reasons of linguistic rhythm.

Sardis

(*Rev. 3:1-6*)

1 "And to the angel of the church in Sardis write: 'The words of him who has the seven spirits of God and the seven stars.

" 'I know your works; you have the name of being alive, and you are dead. 2 Awake, and strengthen what remains and is on the point of death, for I have not found your works perfect in the sight of my God. 3 Remember then what you received and heard; keep that, and repent. If you will not awake, I will come like a thief, and you will not know at what hour I will come upon you. 4 Yet you have still a few names in Sardis, people who have not soiled their garments; and they shall walk with me in white, for they are worthy. 5 He who conquers shall be clad thus in white garments, and I will not blot his name out of the book of life; I will confess his name before my Father and before his angels. 6 He who has an ear, let him hear what the Spirit says to the churches.'

The road which connects the seven churches now turns southwards. After the generous words of praise lavished upon

[18] *Ibid.*

the church at Thyatira—in spite of the stern call to repentance—there comes a letter which does not contain a word of praise. Sardis, once the famous capital of Lydia, and famed throughout the ancient world as the home of Croesus of great wealth, had long fallen into a state of insignificance. Sardis only *seemed* to be alive; in reality it was living on a dead past. It carried on an insignificant existence as a place of exchange for woolen goods from the East; perhaps this accounts for the picture of the white garments (verse 5).

The state of the church corresponded to the external state of the city. It too seemed to be sinking into decay. Here we hear of it for the first time. Later on there was a learned bishop, Melito of Sardis, who kept the name of Sardis alive, but Ignatius does not mention this place in his letters to the churches in Asia Minor.

Thus we already see the spiritual destiny of this church. It represents a piety which is declining, whose strength is slowly ebbing away. It is evident that the exhortation is meant to express this through a clever play on words. Perhaps the bishop of this church bore the name of Zosimus, which recalls the Greek word for "life": "Zosimus! your name means 'Thou livest'; but thou art dead." "This is a terrible saying, which is only tolerable because it is said while there is still some life left." [19] Bengel, who first of all drew our attention to the connection with the name adds, "The little saying contains much that is painful." [20]

But of course this exhortation is addressed to the church.

The short vigorous phrases of the opening section sound like echoing cries to awaken someone from sleep. Serious as the words of command are in the second verse, they do contain a ray of gospel light. For if we are told to "wake up," death has not yet the last word. And so long as the Lord gives us a mission, he gives us the strength to do it. As Bengel says,

[19] Hermann Bezzel, *Die Offenbarung Johannis.*

[20] Bengel, *op. cit.*

"When the Lord Jesus commands us to do something, this command carries with it the strength to do it, just as it did when He told a cripple to stand up and walk, or a blind man to see." [21]

The exhortation is twofold, and includes both retrospect and warning: "Remember then what you received and heard." This verse recalls plainly, for instance, John 1:12; "receive and hear" are typical Johannine expressions for the approach to faith. Repentance begins with the fact that we remember our beginning. There is nothing so humbling or so strengthening as the fact of returning to the beginning set by God, when faith began. It is the exact opposite of a "historizing" piety, a rigid orthodoxy, and a worldly ecclesiastical conservatism. It is not the memories of church history which keep the faith and love of the church alive, but rather the recollection of "what God has done for me." Against this background the summons to keep the commandments has meaning, and the call to repentance is a promise.

At this point, in the middle of the third verse, it looks as though we ought to insert the verse from Rev. 16:15, which seems out of place there; while here it fits in well.[22] This intensifies the call to repentance.

The Lord comes like a thief in the night, that is, secretly, suddenly, unexpectedly. This figure of speech is wholly eschatological: when night falls over the world, the hour of Jesus Christ comes nearer. From the human point of view we only know that it is night; but at any moment his coming may shine out of the darkness. Time becomes transparent.

In a remarkably urgent and yet moving way, which makes us ashamed, the church is reminded that even in the stagnation of Sardis there are still some whose spiritual life has remained fresh and watchful. The praise bestowed by the Lord upon

[21] *Ibid.*

[22] In his modern German translation, the author has verse 3b read: "If you do not awake, I will come like a thief; you will never know at what hour I will come upon you." (Translator's note.)

them is a hidden warning to the others to return to the point which their more faithful brethren have never abandoned.

So the promise of victory already begins in the second half of the fourth verse, in order to be completed in the next one. Both images refer to the world beyond. White garments are signs of victory, and indeed of future victory, and the names of those who have overcome are written in heaven. In a solemn hour the exalted Lord himself will fulfil the promise which he once gave to the circle of his disciples on earth (Matt. 10:32), a promise which now applies to all the disciples of Christ. In an impressive scene in Dostoevsky's writings it is said of those who have been thus rejected that "God Himself had forgotten them." Here we have the exact opposite: the glowing assurance given to those whom the eternal Lord will never forget, unto all eternity.

NOTES

Revelation 16:15 will only become intelligible when we know that it presupposes the ancient custom of sleeping without any clothes on. In the traditional sense to be "naked" means to be laid bare to the judgment of God.

In the ancient world many things were written down upon tablets of wax, so that what was written could more easily be removed. In the "book of life" (verse 5) the names of the victors were written in indelible ink.

Philadelphia

(*Rev. 3:7-13*)

7 "And to the angel of the church in Philadelphia write: 'The words of the holy one, the true one, who has the key of David, who opens and no one shall shut, who shuts and no one opens.

8 " 'I know your works. Behold, I have set before you an open door, which no one is able to shut; I know that you have but little power, and yet you have kept my word and have not denied my name. 9 Behold, I will make those of the synagogue of Satan who say that they are Jews and are not, but lie—behold, I will make them

> come and bow down before your feet, and learn that I have loved you. 10 Because you have kept my word of patient endurance, I will keep you from the hour of trial which is coming on the whole world, to try those who dwell upon the earth. 11 I am coming soon; hold fast what you have, so that no one may seize your crown. 12 He who conquers, I will make him a pillar in the temple of my God; never shall he go out of it, and I will write on him the name of my God, and the name of the city of my God, the New Jerusalem which comes down from my God out of heaven, and my own new name. 13 He who has an ear, let him hear what the Spirit says to the churches.'

One of the outstanding literary characteristics of the Apocalypse is the fact that all its impressions and truths are intensified the nearer the end approaches. This is true of every series of seven, even of the letters to the seven churches. The highest praise and the severest blame come at the end of the series.

The letter to the church at Philadelphia has always been regarded as one of the most encouraging and consoling parts of the Apocalypse. We cannot conceive how many generations of Christians have drawn comfort and strength from this passage. As the massive walls of ancient cathedrals within which praise and prayer have been offered to God in worship become mellowed with a wonderful beauty which age alone can give, so this passage shines with a quiet light, distilled from the experience of many Christian generations who in the midst of distress and tribulation have been upheld by these words.

In their individual form also the last two letters are the freest in style, and yet, as a whole, the most condensed.

The exhortation to Philadelphia breathes a spirit of pastoral tenderness which does not lessen the majesty of mercy or of promise. This becomes very evident in the echoes from the

Old Testament, which are here far more important than in the previous letters, and light up the fundamental spiritual character of this letter in an unmistakable way. Here we breathe the air of the Old Testament passages about the "Servant of the Lord," especially that of Isaiah 53; and just as in the letter to Smyrna, the parallel with the way of the cross of Jesus himself stands out clearly. The church at Philadelphia receives the warmest praise and the tenderest pastoral counsels. Perhaps this church is so carefully and kindly treated because among all these churches its lot was the hardest to bear. And this too is the way of the exalted Lord, as it was the way of Jesus in his life on earth.

The outward picture of the church makes us immediately aware of a significant contrast. Among the seven cities, Philadelphia was probably the youngest, and in a certain sense also the least important. We hear of it after it had been founded by Attalus II of Pergamum (*circa* 138 B.C.) who also bore the name of Philadelphos. It was frequently shaken by earthquakes, and often needed relief from the state to meet the distress caused by them. This early Christian church, here praised so highly, was as flourishing as ever fifty years later when Ignatius wrote to it. Eleven of its members died a martyr's death, along with Polycarp of Smyrna (*Mart. Polyk.* XIX). Its "first love" never faded (Rev. 2:4).

The hostility which caused this church so much suffering was not due to its relation to the state in its public capacity. Here, just as in the earthly life of Jesus, the Jews were its bitterest enemies. The expression in verse eight shows quite clearly that this was the background of the life of this community. It is difficult to estimate which conflict was more difficult or more bloody for the early Christians—the struggle against emperor worship and the growing conflict with the Hellenistic world of their environment, or the severance from Judaism. In the early years of Christendom it cannot be denied that it was the Jews who struck the heaviest blows at the nascent church. During those years, the conflict with those whose religious heritage they shared, must have been harder for the Christians to bear than the struggle against emperor worship. But in any case, it was the struggle of the true faith against a false one.

Consciously or unconsciously therefore the Old Testament influence becomes evident. In the introit the exalted Lord speaks in phrases in which messianic dignity and royal claims are combined. "The Holy One of God" (John 6:69), Jesus allowed himself to be called in his days on earth when he asserted his full messianic claim over against the Jews. The image of the power of the keys surely comes from Isaiah 22, from the court of the King of Israel, and implies the royal authority whose official insignia consisted in a special circlet on the brow ("crown") and the key of the royal house.

In virtue of this royal authority and the heavenly "power of the keys," the Lord has opened the door. In virtue of the same authority he prevents any hostile power from closing it again. This means the plans and possibilities of God with humanity are greater than the resistance of his enemies. Even under the obvious limitations of the missionary possibilities of this church, which is expressed in the phrase, "you have but little power" (verse 8), God's commission remains great and undiminished. If he gives a commission, then he can give the power to fulfil it.[23] Believing in this heavenly authority the church at Philadelphia has held on in utter fidelity, as a shining example to her sister churches.

But the "power of the keys" of the heavenly Lord extends

[23] Bengel, *op. cit.* "No enemy can hold up the progress of the work of Jesus and his servants; nor can any well-meaning person either, who now and again wants to go in another direction than that which God wills. . . . Where Jesus allows hindrances to prevail, no one can remove them; and where he creates an opening for good, no secular power can prevent it. Others often say: 'There is nothing to be done—let things be—you won't gain anything! and people will only laugh at you!' Then we must stand firm. Each of us, however small may be our post, must stick to it manfully, and not allow ourselves to be frightened away. Often all we can do is to protest; but even that we must not omit, until the right times comes, to come through the difficulty."

far beyond this world of time. At the end of all history and of all missionary history, he will open the door to those who have been faithful. The word "door," which oscillates with an unexpressed double meaning, expresses that transparence in which all that is earthly lets through the light of the eternal world.

The enemies are the Jews. Here too it becomes evident that their historical religious privileges have passed to the new Israel, the new "people of God." The Jews are no longer the "people of God" but only a "synagogue of Satan" (Rev. 2:9; 3:9). But apart from this short and sharp observation, no further attention is paid to the enemies of the church. The Lord remains the One who acts. "Behold, I give . . ."—even this enmity has its place in God's plan; it too stands under the mighty power, overshadowing all that is of this transitory world, implied in the words, "I come quickly." This End is not pitiable and mean, it is not a goal which is reached with much toil and trouble after a conflict which seemed almost hopeless, but it is the expression of the divine majesty. The expectation which Israel once had, and which its apostate sons still cherished—namely, that one day the nations of the earth would pay homage to Israel—now comes out in majestic inversion against Israel itself.

The Israel which has fallen away, which is now the persecutor of the church of God, will one day come and pay homage to the spiritual "people of God," the church of Christ which Israel now persecutes. The most beautiful promise which was once given to the Servant of the Lord (Isa. 43:4) is fulfilled in the spiritual Israel: "I have loved thee." There is a magnificent New Testament fulfilment of this promise. It will not fulfil the rigid nationalistic dreams of ancient Judaism, but it does fulfil them in the New Testament sense, with all the fulness and breadth of the gospel: even the enemies of God will at last bow in homage before the true people of God, because inwardly they have been conquered.

This not because of any claim that the church makes, but simply because this people of God communicates the word of life. The exalted Lord, who has the authority to fulfil the eternal saving plan of God without any depreciation, and against all human expectation, can bring it to completion in such a divinely ordered way that even God's enemies are inwardly conquered.[24] In this too this letter reflects the way of the Lord, and his mystery of the cross.

The next verse (10), with its great promise, is equally important. "An hour of trial" is at hand, probably a wave of persecution. This "trial" refers to the difficult time when the great final conflict between God and the world, which is to precede the return of the Lord, will take place. Already the shadows of the bloody conflict with the Roman Empire are gathering. But when the "hour of trial" comes, the Christians are to know that it is ordered by their Lord. Those who take the words of Jesus seriously will find that "the world will turn again and rend them." [25] But in the time of trial the high priestly prayer of Jesus will be fulfilled that his disciples will not be taken out of the world but that they will be preserved from the evil. "As we deal with the Word of God so also God deals with us." Thus obviously the church at Philadelphia is being promised no less than that the coming distress will no longer touch it. It is already so deeply rooted in God that in the storm of history it will experience his "keeping" power. On the same passage Bengel says: "This may be a *salvus conductus*: Noah in his ark floated gently on the face of the waters when all the world round him were being drowned in the sea." [26]

This great promise is also behind the command which is addressed to the church, "Hold fast that which thou hast, that no one take thy crown." Even the wealth of praise and pas-

[24] Bengel, *op. cit.* "How often people's views change when the Lord looks at them!"
[25] *Ibid.*
[26] *Ibid.*

toral warmth in this letter is not without the seriousness of eternity; from the human point of view it is still possible for Philadelphia to fail. "A lifetime of faith will be of no advantage to you unless you prove perfect at the very last," says one of the earliest Christian writings.[27]

The promise of victory rises to a height of solemn greatness and beauty. The victor will be integrated into the heavenly Temple of God like a pillar which is firmly established, and carved out of marble. The image is drawn from the environment; it refers to a Hellenistic custom: the provincial chief priest of the cult of emperor worship, when his period of office was finished, set up in the temple courts a statue of himself with his own name and that of his father and his birthplace inscribed beneath it. Here again the earthly custom is contrasted with the action of the heavenly ruler, who himself, in eternity, where our names are written (Luke 10:20), sets up this statue of remembrance. The name of God is incised there, the name of the heavenly city, the new name of Christ, who one day at the end of all things will visibly manifest his glory before the whole world.

The letter to the church at Philadelphia emphasizes a truth which is essential for the understanding of the Apocalypse as a whole. The theology of the cross must not be treated in a one-sided way, but it needs to be continually enlarged by the expectation of the Lord's return. The way of the church through cross and weakness, humiliation and persecution is not the final way. Its aim will be fulfilled when God in his glory has attained his End. This is the great consolation of this most beautiful of all the letters to the seven churches, in its message which spans the centuries.

[27] *Didache* XVI:2. In the Furche edition, pp. 37, 79, the comment is made: "How great an impression this sentence made upon the early church is shown by the fact that it is frequently quoted."

Laodicea

(*Rev. 3:14-22*)

14 "And to the angel of the church in Laodicea write: 'The words of the Amen, the faithful and true witness, the beginning of God's creation.

15 " 'I know your works: you are neither cold nor hot. Would that you were cold or hot! 16 So, because you are lukewarm, and neither cold nor hot, I will spew you out of my mouth. 17 For you say, I am rich, I have prospered, and I need nothing; not knowing that you are wretched, pitiable, poor, blind, and naked. 18 Therefore I counsel you to buy from me gold refined by fire, that you may be rich, and white garments to clothe you and to keep the shame of your nakedness from being seen, and salve to anoint your eyes, that you may see. 19 Those whom I love, I reprove and chasten; so be zealous and repent. 20 Behold, I stand at the door and knock; if any one hears my voice and opens the door, I will come in to him and eat with him, and he with me. 21 He who conquers, I will grant him to sit with me on my throne, as I myself conquered and sat down with my Father on his throne. 22 He who has an ear, let him hear what the Spirit says to the churches.' "

The external setting of these churches comes out more clearly in this letter than in any of the preceding ones.

As the seer finishes his journey in imagination, round the circular route of the seven churches, he reaches the most south-easterly point at Laodicea, a Phrygian town on the Lycus, which was at the junction of several branches of the great trade road from Ephesus to the East. It was named after the wife of King Antiochus II, Laodice. It was destroyed at the same time as Colossae—in the year 60—but swiftly recovered. Its economic prosperity was due to its good situation; and its wealth was its main characteristic. It carried on a flourishing trade in linen and in wool and was also a center of banking operations; even Cicero recommended the banks of Laodicea. Finally, more recently a medical school had been opened which became famous throughout the Roman Empire for its medicinal preparations, and also rejoiced in the fame of the greatest medical man of antiquity, Galen, who came from Pergamum.

The Christian church in this remarkable neighborhood, calls for our special consideration because it is directly connected with the personal missionary activity of Paul, and the period of his three-year residence in Ephesus. From an allusion in the epistle to the Colossians (which was also intended for Laodicea, as stated in Col. 4:16) we may surmise that the church at Laodicea had been founded at that time by Paul's follower, Epaphras (Col. 4:12).

The difficult spiritual problem of this church consisted in the danger of becoming conformed to the surrounding environment.

In the history of the church this danger appears under different forms, but its underlying permanent element persists, and leads to the same result. The last difficult crisis of this kind took place towards the end of the nineteenth century, that is, when the Christian church seemed about to succumb to that attitude of bourgeois "security" characteristic of the age, when Kierkegaard began his great struggle against the "bourgeois" mentality in the church, and its compromise with the ideals of this world. Our letter shows how early the danger of worldliness and of compromise with a secular environment arose in church history.

In the light of this situation even the introduction to this severely-expressed letter has great significance. The exalted Lord here speaks of himself with one of the highest names of God in the Old Testament, one which God himself has chosen (Isa. 65:16). Later, this became one of the names of Christ (II Cor. 1:18ff); the phrase "faithful and true," is, at bottom, only a translation of this Hebrew name. Thus the one real standard is here contrasted with the increasing lack of principle in a church which is becoming increasingly conformed to the spirit of this world. Even the allusion to "the beginning of the creation of God" has its own significance; the exalted Lord is not *part* of creation, but its Lord. He is not a sector of the world in which we live, but he is its origin, and thus he is its LORD, in the strict sense of the word, which in all our dealings with the world we must never be prone to forget or overlook.

The description of the spiritual situation of the church is presented in a very concrete way, which is probably due to the geographical situation of Laodicea. The great geographer of the ancient world, Strabo, once described the hot carbonic spring at Hierapolis which rose in a pond and had enabled the city to become a brilliantly endowed spa, or "watering-place" to which people came to "take the waters." The water flows over a rocky ledge exactly opposite Laodicea, leaving behind it deposits of lime which turn into shining cascades of pure white stone; in its fall the river loses its heat, and the water becomes lukewarm. The words of blame (verses 15ff) remind us of this natural phenomenon, which was famous in the ancient world.[28]

The spiritual life in Laodicea is not like a clear draught of spring water, fresh from its source, but it is insipid, lukewarm water, which is so unpleasant that involuntarily one spits it out again. The inner life of the church in Laodicea is characterized by this miserable, despicable "mediocrity," in which no great ardent decisions are ever made. The prevailing temper is not the spiritual coldness of entire loss of faith, but still less is it the glowing fervor of a life with God. "Glowing" is one of the great words of early Christianity, above all of the Apocalypse. The truly Christian life should be illumined by a steady "glow"; without the glow of living faith and living expectancy of the End, all Christian life is only a matter of

[28] Cf. J. B. Lightfoot, *St. Paul's Epistles to the Colossians and to Philemon*, pp. 10ff. (Translator's note.)

tepid spiritual mediocrity.[29]

The terrible words of censure in verse sixteen are to some extent softened by the fact that at first they only threaten judgment; the reproach does not amount to a hard and fast statement about carrying it out. "The phrase, 'I will spew thee out . . .' moderates the language, and makes an *oratio categorica* into an *oratio modalis,* which still leaves some hope." [30]

These words of blame are so strong, and the force of the accusation is so urgent, that the next two verses sound like a lively conversation which is full of holy irony.

The church may say: "I am rich, I have prospered, I need nothing"; but the reality is the exact opposite. The inevitable result of spiritual complacency and self-satisfaction is the loss of all true self-knowledge. Self-sufficiency leads without exception to self-deception. When one who is living in spiritual self-deception comes to see the true state of his own life, he is being confronted by a final urgent appeal from the grace of God. This hidden grace, which is still seeking man, speaks through the verdict pronounced upon the spiritual state of the church: "wretched, pitiable, poor, blind, and naked!" (verse 17). Above all it comes out in the cutting irony of the following sentences.

These sentences are a sarcastic imitation of the commercial spirit which has invaded the church. "I counsel thee"—that is the way the cloth sellers and bankers of Laodicea often talked to their worldly Christian customers; "*I* counsel you" —in the opposite way, says the Lord. "You are thinking about the state of your possessions? Buy from me pure gold 'refined by fire.' You are choosing fine material for a new garment? Take the white robe of righteousness which will conceal your nakedness and unrighteousness. You are look-

[29] Edmond de Pressensé (d. 1891) says in his *Life of Jesus:* "The most dangerous Christian life is that of the 'Dead Sea,' over which no bird flies, on whose shores no flower blooms—lukewarmness."

[30] Bengel, *op. cit.*

ing for the best and most expensive eye salve you can find in the chemists' shops of Laodicea? Don't look at your own good appearance! Buy my eye salve, in order that at last your own eyes may be open to your own true state!"

There is a whole divine method of education in these sentences.

The fact that the Lord can speak so sternly to this church shows that all is not lost. This is the point of verse 19, which is a quotation from the Book of Proverbs (3:12), and also a reminder of the high aim of Heb. 12:10: "that we may be partakers of His holiness." The Lord's censure is always a token of his seeking love; only those for whom no one cares are lost. Therefore: "Repent of your lukewarmness and mediocrity! and come back to the Lord! with ardor and desire!"

The closing saying (verse 20) combines, in a very beautiful way, the Johannine language of the Fourth Gospel with the vivid pictorial language of the earlier Gospels. Here Jesus, the Coming One, is speaking. Not only the One who will return sometime, at the end of all things, but he whose coming takes place continually, who comes to us in everything that happens, even in blame, and stands at the door, and knocks. What a picture of urgent pleading! It speaks of the loving care of the Lord, which spans all the generations with his longing over his human family, whether they will listen to him or not! Behind it there is not only censure on a mediocre and imperfect present, not only the threat of a future judgment, but more pleading and urgent than all this is the promise of holy communion with God: the joy of the messianic banquet, the age-long image of man's full communion with God, awaits his people.

For it is not culture, or the pleasures of art and knowledge which will save us, but only the gospel; not the cleverness of the world, but the simplicity of the cross; not our astuteness, but the mercy of the Lord. The message of the gospel sounds powerfully in these words, in spite of their shattering severity.

For the church, as well as for the individual Christian, even if they have been sunk in spiritual sleep for years, there is still the possibility of awakening, and a return to unconditional obedience.

The promise of victory closes not only this letter but all the seven. Therefore it rings out here most clearly and powerfully. The victor in the eternal world will have a share in the dominion of the risen and exalted Lord. He who has conquered death and the powers of this world will guide us through all the dangers of this life, through heights and depths, and also through the deadly danger of mediocrity and spiritual sloth, to the eternal joy of victory.

NOTE

The phrase "the beginning of God's creation" (verse 14) reminds us in a remarkable way of Col. 1:15; Colossae and Laodicea were neighboring towns.

Chapter 7

The Sevenfold Prophecy

(Rev. 4:1—5:14)

THE ONE ON THE THRONE

(Rev. 4:1-11)

1 After this I looked, and lo, in heaven an open door! And the first voice, which I had heard speaking to me like a trumpet, said, "Come up hither, and I will show you what must take place after this." 2 At once I was in the Spirit, and lo, a throne stood in heaven, with one seated on the throne! 3 And he who sat there appeared like jasper and carnelian, and round the throne was a rainbow that looked like an emerald. 4 Round the throne were twenty-four thrones, and seated on the thrones were twenty-four elders, clad in white garments, with golden crowns upon their heads. 5 From the throne issue flashes of lightning, and voices and peals of thunder, and before the throne burn seven torches of fire, which are the seven spirits of God; 6 and before the throne there is as it were a sea of glass, like crystal.

And round the throne, on each side of the throne, are four living creatures, full of eyes in front and behind: 7 the first living creature like a lion, the second living creature like an ox, the third living creature with the face of a man, and the fourth living creature like a flying eagle. 8 And the four living creatures, each of them with six wings, are full of eyes all round and within, and day and night they never cease to sing,

"Holy, holy, holy, is the Lord God Almighty,
who was and is and is to come!"

9 And whenever the living creatures give glory and honor and thanks to him who is seated on the throne, who

lives for ever and ever, 10 the twenty-four elders fall down before him who is seated on the throne and worship him who lives for ever and ever; they cast their crowns before the throne, singing,

11 "Worthy art thou, our Lord and God,
to receive glory and honor and power,
for thou didst create all things,
and by thy will they existed and were created."

In his vision the seer is standing at the gate of the celestial palace. Suddenly, the door opens, and from within comes a voice, the same voice, "like a trumpet," which he had heard in his earlier vision, summoning him to come right up to the open door at the entrance to the palace. This mysterious summons symbolizes a sudden plunge into the heart of the Apocalypse. The actual vision now begins; the seer is called to the place where the heavenly vision is disclosed. At this point the sevenfold prophecy begins, which is developed in the following chapters.

The phrase, "after this I looked," always denotes an important section. The beginning of a new vision is always described with the words, "I looked." It might equally well be translated: "I had a vision." But when this simple expression is given in an expanded form, as it is here: "After this I looked, and lo . . . ," it means that this is a very important section, or a particularly important vision. In this instance too the seer makes it quite clear, when he says, "I was in the Spirit," that is, I fell into an ecstasy.[1]

Thus the introduction to the long series of visions which now begins is arranged in a very imposing manner. In comparison with the following scenes this one is particularly impressive and complete in itself. It contains several details which sound very strange to the modern reader who is not familiar with apocalyptic thought and language. But their significance is summed up pictorially in the radiant majestic center of the

[1] This fuller phrase occurs in Rev. 7:9; 15:5; 18:1; 19:1.

picture, which expresses the adoring vision of the Lord of the universe who is seated upon the throne. The first glimpse of the secrets of world history, as of eternity, is given here, which heaven will make quite plain and clear later on. Here the picture of the celestial throne room suggests the glowing radiance which streams through the open door of the celestial palace. Color and pictures, candelabra and peals of thunder, elders and heavenly beings gathered round the throne. All this is only the reflection which shines from the center of the picture, where the Lord of the universe whose name none dare utter, the All-Ruler is enthroned (verse 8).

Almost each individual feature of this vision has a significance derived from ancient religious symbolism; images drawn from the rich sources of apocalyptic, and above all from the prophetic visions of the Old Testament, echo and re-echo in these lines. But in a masterly way, the traditional images have been transformed into a new picture. The interest in fantastic detail, which was predominant in the earlier apocalypses, has disappeared. The wealth of color and pictorial detail is now only used as a way of trying to express the inexpressible. "The unseen background of world history is unveiled." [2]

We have no right therefore to destroy the meaning of this great vision by a pedestrian explanation of the details. The Lord of the universe is seated in majesty upon his throne in the midst of the sparkling radiance of precious stones: in the majestic whiteness of jasper, in the shimmering crimson of the carnelian, and in the radiant glow of the emerald, which ranges from a light blue aquamarine to a deep translucent green. There is no need to inquire into the origin of these illustrations; it is far more important to try to understand what they mean apart from all literary allusions. Thunder and lightning are the most powerful cosmic phenomena known to primitive man, and they still have a very powerful

[2] Beck, *op. cit.*

effect upon him. So the seer does not make a clumsy effort to describe the majesty of the Lord of the universe. The radiance of the divine glory which surrounds him, and the praises of the heavenly beings reflect his glory.

As the rainbow encircles the throne with its glowing colors, so there stand around the throne the *curia coelestis,* the members of the celestial court. The radiance of this picture is enhanced by the seven torches of fire which burn before the throne and are reflected in the "sea of glass, like crystal." "Like a sea," says the seer, and in so doing he denudes the image of all "representational" significance. The language he uses is not that of a rather clumsy eschatology which merely intensifies impressions of earthly things, but it suggests the "wholly other." When, later on, one of these "elders" gives an explanation to the seer, and is therefore addressed as "Sir," we see that here he is speaking of heavenly beings who surround the throne of the Lord of the universe, not the spirits of just men made perfect, but—angels.

Possibly here as elsewhere, the numbers mentioned are influenced by astrological ideas: for instance, the twenty-four hours of the day, which were also represented pictorially in the ancient world. If such influences have colored the picture in any way—this is not at all certain—then they are used wholly in order to serve the greater concern which here determines the meaning of the pictorial language.

In the other group which surrounds the throne, that of the four heavenly creatures, this astrological background comes out more clearly. There was an ancient notion, according to which the four groups of stars, Taurus, Leo and Scorpio (which were always thought of in a human way) and Aquila, supported the vault of heaven which, as we know, was regarded by the ancients as a kind of tent roof spread over the earth. This ancient imagery is used here. It does not matter whether this was done deliberately or not. The throne of God is upheld by more than the glory of the stars, that is, by heavenly beings.

Luther's translation, "*Tiere*" (beasts), is wrong. They are noble heavenly beings who offer eternal worship before the throne of heaven.

This first scene is full of a majestic radiance and a sublime repose. No echo of the dramatic events which the latter chapters will disclose penetrates into the solemn stillness of the heavenly throne room. One thing only is fitting in this sublime setting: the liturgy. The seer describes this heavenly worship in an unforgettable vision.

First of all, the four living creatures sing the *Sanctus* which the prophet Isaiah had already heard from the lips of the heavenly host (Isa. 6:3). Here this act of adoration is more fully developed and more richly articulated (in sub-sections three times three); the language is still more majestic ("the Lord God Almighty, who was and is and is to come"). This *Trisagion* has been absorbed into the liturgy of all Christian confessions, so that already a ray of future glory and unity falls upon the divided church.

After this song of praise, the celestial "elders" fall down in worship, and with the ancient gesture of oriental and late-Roman court ceremonial, they cast their crowns before the throne. Thus the celestial elders begin the song of praise to the Creator and Lord of the universe.

This song of praise is the key to the deeper understanding of this impressive introductory vision.

The attentive reader in the early church could be in no doubt that the majestic atmosphere of this vision was not accidental. For the first words of the hymn of the elders are derived literally from the political language of the day. *Vere dignus*—"worthy art Thou"—were the first words of the ritual, the solemn *acclamatio,* with which the emperor's entrance was greeted in triumphal processions. The formula "our Lord and God," as we learn from the imperial biographies of Suetonius, was introduced by Domitian into the cult of emperor worship as an expression of homage. First of all he arranged that his procurators should introduce the formula, "our Lord and God commands," into their official documents. After that it became the custom also to address him as *Deus ac Dominus noster*.[3]

Thus it is impossible to assert that the seer is here using liturgical language which is remote from life, and out of touch with the world of his own day. When we look back at this chapter from the standpoint of these unambiguous phrases, we can see still more features drawn from the cult of emperor worship. The "torches of fire" belong to it, as well as the precious stones, which were always symbols of political dominion. The representation of the seat of the throne also reminds us of the Hellenistic-Roman custom of paying homage to the empty throne of the emperor, and thus worshiping the present numen of the emperor, that is, his religious presence. The significance of even such small details, and the light they throw upon the political religion of the day, comes out in the fact that these gestures appear very early in the cult of emperor worship. Tacitus reports that the Persian King Tiridates approached the picture of Nero, took his royal diadem from his head and laid it at the feet of the portrait (*Ann.* XV:28).

Although the fact of conflict is clearly suggested in the majestic solemnity of this vision, there is also another conviction, namely, that this conflict is inevitable. This is the situation, as Luther puts it in his great document of the unfree will: "The world and its god cannot endure the word of the true God, and will not endure it; the true God cannot be silent and will not be silent—thus when these two gods come into conflict with one another, how can there be anything other than discord in the world?" [4]

[3] Bousset's contention that Domitian merely permitted this mode of address only in letters to himself, is not in correspondence with the facts; in later excavations a statue of Domitian has been found which was intended to be worshiped (at that time no other kind of memorials were erected), and it bears this deifying inscription upon it.

[4] *WA* 18, 526. Cf. also II Cor. 4:4.

The glory of the worldly power which opposes the true God is only a borrowed radiance. Behind it there is hidden none other than the "prince of this world." This, however, will only become plain in the course of the revelation.

Now however, in contrast to the Hellenistic-Roman custom, *this throne is not empty.* He who sits upon the throne, and reigns, is already known, even though out of reverence and awe his name is not uttered. So this first vision of the seer of the heavenly throne room is both a confession of faith and a mighty challenge. The fact that this pictorial imagery has been taken over at once empties it of all its power; its illegitimate use is ended, and the solemn words, "worthy art thou our Lord and our God," are severed from the false worship and offered to him to whom alone it belongs, and who is alone worthy to receive this name.

This is the true background of world history. The world does not know it; very often even the church is not aware of it, when it gives way to unbelief; but here the church is reassured in a very solemn yet comforting way, that "the Lord is King," and "there is none else."

An important feature of this chapter is that this conflict symbolism contains no traces of that stormy struggle which the later chapters of this book will describe. The whole point of this vision, described with such dignity, majesty, and calmness, is the absolute claim of the First Commandment. The seer's eyes are fixed so exclusively upon God—the Creator and Lord of the universe—that not even the figure of Jesus Christ appears at this point.

This is the beginning of the visions. It is not an overture, anticipating, with great artistic power, some of the great or terrible events which will usher in the last day; but it is a hymn of praise to the divine majesty. Whatever there will be to say about the trials of the last days, all is controlled by the call to "Look up and raise your heads" (Luke 21:28). *Sursum corda*—"Lift up your hearts!" Whatever there may be to say about the final hour of the course of world history, it is all seen in the clear calm light of faith in him who is the Creator and Lord of the world. The heavenly music proclaims that "God is in his temple." So when the terrible pictures which depict the horrors of the last days begin to be shown, the church is not to forget that behind and above all events the eternal Lord and Savior is on the throne. "We are to learn here what a great God we have, and humble ourselves before him with all our hearts." [5]

NOTES

The summons of the angel to the seer to come to the threshold of the gate of the heavenly palace holds good till Rev. 10:1; evidently until then he does not change his position. It is a fine picture: the obedient seer who receives God's instructions, waiting at the gate of the heavenly palace. It was thus that Dürer saw him—the essential example of an obedient messenger of the divine revelation about the last days.

The same colors as in verse three are also found in Grünewald's picture of the resurrection, in the halo around the head of Christ. Cf. also Ps. 104:2; I John 1:5.

The twenty-four elders (verse 4) must signify a full or complete number: the day has twenty-four hours, the alphabet twenty-four letters; there are twenty-four signs of the zodiac; in the Bible there were twenty-four classes of priests and twenty-four of the Levites; the chosen people numbered twelve tribes, and twelve apostles constitute the leaders of the church in the New Testament. All these numbers signify completeness; in the great hall of heaven no servant is absent whom the Lord has called.

The sea of glass (verse 6) recalls the "molten sea" in Solomon's temple (I Kings 7:23), which it excels. Other ancient conceptions may well be included here. Here all it means is the unimaginable purity and otherworldliness of the heavenly world.

The four living creatures (verse 6) have their counterpart in the Old Testament in Ezekiel 1:4-14. Irenaeus was the first to suggest that they represented the four Evangelists. St. Augustine adopted this comparison, although in another context than that with which we are familiar, and made it part of the heritage of the church. The Bible itself has no such conception.

[5] Bengel, *op. cit.*

THE LAMB

(*Rev. 5:1-14*)

1 And I saw in the right hand of him who was seated on the throne a scroll written within and on the back, sealed with seven seals; 2 and I saw a strong angel proclaiming with a loud voice, "Who is worthy to open the scroll and break its seals?" 3 And no one in heaven or on earth or under the earth was able to open the scroll or to look into it, 4 and I wept much that no one was found worthy to open the scroll or to look into it. 5 Then one of the elders said to me, "Weep not; lo, the Lion of the tribe of Judah, the Root of David, has conquered, so that he can open the scroll and its seven seals."

6 And between the throne and the four living creatures and among the elders, I saw a Lamb standing, as though it had been slain, with seven horns and with seven eyes, which are the seven spirits of God sent out into all the earth; 7 and he went and took the scroll from the right hand of him who was seated on the throne. 8 And when he had taken the scroll, the four living creatures and the twenty-four elders fell down before the Lamb, each holding a harp, and with golden bowls full of incense, which are the prayers of the saints; 9 and they sang a new song, saying,

"Worthy art thou to take the scroll and to open its
seals,
for thou wast slain and by thy blood didst ransom
men for God
from every tribe and tongue and people and nation,
10 and hast made them a kingdom and priests to our
God,
and they shall reign on earth."

11 Then I looked, and I heard around the throne and the living creatures and the elders the voice of many angels, numbering myriads of myriads and thousands of thousands, 12 saying with a loud voice, "Worthy is the Lamb who was slain, to receive power and wealth and wisdom and might and honor and glory and blessing!" 13 And

> I heard every creature in heaven and on earth and under the earth and in the sea, and all therein, saying, "To him who sits upon the throne and to the Lamb be blessing and honor and glory and might for ever and ever!" 14 And the four living creatures said, "Amen!" and the elders fell down and worshiped.

The heavenly worship continues. A still fuller liturgy is added to the first one. The development of the theme becomes still more vital, arising out of the profoundly moving dialogue between the seer and the angel or the elders. When the decisive act of the Lamb takes place, the threefold song of adoration of the celestial choirs breaks forth with still more power than in the previous chapter.

There are three acts in which the heavenly liturgy is fulfilled. First of all the antiphonal converse, in which the mighty angel, the seer and one of the elders take part (verses 1-5), then the climax of the ceremony, as the Lamb steps forth and opens the sealed roll of the book (verses 6-7), and finally, as the conclusion, the threefold song of adoration (verses 8-14).

The first verses sound like the preparation for an important political event, such as, the enthronement of a ruler. The "One who sitteth on the throne" holds a scroll in his hand. In the solemn court ceremonial the ruler used to hand over a sealed scroll to one of the court officials, from which the royal speech (from the throne) was read aloud. If such a scroll was a testament, then, as everyone who is familiar with Roman customs knows, it was sealed with seven seals. That is the case here. Thus this picture is meant to express the fact of the authority of the Ruler, and that his will cannot be reversed or broken.

The loud cry of the angel intensifies the excitement of the scene: "Who is worthy to open the scroll, and to read it aloud?" If, where an earthly ruler was concerned not everyone was considered fit for such an office, but only one who was allowed to do it by favor of the sovereign himself, still more must this rule hold good in the celestial scene, and to a far greater extent. The world, broad as it is, has no one who could claim to be worthy of this honor.

As the angel's question echoes and re-echoes through the illimitable spaces and no one in the whole universe dares to respond, the seer bursts into tears. It is plain that this moment is beyond human capacity. Greater than the majesty of earthly rulers is the majesty of God. He does not impart the secret of his plan for the world to earthly courts. The angel's cry and the tense silence of the universe mean that it is not given to men to understand God's purpose beyond the light of their own reason, or in their own strength. This royal privilege however, is granted to the church in order that through the service of the seer, it may become sure of the mysteries of God! The moment at which the seer bursts into tears, because the mystery of the divine meaning of history is hidden from man, symbolizes the primal need of humanity. "Without tears the divine revelation is not written; without tears it will not be understood." [6] Curiosity and arrogant speculation will never ferret out the deep meaning of history. But where men suffer from the sense of the meaninglessness of the universe, the possibility which the seer represents still remains to lead them out of suffering and uncertainty.

But before the Lamb steps forth and removes the difficulty, the certainty of the heavenly solution is already anticipated in a consoling way. One of the celestial elders is allowed to comfort the seer with the promise of the victory of Christ. The imposing names which the Old Testament gave to the Messiah—the Lion of the tribe of Judah, the Root of David (Gen. 49; Isa. 11)—are fulfilled in Christ. He has conquered. It is no accident that in the Apocalypse the word victory always stands alone, and absolutely. Jesus is the victor in a far more complete sense than was ever true of the emperors

[6] Bengel, *op. cit.*

when in an official triumph among the roll of titles which were proclaimed was *Semper Victor.* Jesus Christ is absolute victor; for in this one word the Apocalypse always sums up his whole saving work. The victory of Christ, completed in the resurrection from the dead, embraces the universe, world history as well as the created universe. And the triumphant consciousness of the early church resounds from the confession of this short passage: Christ is victor.

The central scene of this chapter, which is sketched in lightly with a few strokes, forms both outwardly and actually the climax. The seer sees before the throne the Lamb, which is immediately recognized by the deadly wound in its throat. The seven horns symbolize his power, and the seven eyes his insight into God's wisdom. Scarcely has the seer looked up, when the Lamb steps forward, and takes the scroll into his own hands. The simple, swift action testifies to the fact that he is worthy, and is therefore called to disclose the mysteries of God. The very brevity of the description makes this scene most impressive.

Why, however, is Christ called "the Lamb"? What does this mean? To many people this expression is either incomprehensible or repellent. How has it come to be used of Christ and his work?

The metaphor of the "Lamb of God" is one of the most ancient and definite theological statements of the early church about Christ and his work. Although many traces of this idea in primitive Christianity have disappeared, it certainly played a greater part there than the Pauline preaching of the cross. There are certain external reasons for this fact.

The Aramaic word for "lamb" can also be translated by the Greek word *pais,* which can mean either son or servant. Then we remember that primitive Christianity regarded Jesus in a special sense as the Servant of the Lord (cf. Acts 3:13; 4:27, 30). In so doing the nascent church was quite deliberately referring to the great picture of the Servant of the

Lord in Isaiah 53, which summed up the hope of salvation of the old dispensation. So when the primitive church described Jesus as the "Servant of the Lord" it was gathering up the highest Old Testament expression of the hope of salvation in him as its fulfilment. This was the first conscious theological action of the early church; the proclamation of the suffering and dying Servant of the Lord, Jesus Christ, was without doubt the heart of the whole message of the New Testament, as indeed we can see from many New Testament passages.

The fifty-third chapter of Isaiah described the Servant of the Lord as the suffering Lamb of God. The Lamb as a sacrifice, dumb and silent, who can do nothing but suffer in silence, became the most poignant image of the death on the cross, in which the Lord of the world allowed himself to be sacrificed as one who was completely defenseless. The whole paradox of the Christian message of Jesus Christ, who went to death in order to conquer death, the devil and the world, was doubtless expressed as strongly in this imagery as in the Pauline theology of the cross. The fact that this chapter of the Old Testament was so often used in this way, shows that the Christian church set great store on this connection.

It is perhaps not quite easy to decide to what extent this precious primitive element in the Christian message lies behind this passage. For the language is not uniform. But it is important to note that no other book in the Bible makes so extensive and so deliberate a use of this idea as the Apocalypse.

Even to Judaism, with its expectation of the Deliverer, this image of the Lamb as denoting the Messiah was known. But the seer is not expressing an ancient religious idea in a traditional image in a new way; when he speaks of the "Lamb as though it had been slain," he is pointing to the historical figure, the historical work of Jesus himself.

In the Apocalypse, therefore, the witness to the Lamb of

God may be said to occupy the position comparable to that of the "word of the cross" in Pauline thought. Both forms of this testimony suggest the greatest mystery of the Christian faith: the fact that God "came down" from heaven in human form, and his self-offering in the humiliation of his saving death. The fact that this thought was not remote from St. Paul comes out when he speaks of Christ as the paschal Lamb who has been sacrificed for us. (I Cor. 5:7; cf. also John 1:29; I Pet. 1:19).

So the Apocalypse, with its witness to the Lamb, is in agreement with the fundamental witness to Christ of the primitive church, to God hidden in the flesh, known by his church alone.

The Apocalypse does not seem to mention the Jesus of history at all. Actually, Rev. 2:8 alone suggests a direct reference to him, but when it speaks of the Lamb of God it bears witness to the Lord who in his life, teaching and passion fulfilled the will of God as an obedient servant, and thus testifies to the saving significance of his death. It does this in such a way that it complements the Pauline theology; alongside the theology of the cross there is also the theology of expectation. The certainty of the final victory of Christ must be added to belief in the saving significance of his death; limitation to the theology of the cross alone would restrict the fulness of the primitive Christian testimony. Both the theology of the cross and the theology of the expectation of the end are gathered up and combined in the theology of the Apocalypse.

The One whom the world can only understand as the Lamb, and where it does not understand, can only mock, is alone able to break the seal and disclose the meaning of the end of history. He sees the hidden mysteries of history because he has experienced and suffered them in his own person. Hence for Christendom there is no knowledge of Jesus Christ apart from knowledge of the end of history. So the fourth and the fifth chapters end in a marvelous unity. Moreover, the vision of the supernatural, eternal, and timeless world sinks once more to the plane of human history: the whole meaning of world history is summed up in the historical form of the lowly Son of God. He can estimate it aright. Jesus Christ is the Lord of history, unto the end of the world, and his cross is its center and its turning point.

Gazing at that royal gesture with which the Lamb of God introduces the conclusion of the course of history, once more the impressive threefold song of praise breaks out.

First of all, the four "living creatures" and the four and twenty elders again fall down in worship, and raise their voices in praise to the music of harps, and the fragrance of incense, rising from golden bowls (verses 8-10), joined by the countless host of heaven (verses 11-12), and finally, the whole creation breaks out into the song of the mighty final chorus (verse 13), until at last there floats from the lips of the four living creatures alone, the celebrants of this celestial liturgy, the sound of the amen, which is taken up and re-echoed by the elders in adoration.

Once more, each feature of this scene reminds us of political ceremonial. Incense was not only used in Jewish worship; what a significant part it played in emperor worship! A whole chapter of the history of the persecution of the Christians indeed turns on the question of whether the Christian may offer a few grains of incense before the image of the emperor without denying the true God. And the act of homage, here as well as in Rev. 1:5ff, is a parallel to the *acclamatio* in emperor worship. It is the festal cry with which the church accompanies the enthronement of her exalted Lord. Here again, as in Rev. 1:5ff, there resounds the jubilant cry, which might be the title of the whole Apocalypse: *Christus Imperator*.

But this outburst of praise, in honor of the victory of the Lion of Judah and of the Lamb presupposes a line of thought which goes far beyond any political metaphysic. It is not a solemn liturgical language, remote from the life of the world;

we might indeed call it a "polemical song" were it not for the fact that this song of praise is far more imposing and natural than any polemic could ever be. These choruses also begin with the phrase *vere dignus*, "worthy art Thou." But it is a new song, the old has been superseded, for it belongs to a new order greater than all previous political orders. Its dominion is openly manifested in him we call the "Lamb of God," who yet was the only one worthy to fulfil the meaning of history as a whole.

The first song of praise has three characteristics. It is called: "the new song." Man cannot learn this song by his own effort. God must show his church, and through it the world, to whom power and honor in the world belong. The church, however, dwells in this "new order"; thus this phrase has become one of the slogans of the primitive Christian understanding of the world and of history.

Secondly, this song is universal. The universe had no one who could open the scroll and break the seals (verse 3); but one day this same universe will worship and adore God and the Lamb. This song of adoration, which includes the whole creation, is reflected in the consciousness of the church on earth that before the Lamb, who is victor, there are no distinctions of nation, race, or tongue.

Thirdly, as almost everywhere in the Apocalypse, the adoration of the exalted Christ as the eternal ruler, is always connected with the witness of the life of the Jesus of history. The meaning of the death of Jesus on the cross (John 11:51ff) is that he should "gather into one the children of God who are scattered abroad." Resurrection and eternal glory are indissolubly connected with this historical act.

Three times this song of praise is repeated. First of all it was sung by the four living creatures and the four and twenty elders. Then it was taken up by countless numbers of the heavenly host. Finally, the hymn of praise resounds through the universe. Again, this is no merely empty symbolism.

Those who are able to offer this praise will one day have a share in the dominion of Christ, as he promised to his disciples (Matt. 19:28; Luke 22:30), and the seer has assured the church that this will happen when the end comes (Rev. 22:5). Thus the great scenes of the fourth and fifth chapters close on the same note. At the end of time, both creation and redemption will have been visibly completed. Alongside the majesty of God stands almost directly, distinguished from him by his saving historical work, and yet with him connected by the same divine authority, the Lamb who has taken away the sins of the world, and now in eternity sees in anticipation the result of his sacrifice (verses 9ff). His sacrificial death was not in vain: from all nations, from the ends of the earth, and indeed from every sphere of creation, they will come, and they will bear witness to the royal kingship of Jesus Christ in songs of praise. So a wide view of the future opens out before us. The twentieth chapter of the Apocalypse will bring the conclusion of this triumphal vision, now celebrated in anticipation.

Once again, how consoling is this certainty of the outcome of history! Both chapters seem to describe a great moment of suspense: when will the final conflict break out? The next chapter describes how it begins. But this magnificent testimony to the power of God and the power of Jesus Christ precedes it.

More and more, the path of the church on earth will lead through a "dark wood" of extremely difficult historical decisions, until the end comes. But the darkness of its journey through history is illuminated by the supernatural light of these two chapters, which transform terror and foreboding into strong consolation, both for the church and for the individual: "Thus saith the Lord, thy redeemer, the Holy One of Israel: I am the Lord thy God, which teacheth thee to profit, which leadeth thee by the way that thou shouldest go." (Isa. 48:17).

NOTES

The "scroll written within and on the back" (verse 1) was probably a roll of parchment on which the writing was not only on the smooth inner side, as was usual, but also on the outer side, on the back. This phenomenon was unusual in antiquity, but it was sufficiently often done to be described by a special technical term: *opisthographon.* Here this probably means that the revelation contained in the scroll of God's purpose about the End is complete and conclusive. Zahn, however, suggests that the phrase would mean something different if in the sentence, "a scroll written within and on the back, sealed with seven seals," the comma (which, as we know, was not written in the ancient text), were placed elsewhere, e.g., "a scroll written within, and sealed on the back." This rendering is quite possible. From a study of ancient documents we know that the so-called "Pretorian testament" was sealed with seven seals.

The designation of Jesus Christ as the Lamb (Greek: *arnion*) occurs twenty-eight times in the Apocalypse. F. C. Burney long ago suggested that the New Testament expressions, "Servant," "Holy Child," "Lamb," and perhaps also "Son of God" were derived from a common Aramaic source (*taljah*).

The bowls of incense (verse 8) are the *turibula* used in emperor worship.

Instead of "they shall reign" (verse 10), several manuscripts read "they reign." This expresses the idea that the Christians reign already, and are no longer suffering; "the persecuted are now already kings over their persecutors." [7] But the expression in the future tense is not only better attested in the manuscripts, but it is actually more likely to be correct. The End will disclose what is not yet visible (Rev. 22:5).

[7] Lohmeyer, *op. cit.*

Chapter 8

The Seven Seals

(Rev. 6:1—7:17)

FIRST FOUR SEALS: RIDERS OF THE APOCALYPSE
(*Rev. 6:1-8*)

In the construction of the following sections the art form of the Apocalypse stands out very clearly. We can see how the law of "sevens" determines the series of pictures. As one seal after another is broken, the seven visions disclose their meaning with increasing intensity. Before the last seal is broken, an intermediate section is inserted; then, when the vision of the seventh seal opens, the new series of seven begins at the same moment, that of the seven trumpets, just as the calyx of a seven-leaved flower opens, and a seven-leaved bud emerges out of the last sepal. The same scheme reappears later on. It is from such observations of design that the compact literary construction of the book becomes evident.

> 1 Now I saw when the Lamb opened one of the seven seals, and I heard one of the four living creatures say, as with a voice of thunder, "Come!" 2 And I saw, and behold, a white horse, and its rider had a bow; and a crown was given to him, and he went out conquering and to conquer.
>
> 3 When he opened the second seal, I heard the second living creature say, "Come!" 4 And out came another horse, bright red; its rider was permitted to take peace from the earth, so that men should slay one another; and he was given a great sword.
>
> 5 When he opened the third seal, I heard the third

> living creature say, "Come!" And I saw, and behold, a black horse, and its rider had a balance in his hand; 6 and I heard what seemed to be a voice in the midst of the four living creatures saying, "A quart of wheat for a denarius, and three quarts of barley for a denarius; but do not harm oil and wine!"
>
> 7 When he opened the fourth seal, I heard the voice of the fourth living creature say, "Come!" 8 And I saw, and behold, a pale horse, and its rider's name was Death, and Hades followed him; and they were given power over a fourth of the earth, to kill with sword and with famine and with pestilence and by wild beasts of the earth.

"In all religious literature a more impressive picture has scarcely ever been painted with so few strokes." [1] As the first septenary unfolds, a scene from the life of the ancient world, which St. Paul had already used (I Cor. 9:24) passes before the eyes of the seer. It is true of course that the classic poetic example of these visions is found in the visions of Zechariah: "I saw in the night, and behold, a man riding upon a red horse! He was standing among the myrtle trees in the glen; and behind him were red, sorrel, and white horses." (Zech. 1:8; cf. Zech. 6). But something wholly new has been created out of the Old Testament picture; in its place there is an extremely concrete dramatic scene.

The games in the circus are beginning, as was usual at the solemn opening of the official reign of an emperor. "The beginning of the dominion of Christ is introduced by cosmic games in the circus, which represent the prelude to the end of this world." [2] The colors of the horses, which originally symbolized the four winds, are the colors of the different charioteers and their supporters. With a "voice of thunder" (verse 1), one of the living creatures gives the signal to start

[1] Bousset, *op. cit.*

[2] Peterson.

the race: "Go!" [3] Then follows that impressive scene which has interested representational artists, and has inspired great pictures. The conflict symbolism is quite clear. As these games in the circus usually accompanied the official opening of an emperor's reign, so the racing of the four apocalytic riders indicates the final assumption of sovereignty by Christ, and the beginning of his rule. Albrecht Dürer in his well-known engraving has drawn the stormy galloping of the wild riders, spreading fear and terror wherever they went. But the gaze of the seer is not mainly directed to these terrible scenes, but to the divine commission of which they are the instruments.

The fact that the first four seals are placed together, apart, and contrasted with the following ones, is probably due to the ancient tradition of apocalyptic, which is also represented in Mark 13. There too the first four plagues of the End-period are strung together under the heading the "beginning of woes." Although the seer follows the rich tradition of this apocalyptic literature more closely than is at first evident, yet he writes in a very independent way. The fact that horses are mentioned, too, is a significant point, for the horse provoked much speculation and wonder among primitive people. We find traces of this in the Old Testament. Solomon's magnificence and superiority is characterized by the fact that he introduced horses—hitherto unknown—into Israel (II Chron. 1:14-17). And in Ezekiel (23:20) the horse is a symbol of that worldly power whose political metaphysic was denied to Israel the people of God, who had to depend upon God alone.

In spite of some obscurity, the general meaning of the scenes, and the commission of the individual riders, is quite clear. They all announce the first great acts of judgment with which God introduces the end of history.

The first rider comes from the east, upon a white horse.

[3] In later Greek "come" can also mean "go"; so we could just as well render this word here as "go!" or "run!" Luther's translation "come and see" is derived from a faulty text of Erasmus, who simply based his rendering on the Vulgate.

According to expressions used in ancient literature (Virgil, etc.) we may surmise that white is the color of the east. Its signs are the bow and the crown of the conqueror. These features are derived from contemporary history. Every member of the far-flung Roman Empire knew that the "bow" meant the Parthians who were a constant cause of unrest upon the eastern frontier of the Empire; they were as much feared by the Romans as the Huns, and as later on, the Turks were feared in the Middle Ages (and they too came from the east). This first rider has a terrible task to fulfil—war among the nations—and his whole appearance suggests irresistible victorious power. We must on no account confuse this figure with the rider in Rev. 19:11ff, although this is often done in devotional expositions of this passage.

The second rider, whose appearance follows directly upon the heels of the previous one (without any introductory formula), rides from the north on a bright red horse. As the sword that is given to him denotes, his commission is that which the Lord Jesus had already described in Matt. 10:34—civil war, indiscriminate fighting and bloodshed, every man against everyone else, ruin and collapse.

The third rider comes from the south, upon a black horse, and holds scales in his hands. Scales is a symbol which has many different meanings. What it means here is made clear by a mysterious utterance, "as it were a voice." In a supremely casual, yet masterly way, we are not told whence the voice comes. It is enough that the message once more makes it clear that here it is not arbitrary forces from the depths of history which are being released, but that God himself gives a definite commission to each of the four riders. Whether this metaphor of the scales is derived from astrology and signifies a "bad" year in the agricultural sense (in the East such years of poor corn harvests were often good years for oil and wine) (verse 6), or whether the scales is only a metaphor of the market place, in any case this rider personifies famine. For a denarius, the average day's wage for an agricultural laborer at that time, there will only be a meager daily ration of wheat or barley. It is not quite certain what the order "not to hurt the oil and the wine" signifies; it may have a deeper meaning. Oil and wine belong to the sacrament (James 5:14). Anyone who uses them belongs to the family of "believers." These words may be meant to convey a message to Christian believers, assuring them that they will not suffer from the famine, but that they will experience the wonderful assistance of their Lord.

Finally, the fourth rider rides upon a pale horse and come from the west. The shadow of the underworld accompanies him like a sinister "hanger-on." At first sight it is not easy to recognize his commission. The most probable meaning is that he is the minister of God's judgment, who brings great epidemics upon the earth; the Greek word for "death" can also mean plague, as for instance in the Middle Ages the dreaded plague was called the "Black Death." This fourth rider must bring the misery which always follows great epidemics, famine, death, and dangers from wild beasts.

The closing sentence, based on some words from Ezek. 14:21, sums up the terrible effect of the four riders. It is a striking fact that each of the four has a limited task: none of them is allowed to go as far as complete annihilation. The judgments with which the End-period begins are above all finger-points of God, which call our attention to the end of all history. As soon as the period of the last things begins, the reality of God's wrath, which lies like a shadow over all historical life, becomes visible. So long as history goes on its way without apparent interruption, the "natural man's" interpretation of history consists in denying the reality of the wrath of God. But when the end is in sight, this illusion is no longer possible.

Thus we are still only at the beginning of the events of the end of history. At all times men have probably understood the simple urgent language of this picture of judgment, as ballads and hymns and art testify.

NOTES

Many commentators, especially "devotional" writers, take the rider on the white horse to signify Christ. But that is quite impossible, if the Apocalypse is to have any order at all. Those who regard the first rider as Christ himself, and then, as they usually do, speak of the "victory of the gospel," are following a method of exposition which is out of place here; for if we follow this line further, it is impossible to understand why the three other riders are mentioned, and what they are supposed to have to do with the victory of the gospel. In Rev. 19:11 however, the sense is clear, and fits into the context. But it is not connected with this passage.

On verse 6 Salomon Reinach, a French commentator, has drawn our attention to an edict of Domitian from the year A.D. 92-93, which in a time of famine introduced very high prices and a kind of food rationing.

FIFTH SEAL: SOULS OF THE MARTYRS
(*Rev. 6:9-11*)

9 When he opened the fifth seal, I saw under the altar the souls of those who had been slain for the word of God and for the witness they had borne; 10 they cried out with a loud voice, "O Sovereign Lord, holy and true, how long before thou wilt judge and avenge our blood on those who dwell upon the earth?" 11 Then they were each given a white robe and told to rest a little longer, until the number of their fellow servants and their brethren should be complete, who were to be killed as they themselves had been.

As the Lamb opens the fifth seal, after the dramatically moving scene of the four riders, another striking picture follows, which is one of the most profound in the Apocalypse.

In this vision, which has very little prophecy in it, but a great deal of description, the theme which plays so great a part in the older apocalyptic tradition emerges: that of persecution. We are at once aware that this subject is of more than literary interest, and that the seer himself is personally deeply concerned. When he refers to it, he is answering one of the most difficult questions for the primitive church, which has never ceased to concern later Christian generations, and is still a problem for us at the present day. Two painful experiences were pressing on the heart and mind of the church: the severity of the first persecutions, on the one hand, and the disquieting fact of the delay of the Lord's return, on the other. Out of this pressure the difficult problem arose of the relation between the fulfilment of the individual, and the fulfilment of the world.

The firm belief of the early church in the coming of the end presupposed that time, under God's guidance, was moving towards a goal. But meanwhile Christians died, many of them the sacrificial death of the martyr. The ninth verse literally says that they were "slain" or "killed," that is, that they were "sacrificed." Thus the Christian church was forced to face the question: after all, is this death by martyrdom in vain? since in the course of history there was still no visible answer to the silent question of the meaning of their sufferings.

This question determines what follows. Here traditional pictorial material is used rather superficially, and this makes the picture rather indistinct. As in the Old Testament the blood of the animals which had been sacrificed flowed around the foot of the altar, so here the seer sees the blood of the heavenly martyrs mingling at the foot of the heavenly altar of sacrifice. In Hebrew thought, the "blood" is the source of life, or of the soul; in this picture therefore it is the souls of the martyrs which we see at the foot of the altar. There may also be here a remnant of the ancient conception that God keeps the souls of the righteous who have been sacrificed apart, until the resurrection. But the details of the scene are not clear, because they fade out of sight compared with the significance of the great question which here confronts us, and which the dead persons themselves—a bold image—

with a mighty voice cry out to God in prayer: When will it become plain that the sacrifice of our lives has a meaning? When will our death be avenged? Apparently this question contains echoes of the cruel inheritance of the Old Testament psalms of vengeance; but it is lifted on to a new Christian plane. Here the question is not one of personal "revenge," but of the final accomplishment of God's plan, for whose sake they have sacrificed their lives, and thus for the speedy visible assurance that their sacrifice has not been in vain.

That, however, was the question of the whole church which was suffering the pain and sacrifice of persecution. The cry of the martyrs not only recalls the cry in Isa. 21:11 ("Watchman, what of the night?"), but it is also illuminated by the Lord's promise in Luke 18:7 ("And shall not God avenge his elect, which cry to him day and night? . . .") God will exercise "vengeance" for his elect—in his own way—and "that right soon."

We must also note that sensational accounts of martyrdom are quite foreign to the New Testament. The only description of a martyr's death in the New Testament—that of Stephen—is very restrained, and there is no emphasis on the physical details of his suffering. The same applies to the Apocalypse. In the words of Lohmeyer: "This book, which is so full of passion and of bloodshed, has no descriptions of the sufferings of Christians, as there are in later records of martyrdom; it regards suffering and death for the sake of the faith not as an eschatological 'woe,' but as glorification." [4] We may also recall the fine words of Ignatius in his epistle to the Romans, the classic testimony to the enthusiasm for martyrdom in the persecution under Trajan: "Grant me no more than to be a sacrifice for God while there is an altar at hand." [5]

The answer to this difficult question posed by the martyrs

[4] Lohmeyer, *op. cit.*

[5] Ignatius, *To the Romans,* II:2.

is consoling, by the very fact that it is so reserved. It is, it is true, a consoling gesture that the white garment of the victor is to be given to them. It is also comforting to be told that they are to keep quiet a little longer—how brief is the course of the world and of history measured by God's eternal plans! But then the actual meaning of their time of waiting is shown to them: the number of the martyrs must be complete before their "deliverance" can begin. This expresses what St. Paul had already dimly perceived when he was speaking of his own life, the course of which was so often shadowed by danger of death and constant persecution, namely, that through his own sufferings he must "fill up" the sufferings of Christ (Col. 1:24). Christ must suffer—that the early church knew, and they knew that they also must suffer. Every believer in Christ ought to be prepared for martyrdom; for Christians who are called, as members of his body, to be conformed to his death and resurrection, cannot express their priestly communion with their Lord more perfectly than when they accept the suffering and the glory of martyrdom. This promise is an immense comfort to the whole church. But to be allowed to know it is a grace which strengthens their hearts.

Already the great fulfilment gleams on the horizon; the day is not far distant when all the powers of the earth which are hostile to God, which have brought persecution and death upon his own, will be judged (Rev. 18:20). Then their sacrifice will be avenged. In this strong concrete consolation all personal desire for revenge disappears. The Father of an infinite majesty in his unalterable, mysterious, divine direction of the world, holds the goal of history firmly in his hands. This is the abiding consolation of this brief vision. No one who has borne his witness unto death is forgotten before God. Those who are already "completed," as well as those who are to come, all have their place in the plan of God.

Because the main concern in this short section is with this consolation, it is not "prophecy" in the usual sense of the word; but neither is it only a description reflecting the historical situation of the church by means of traditional apocalyptic. It is vision; for what is said here goes far beyond the reality of this world and reality as we know it.

NOTE

It is not possible to say of which martyrs the seer is thinking.

SIXTH SEAL: COSMIC SIGNS
(*Rev. 6:12-17*)

> 12 When he opened the sixth seal, I looked, and behold, there was a great earthquake; and the sun became black as sackcloth, the full moon became like blood, 13 and the stars of the sky fell to the earth as the fig tree sheds its winter fruit when shaken by a gale; 14 the sky vanished like a scroll that is rolled up, and every mountain and island was removed from its place. 15 Then the kings of the earth and the great men and the generals and the rich and the strong, and every one, slave and free, hid in the caves and among the rocks of the mountains, 16 calling to the mountains and rocks, "Fall on us and hide us from the face of him who is seated on the throne, and from the wrath of the Lamb; 17 for the great day of their wrath has come, and who can stand before it?"

The last description in this chapter, the opening of the sixth seal, also seems to be wholly derived from the apocalyptic tradition, since it speaks of earthquakes, and in detail it displays many Old Testament characteristics. Even so, however, this description reveals the hand of the great seer and artist, for it outstrips previous descriptions of such days of judgment.

In a few lines three great movements are combined.

The first vision describes, in glaring colors, a terrible earthquake, which also affects the heavens and the stars: the sun becomes black as sackcloth, the moon blood-red. As the historical storm shakes the firmament (which according to the thought of the ancient world was suspended over the earth like the roof of a tent) the stars fall in heaps from heaven, "as the fig tree sheds its winter fruit when shaken by a gale" (verses 12-13).

The tent of heaven is "rolled up" like a roll of parchment which crumbles in the fire. This is an uncanny idea: the roof of the world simply disappears, and so do the foundations of the earth. Even the mountains, which according to the view of the ancient world support the earth in the depths of the ocean, and form its actual foundation, break down (verse 14).

Elemental terror reigns over the whole earth. The rulers of the earth—described seven times—try to flee into the clefts of the rocks; here the prophecy of Jesus in Luke 23 is fulfilled. The fact that is often expressed in colorless phrases here becomes cosmic reality: men have lost the very foundations of their existence; they have melted away from under their feet. Something has happened which man rarely feels in the course of earthly history. In great catastrophes he awakes to the elemental sense of his powerlessness; here this has become real: this drama of cosmic terror cuts the thread of all earthly progress; the structure of the world itself breaks down. Whatever follows this cannot grow out of earthly presuppositions. But while the cry of distress echoes from those who are terrified by the great day of wrath, without receiving an answer, above the breakdown of the old world there arises the new world of God.

NOTES

Theodor Mommsen suggests the "great men" of verse 15 may be Parthian state officials and courtiers, whereas according to him the "generals" would be Romans. Thus the political metaphysic of the day shines through the language at many points.

The expression "the wrath of the Lamb" (verse 16), which was a great "offence" to D. H. Lawrence,[6] is in point of fact a paradox; but

[6] *Apocalypse* (New York: Viking, 1932).

it recalls the paradoxical expression in the fifth chapter, "the Lamb is victor" (see pp. 114-15).

Lawrence's remarks on this chapter show also how very differently people read the Apocalypse. While Lohmeyer in his exposition of this section describes it as "one of the finest poems of the seer," Lawrence calls it "a muddled cosmic calamity."

CELESTIAL INTERLUDE: SPIRITS OF JUST MEN MADE PERFECT (Rev. 7:1-17)

Number of the Sealed

(Rev. 7:1-8)

> 1 After this I saw four angels standing at the four corners of the earth, holding back the four winds of the earth, that no wind might blow on earth or sea or against any tree. 2 Then I saw another angel ascend from the rising of the sun, with the seal of the living God, and he called with a loud voice to the four angels who had been given power to harm earth and sea, 3 saying, "Do not harm the earth or the sea or the trees, till we have sealed the servants of our God upon their foreheads." 4 And I heard the number of the sealed, a hundred and forty-four thousand sealed, out of every tribe of the sons of Israel, 5 twelve thousand sealed out of the tribe of Judah, twelve thousand of the tribe of Reuben, twelve thousand of the tribe of Gad, 6 twelve thousand of the tribe of Asher, twelve thousand of the tribe of Naphtali, twelve thousand of the tribe of Manasseh, 7 twelve thousand of the tribe of Simeon, twelve thousand of the tribe of Levi, twelve thousand of the tribe of Issachar, 8 twelve thousand of the tribe of Zebulun, twelve thousand of the tribe of Joseph, twelve thousand sealed out of the tribe of Benjamin.

Before the last scene in the septenary which has just begun, an entirely different scene is inserted. Once again there is a scene of deep solemnity and impressiveness. Its poetical character heightens the impression. But the essential meaning of this chapter lies at a deeper level. Before the new conflicts leading to martyrdom are described, the promise is vigorously re-emphasized. From the last terrible scenes of the previous chapter we still catch echoes of the question: "Who then can stand?" The church is assured that all through the increasing terrors of the last days the merciful union of believers with their heavenly Lord will never cease, no, not for a moment. This reassurance is given to the church which is passing through these terrors as a strong consolation and a great certainty.

There are two simple but magnificent scenes, of which the first alone carries the great theme further (verses 1-8; 9-17).

The first scene is introduced by an impressive moment of tension. The storm angels are already at the four ends of the earth—conceived in the ancient manner as a disk—suddenly, a loud cry from a special messenger of God tells them to halt. The universe is still, with the stillness of expectation. The same angel—the one from the east, the Paradise quarter, comes forward, carrying in his hand a divine seal. So before the next divine judgment breaks out, the believers are gathered together, and are sealed with the divine sign. Behind this imagery are motifs from the Old Testament. For instance, the same comparison is used in Ezek. 9:4. As slaves and animals have a mark of identification stamped or burnt in upon them in order that they may be recognized, so the Christians are marked with the divine seal, and thus they will be protected against the deadly dangers, assaults, and temptations of the last days.

How little the seer is concerned with details, or with polemics, comes out in the fact that he does not even suggest *how* this "sealing" is to take place. It is simply taken for granted; God's action is not made visible in a human way; all that matters is that the process takes place. Its result will become known. Neither the number one hundred and forty-four thousand nor the name of Israel should be pressed. Israel is the name of the spiritual people of God.

NOTES

The fact that the four angels who stand at the four corners of the earth are commanded to wait (verses 2ff) is a further sign that the judgments of the last days are not blind outbreaks of wild forces, but that they come under God's holy control.

The mention of trees in verse 3 is probably due to the fact that the force of the storm would affect them first of all. Now they stand motionless in the great stillness.

The expression "I heard the number" (verse 4) increases the restraint of the description. The seer does not see this carried out; he only hears the result.

In the list of the twelve tribes (verses 5-8) it is striking that Judah comes first. This is in the spirit of the New Testament; for it never occurs in the Old Testament. The tribe of Dan is absent, possibly because men thought that the Antichrist would come from this apostate tribe. Thus there is no mechanical guarantee of salvation; falling away is always terribly possible for human beings. Here the tribe of Manasseh takes the place of Dan.

Worship of the Redeemed

(*Rev. 7:9-17*)

9 After this I looked, and behold, a great multitude which no man could number, from every nation, from all tribes and peoples and tongues, standing before the throne and before the Lamb, clothed in white robes, with palm branches in their hands, 10 and crying out with a loud voice, "Salvation belongs to our God who sits upon the throne, and to the Lamb!" 11 And all the angels stood round the throne and round the elders and the four living creatures, and they fell on their faces before the throne and worshiped God, 12 saying, "Amen! Blessing and glory and wisdom and thanksgiving and honor and power and might be to our God for ever and ever! Amen."

13 Then one of the elders addressed me, saying, "Who are these, clothed in white robes, and whence have they come?" 14 I said to him, "Sir, you know." And he said to me, "These are they who have come out of the great tribulation; they have washed their robes and made them white in the blood of the Lamb.

15 Therefore are they before the throne of God,
and serve him day and night within his temple;
and he who sits upon the throne will shelter them with his presence.
16 They shall hunger no more, neither thirst any more;
the sun shall not strike them, nor any scorching heat.
17 For the Lamb in the midst of the throne will be there shepherd,
and he will guide them to springs of living water;
and God will wipe away every tear from their eyes."

The second scene (verses 9-17) confirms this thought. It speaks of the great multitude which no man can number. This statement follows hard on the words of the seer: "I heard their number," and now we hear that no one can count them, nor come to the end of them. What the seer was allowed to perceive, however, has not yet become wisdom for every man. The faith of the church alone can receive what was once made known to the faith of the seer; the wisdom of the world will always regard this as incredible and fantastic. But faith's vision transcends the span of history which still separates it from the end, and sees in anticipation the triumph of Christ, which will also be the triumph of his own.

Moreover the heavenly picture of this scene stands at the end of time. It already sees the moment when all sorrow will cease, and all who have been sealed and perfected will pour into the glory of God in an endless stream carrying palms of victory, and clad in white festal garments, in order to begin the heavenly worship in the celestial throne room. From this "preview" of the end there flows a great river of consolation to those who still are in the midst of the conflict.

Then the choir of martyrs sings its song of victory: "Salvation . . . to our God!," and the choir of angels arrayed in serried ranks around the throne takes up the song of victory in a sevenfold song of praise.

Again, in question and answer, the meaning of this heavenly scene is made clear. The real answer is given in the words: "out of great tribulation" (verse 14). This refers to the special trials and sufferings of the last days (Mark 13:19; Dan. 12:1). The real comfort of this scene consists in the fact that even the terrible sufferings of the last days cannot stop the triumphal procession of the redeemed.

Thus in them all the redeeming work of Christ has been completed, as the scene in verse 14 expresses it; hence they can now offer worship to God day and night, and the glory of God covers them, "tabernacles" over them, as in the Old Testament the "cloud covered the tent of meeting, and the glory of the Lord filled the tabernacle" (Exod. 40:34ff); they are allowed to see God (Lev. 26:11; Ezek. 37:27). God himself will wipe out the tribulations of nature and the sufferings of the last days; and all that the world has always lacked, never understood, often scorned, and rejected, is granted to the redeemed in their fulfilment. Even the creation will fulfil its original God-given task, and in a perfected world the Lamb will be their shepherd—again a daring Johannine paradox—and will lead them to living fountains of waters which will quench all their thirst.

So this whole picture is one of the most glorious in the Apocalypse. The door of heaven is open, and a ray of future glory falls upon the world in its sorrow and its pain.

It is significant that this clarity is mediated through the song of praise. The horrors and sufferings of the last days are not to weigh upon men like a dull unending pain. For the "sealed," that is, for those who have explicitly become God's own people, the tribulations of these days are illuminated by the Passion of Christ, and therefore they have become transparent and intelligible. It is a "spiritualized" tribulation; this comes out plainly in the song of praise, and the explanation given by the elders.

The abiding consolation of this chapter, which is so wonderful, and so often read, is easy to understand. There is an illuminating ray of future glory about it, which is very comforting. The fact remains that this book, which contains more scenes of horror than any other in the Bible, is able to comfort us as no other book can. The terrors of the last days, about which this book leaves us in no doubt whatsoever, will not affect the elect of God. As he has called, gathered, and enlightened them, so also he has the power to keep them in Christ to the end.

The second scene has a great message for our own day, assuring us in trumpet tones: "He who is redeemed by Jesus Christ has perfect assurance of salvation." "He who has begun a good work in you will fulfil it unto the day of Jesus Christ."

NOTES

The fact that in this song of praise the seer again speaks of all nations, makes it plain that he has broken with his Jewish past for the sake of the universality of Christ's kingdom.

In the ancient world palms (verse 9) were always regarded as heroic signs of victory. Virgil calls them *pretium victoribus* (*Aeneid* V:11), "the prize of victory."

The cry "salvation" occurs twice more in the Apocalypse: Rev. 12:10; 19:1.

"Washed in the blood of the Lamb" (verse 14) is a daring image, often used in the New Testament: I John 1:7; Rom. 3:25, 5:9; Heb. 9:14. As an image it is also found in other connections in the Old Testament: Gen. 49:11.

In verse 15 the Old Testament conception of the "cloud of glory overshadowing the mercy seat" is here fulfilled in the New Testament sense.

"Springs of living water" (verse 17) originally meant springs of fresh leaping water, which do not dry up in the heat of the East, and are thus a necessity for life. But here there is profound meaning in the picture! The beauty of the Twenty-third Psalm lies behind the simple, yet bold phrase that the Lamb himself will be their shepherd.

Chapter 9

The Seventh Seal: The Seven Trumpets

(Rev. 8:1—11:14)

CELESTIAL OVERTURE

(Rev. 8:1-5)

1 When the Lamb opened the seventh seal, there was silence in heaven for about half an hour. 2 Then I saw the seven angels who stand before God, and seven trumpets were given to them. 3 And another angel came and stood at the altar with a golden censer; and he was given much incense to mingle with the prayers of all the saints upon the golden altar before the throne; 4 and the smoke of the incense rose with the prayers of the saints from the hand of the angel before God. 5 Then the angel took the censer and filled it with fire from the altar and threw it on the earth; and there were peals of thunder, loud noises, flashes of lightning, and an earthquake.

The seventh seal will now open a new septenary. But before the new series of the visions of the seven trumpets begins, a brief impressive scene marks the opening of the seventh seal. The sense of tension is heightened, swiftly but strongly: a profound expectant stillness falls upon the wide spaces of the celestial palace.

The archangels receive the trumpets, those sacred instruments, which from time immemorial had been used to open ceremonies of divine worship. But still they do not break the silence. In the breathless stillness a heavenly ministrant approaches the altar, bringing the offering of incense, and with it the prayers of the saints before God. This is a striking picture: the prayers of the struggling church, fighting its hard conflict upon earth (verse 3) is the only element which penetrates that strange stillness of expectation, and then only with silent worship and adoration. Yet this does not stay the final judgment. With a mighty gesture the angel who is serving at the altar suddenly fills the censer, which has just been used for adoration, with fire from the altar, and casts it upon the earth. While this bold gesture symbolizes the wrath of God, peals of thunder break the silence. Lightnings flash over the devastated earth below, and the archangels make ready to blow their trumpets which will introduce a new series of trials.

In a silent and yet impressive way, this brief scene suggests that the events of the last days will not pass by the church on earth without the church seeing clearly the way of God. This pause of half an hour means that not only the heavenly host is called to attention, but also the church on earth. The latter will be spiritually enlightened to perceive what God is doing, if not about everything at once, yet step by step.

The most impressive point of all, however, is the fact that this eschatological pause becomes an act of worship; in the midst of the turmoil of the terrible events of the last days suddenly there appears this oasis of worship and adoration. In one of the apocryphal additions to Daniel 3, the so-called Prayer of Azarias, it is said that an angel of the Lord arranged that the men in the fiery furnace were not even singed by the heat; for "an angel of the Lord had gone down into the furnace with Azarias and his companions; and he drove the flames away from it, making a wind blow in the heart of the furnace, like the wind that brings the dew" (Dan. 3:49-50).[1] So in the midst of the terrible events of the last days, God gives to his own the possibility of a worshiping stillness, from which the "prayers of the saints," as the sole earthly element, rise to heaven. Thus the communion of prayer with their heavenly Lord is always possible, when all other earthly help is vain.

[1] *The Old Testament,* II, trans. by Ronald A. Knox (New York: Sheed & Ward, 1950).

NOTES

The "seven angels who stand before God" (verse 2) is the usual designation for the archangels. "To stand before God" is the customary Old Testament term for adoration and service.

Trumpets in the Bible are often mentioned as liturgical instruments. They are used especially when a new period is about to begin, as for instance the jubilee year, the year of forgiveness, but also in connection with announcements of judgment by the prophets (Joel 2:1; Zeph. 1:16; Isa. 27:13). Both Jesus and Paul too speak of the "last trumpet" (Matt. 24:31; I Thess. 4:16; I Cor. 15:52).

The angel who is mentioned in verse 3 who is not one of the seven, has also found a place in the Roman liturgy.[2]

FIRST FOUR TRUMPETS

(*Rev. 8:6-12*)

6 Now the seven angels who had the seven trumpets made ready to blow them.

7 The first angel blew his trumpet, and there followed hail and fire, mixed with blood, which fell on the earth; and a third of the earth was burnt up, and a third of the trees were burnt up, and all green grass was burnt up.

8 The second angel blew his trumpet, and something like a great mountain, burning with fire, was thrown into the sea; 9 and a third of the sea became blood, a third of the living creatures in the sea died, and a third of the ships were destroyed.

10 The third angel blew his trumpet, and a great star fell from heaven, blazing like a torch, and it fell on a third of the rivers and on the fountains of water. 11 The name of the star is Wormwood [German: "Absinthe"]. A third of the waters became wormwood, and many men died of the water, because it was made bitter.

12 The fourth angel blew his trumpet, and a third of the sun was struck, and a third of the moon, and a third of the stars, so that a third of their light was darkened; a third of the day was kept from shining, and likewise a third of the night.

[2] Anselm Schott, *Das Messbuch der hl. Kirche.*

The blasts of the first four trumpets, and the plagues which accompany them, are just as closely connected as the first four seals and the four apocalyptic riders (Rev. 6:1-8). They usher in a new group of the terrors of the last days. The description of the plagues should be closely observed. They are not really prophetic in character. Their pictorial material is drawn from a twofold source: from biblical examples, and from contemporary events; and as they do not contain a particular view of the future, so also the teaching they contain is only loosely connected with the future.

The biblical material is easy to recognize; it includes the plagues of Egypt, recorded in Exodus 8 and 9. This line of thought is extended through the prophecy of Jesus in Luke 21:25ff. In contrast to these two sources, our present passage is a very compact, closely knit, and shorter description. Here everything takes place swiftly and tempestuously.

One natural catastrophe succeeds another. Hail and "fire" (some commentators suggest that this may mean the red sand storm) which to a large extent destroys all the green vegetation, then "something like a great mountain" cleaves the waters and destroys all the sea creatures, the drinking water becomes undrinkable because of the stones which are hurled into it, and finally, partial darkness. The fact that a "third" is constantly mentioned, must mean simply "in part." The literalist efforts to calculate what this "third" might be are terribly wooden.

Although these plagues do not cause complete destruction, but are only permitted to cause a limited amount of harm, they do severely restrict human life and its possibilities. Thus the Lord's words in Luke 21:25ff. are fulfilled: "and upon the earth distress of nations in perplexity at the roaring of the sea and the waves, men fainting with fear and with foreboding of what is coming on the world; for the powers of the heavens will be shaken."

In the account of the second plague there may be a contemporary allusion to a recent event, that is, the eruption of Vesuvius in the year A.D. 79 which completely destroyed Pompeii and Herculaneum. From the best contemporary sources, the *Annals of Tacitus* and the *Letters of the Younger Pliny,* we know what an immense impression this natural catastrophe made on the people of that day, especially as no such event had taken place for generations. Even Jewish writers say a good deal about it, most of them because they regarded it as a divine judgment on Rome for the destruction of Jerusalem. The details of this contemporary description fit in well with these verses, and we may assume that the second plague in particular owes its special coloring to the recollection of this eruption of Vesuvius.

As we have already suggested, this section can scarcely be regarded as prophetic in character, for it contains no reference to the future. In any case, it does not say that this or that particular feature would be an essential element in the history of the end. Its significance must be taken to be more general. It expresses the fact (as was said in verses 1-5) that not only believers, but also all men, are able to see the warning of God's finger and perceive its significance. For every natural catastrophe which suddenly confronts man with his own end reminds him of the last days, and when such terrible events shake the earth, they come to each person as impressive warnings from God. They are storm birds and precursors of ultimate events; those who are not aroused by them to listen to the voice of God will not be roused by anything else, nothing will touch them.

NOTE

"Absinthe" is here given (verse 11) as the proper name of the star whose original meaning is wormwood. This made drinking water bitter and unpleasant, and according to the ideas of the ancient world it poisoned the water. The ancients believed that the constellations were nourished by the vapors which rose from the earth, and that they in turn sent down similar vapors which could do much harm. They were called "effluences," from which we get the word "influenza."

THE EAGLE

(*Rev. 8:13*)

> 13 Then I looked, and I heard an eagle crying with a loud voice, as it flew in midheaven, "Woe, woe, woe to those who dwell on the earth, at the blasts of the other trumpets which the three angels are about to blow!"

The tension which characterizes the whole chapter is intensified by the fact that before the outbreak of the three last plagues, once more a very unusual messenger of God appears. An eagle, flying high up in the sky, proclaims with a hoarse loud cry the following three plagues as three "woes." This picture is probably derived from an ancient Jewish expectation that in the last days an eagle will be the messenger of coming disaster. Possibly this eschatological element lies behind the words of Jesus: "Wherever the body is, there the eagles will be gathered together" (Matt. 24:28).

All these allusions have a profound significance: the whole universe will be involved in the completion of history. As history hastens towards its end, "the eager longing of the creation" will become still more evident. All those visions of the apocalyptic seer, in which animals play a part, often in a seemingly fantastic exaggeration of their qualities and powers, contain the hope that finally the creation itself will be set free from its bondage to decay (Rom. 8:21). As the animal world is often more quickly aware of the approach of natural catastrophes than man, so also in all apocalyptic descriptions it is evident that the animals are aware of the coming catastrophes. We have lost the sense of this connection, but St. Paul himself has said that the whole creation is involved in the fall of man (Rom. 8:20ff). So when Jesus speaks of this (characteristically in an eschatological context) (Matt. 24:28) it is more than a metaphor; it is a "sign" of the beginning of the End. Those who regard the seer simply as a figure sitting at his desk, writing fluently, with a remarkable knowledge of the religious world of his day and of the recent past, and making use of his knowledge, will hardly be able to understand this.

In point of fact, there now follows a series of three visions which bring horror upon the earth.

NOTES

Several later Greek manuscripts have altered the word for "eagle" into the similar sounding word (in Greek) "angel"—led by the usage in Rev. 14:6. This cannot be correct, for it destroys the imagery.

The hoarse cry of the eagle is well rendered by the threefold "woe." (The woes proclaimed occur in Rev. 9:12, 11:14, and 12:12.)

Further, the eagle is an element in political metaphysics. Upon a Roman coin for Hadrian of the year 119 we see the eagle of Jupiter, who hands the scepter to Hadrian.[3]

FIFTH AND SIXTH TRUMPETS
(Rev. 9:1-21)

Fifth Trumpet

(*Rev. 9:1-12*)

1 And the fifth angel blew his trumpet, and I saw a star fallen from heaven to earth, and he was given the key of the shaft of the bottomless pit; 2 he opened the shaft of the bottomless pit, and from the shaft rose smoke like the smoke of a great furnace, and the sun and the air were darkened with the smoke from the shaft. 3 Then from the smoke came locusts on the earth, and they were given power like the power of scorpions of the earth; 4 they were told not to harm the grass of the earth or any green growth or any tree, but only those of mankind who have not the seal of God upon their foreheads; 5 they were allowed to torture them for five months, but not to kill them, and their torture was like the torture of a scorpion, when it stings a man. 6 And in those days men will seek death and will not find it; they will long to die, and death flies from them.

7 In appearance the locusts were like horses arrayed

[3] Hermann Strack, *Die Römische Reichsprägung,* II, pp. 44ff., 97ff.

for battle; on their heads were what looked like crowns of gold; their faces were like human faces, 8 their hair like women's hair, and their teeth like lions' teeth; 9 they had scales like iron breastplates, and the noise of their wings was like the noise of many chariots with horses rushing into battle; 10 they have tails like scorpions, and stings, and their power of hurting men for five months lies in their tails. 11 They have as king over them the angel of the bottomless pit; his name in Hebrew is Abaddon, and in Greek he is called Apollyon.

12 The first woe has passed; behold, two woes are still to come.

At first sight this vision of the fifth trumpet—and at the same time the first "woe"—makes a very confused impression. Here everything seems to be intensified to an incredible, almost unhealthy degree. And yet the picture it presents is one that is closely knit and most impressive. Here we simply need to remember that these visions of the future pass before the eyes of the seer like a powerful drama, after he has become aware of the fifth fanfare of trumpets.

A great meteor falls on the earth; as the meteor flashes past the seer he thinks he sees a great key. At once the terrible significance of this key becomes clear. It is there in order to open the door into the shaft of the bottomless pit. The star which fell to the ground like a fallen angel itself opens the "shaft"; and as soon as it does so clouds of smoke rise into the air, like smoke from a great furnace—as clouds of smoke once hung over Sodom and Gomorrah (Gen. 19:28) —so that the light of day is completely blotted out. But when the seer looks more closely he notices that gigantic swarms of locusts are emerging out of the smoke, and, as once before Pharaoh (Exod. 10:14-15), they darken the sky.

The drama becomes more impressive. The forms of the locusts get larger and larger—now they are "like horses arrayed for battle," and again there are sudden gleams of dazzling light which seem to flash from something that looks like "crowns of gold" such as are worn by victorious warriors. Their faces look hard and ruthless, like fighters who are determined to fight to the death. And then their hair streams in the wind like women's hair; their teeth gleam like the teeth of lions, and on their breasts shine great brazen breast-plates. They are like gigantic centaurs belonging to some demonic sphere; in ancient astrology people used to speak of "scorpion centaurs."

And while the seer is still gazing at this strange vision, suddenly he hears loud noises. He hears the wings of the locusts beat as they rush past him, and even the sound changes as quickly as the picture itself. Now it is no longer as though countless wings were sweeping through the air but as if the air were full of the noise of many chariots, with horses rushing into battle so that the very ground trembles with the trampling of their hoofs.

This is a very compact picture; the particular scenes succeed one another with tremendous power. Recollections from the Old Testament have colored the picture, as for instance the plague of locusts before Pharaoh (Exodus 10), and the prophetic visions of Joel 1. But the individual details can also be found in contemporary descriptions. They may have been so familiar that the rapidly changing scenes were welded together in the receptive mind of the seer. For the whole picture is so living that we must assume that the seer had himself experienced a plague of locusts, and that he has woven personal reminiscences into his picture. In spite of all that is cruel and terrible, the picture is one of compressed force.

This description almost speaks for itself: the horrors of this plague are on a more than human scale. Every one who lives in the East knows the terrible effects of these armies of locusts, and the acute pain caused by the sting of the scorpion. In this vision all this torture is intensified to the nth degree. The final intensification consists in the fact that the people who long for death to release them from their pain cannot find it, but must continue to suffer. This is the highest degree of horror: "they long to die, and death flies from them" (verse 6).

This passage contains another hint that all these plagues suggest a meaning which lies beyond that of natural catastrophes, as was the case with the four preceding plagues. The star angel who fell from heaven to earth was "given the key of the shaft of the bottomless pit," and forces from the abyss of the underworld invade the earth with their horror. Here too we might put all this down to natural catastrophes; yet there is more in them than this. The whole universe is involved in these eschatological events. We know of course that all great catastrophes have something superhuman or "inhuman" about them. Even the organized efforts of modern science to avoid them cannot altogether escape this impression. There is something uncanny about the darker side of existence, something almost ghostly, just as for Faust it seemed that vermin were the suitable companions of the Devil. This is the dark shadow of the view of nature in Paul's thought (Rom. 8:17ff).

In this passage we see again very clearly that pure intellectualism cannot explain the Apocalypse, for catastrophes may indeed be tokens of the majesty of God, as in the classic description of Max Eyth when the bridge had broken down: "The Lord of life and of death hovered over the waters in silent majesty. We felt him, as one feels the touch of a human hand." But in every great catastrophe we may feel the very opposite: as though God himself were powerless, as though the earth which was once his creation had slipped out of his hands. And this applies not only to the troubles of the last days. Every catastrophe can have this effect. In every epidemic, in every earthquake, in every time of flood, it seems as though demonic forces had been let loose which dispute God's right to control this world.

This flash of eschatological truth gleams again and again out of the conflict of Jesus with sickness, death, and demon possession. The world must again become what it once was, and is no longer: the Paradise of God. In the last days, however, that which we can only dimly perceive in rare glimpses will become plain and clear for all to see.

The torture of senseless annihilation will once more visit the earth, to such an extent that for the moment men will no longer be able to believe that this is God's world at all. It will be a world in which men will desire to be quit of the noblest possession of this world, even life itself, but they will seek death—and they will not be able to die. We might put it like this: one day it will become clear what it means that men have lived in this world with its catastrophes without seeking God. Then they will have what in their careless ignorance they have always wanted: a world without God; but it will be a terrible world.

Since this chapter deals with demonic assaults upon the earth, in our exposition we may possibly go a step further. What is possible in the natural sphere can also take place in the spiritual sphere. Spiritual catastrophes can rise out of the "bottomless pit," and break into this world; spiritual earthquakes can shake the very foundations of existence; spiritual epidemics can poison the whole of life; swarms of spiritual destruction, as dense as clouds of locusts, can deny that this is God's world. Indeed, this is always a possibility. The last days will simply intensify this and bring it to a head. Before history ends it must become plain what terrible force there can be in these spiritual catastrophes, these ideological epidemics which drive men away from God; it has to become evident to all what they were doing to the earth which ought to be God's world.

The result will be the same as in the case of natural catastrophes: men will seek death, and will not find it. Life will no longer be worth living; a grim, vast restlessness will pervade the world, bringing horror with it. The truth must be made clear to all men—a truth that they could have known long ago—that without God, and against God, we cannot live in this world of ours.

But alongside of this horror there is also a quiet consolation. This terror will not be allowed to hurt the people who bear the mark of God upon their foreheads; it will pass them by (verse 4). The mercy of God hovers over them, with protecting love and power. Even in the midst of the horrors of destruction and of spiritual devastation there will still be the church of Jesus Christ, preserved by the grace of God. Without the grace of God it would be impossible to come through the horrors of the last days. But indeed without the grace of God even the present could not be endured.

NOTES

The "abyss" or the "bottomless pit" is the lowest sphere of hell which is mentioned in the Bible now and again (Job 28:22; 31:12; Ps. 107:26). According to the ancient view of the Book of Enoch the fire of hell burns there whence a shaft leads to the surface, like a well, which here the angel opens.

In 1917 the German Palestine Society took photographs of the dreadful devastation caused by a plague of locusts (verse 3).

The term "five months" (verse 5) can only be meant as a round number. But it tallies remarkably with the lifespan of locusts which live and do harm for a whole summer, for instance from May to September.

Apollyon (verse 11): This is the way in which the Hebrew name for the underworld is translated in the Greek version of the Old Testament (Job 26:6; Ps. 88:12; Prov. 15:11). It is an open question whether the Greek name recalls Apollo. Yet this suggestion which came first from Grotius, may well be true; Aeschylus derives the name of the god Apollo (whose token among others is the locust) from the verb for "ruin" or devastation.

How careful one has to be in exposition comes out in the fact that the locusts are "interpreted" in the most fantastic ways: Luther wanted to think they represented the Arians, and Calovius, the champion of Lutheran orthodoxy, simply applied this term to the Calvinists!

Sixth Trumpet

(*Rev. 9:13-21*)

13 Then the sixth angel blew his trumpet, and I heard a voice from the four horns of the golden altar before God, 14 saying to the sixth angel who had the trumpet, "Release the four angels who are bound at the great river Euphrates." 15 So the four angels were released, who had been held ready for the hour, the day, the month, and the year, to kill a third of mankind. 16 The number of the troops of cavalry was twice ten thousand times ten thousand; I heard their number. 17 And this was how I saw the horses in my vision: the riders wore breastplates the color of fire and of sapphire and of sulphur, and the heads of the horses were like lions' heads, and fire and smoke and sulphur issued from their mouths. 18 By these three plagues a third of mankind was killed, by the fire and smoke and sulphur issuing from their mouths. 19 For the power of the horses is in their mouths and in their tails; their tails are like serpents, with heads, and by means of them they wound.

20 The rest of mankind, who were not killed by these plagues, did not repent of the works of their hands nor give up worshiping demons and idols of gold and silver and bronze and stone and wood, which cannot either see or hear or walk; 21 nor did they repent of their murders or their sorceries or their immorality or their thefts.

Once more, these terrible events do not break out blindly and suddenly, but after a brief descriptive introduction: A mighty voice resounds from the golden altar of God, and fills the spaces of heaven. A command is issued: the four angels who are bound at the Euphrates, are to be released in order to carry out their commissions.

For Eastern people the name of the Euphrates was connected with great and terrible historical events. Beyond this ancient frontier, which marked off the frontiers of the historical region of the Holy Land, there lived the restless peoples of the East, the Parthians and the Medes. During the whole period of Roman history men looked anxiously towards this eastern frontier, from which there came continual threats of invasion by fresh hordes of warriors. So here in this passage, which is now wholly eschatological in content and has nothing to do with history as we know it, the storm breaks loose—at the hour and the moment which God appoints! This mark of time bears witness to the belief that in the apparent chaos of the last days nothing but God's plan will be achieved, and indeed God's plan as a whole, down to the last detail.

The picture flashes past very swiftly in scenes which increase in intensity as they mount to a climax. John may have begun by seeing the four points at the ends of the golden altar, and these four points (or horns) then suddenly turned into the four storm angels of the Euphrates. Then, equally suddenly, this glowing rectangle of gold turns into the rush of Eastern warrior hosts, more than two hundred million, a countless host. "I heard their number" means that the incredible is explicitly confirmed by God himself. The pictures flash past: the mounted men wore breastplates of the color of fire and sapphire and sulphur, that is, red and blue and yellow—not heraldic colors, but elemental primary colors, succeeding one another in the fashion of a vivid dream. The scene becomes still more stormy. Suddenly the horses have lions' heads, and clouds of smoke and sulphur come out of their mouths, their tails are like serpents—they are eschatological monsters, beyond human imagination. And once more a "third," that is, a great part of mankind, is killed.

When this terrible picture is over, a final remark follows, which is not part of the scene at all, but which heightens its significance: even this terrible visitation does not change men. After the first woe everything ended in despair, but here it all ends in complete hardening of heart. The phrases the writer uses to castigate the folly and error of this pagan behavior are echoes of the prophetic writings of the Old Testament. It is frightening to see the result of all these events —that is what these words seem to mean. Even under such visitations and judgments man is still capable of hardening his heart! This reminds us of the words of H. F. Kohlbrügge: "Everything breaks down, save the heart of man!"

NOTES

The fourfold note of time in verse 15 has been influenced by Old Testament examples: Hag. 1:15; Zech 1:7.

In verse 17 some commentators translate thus: ". . . I saw the horses in my vision." Although this translation is possible I believe that we should translate the Greek word exactly as in Rev. 4:3. Here we are not dealing with the supernatural vision of the seer, who never uses such expressions, but with the "appearance" of the horses.

CELESTIAL INTERLUDE
(Rev. 10:1—11:14)

Angel with the Book

(Rev. 10:1-11)

1 Then I saw another mighty angel coming down from heaven, wrapped in a cloud, with a rainbow over his head, and his face was like the sun, and his legs like pillars of fire. 2 He had a little scroll open in his hand. And he set his right foot on the sea, and his left foot on the land, 3 and called out with a loud voice, like a lion roaring; when he called out, the seven thunders sounded. 4 And when the seven thunders had sounded, I was about to write, but I heard a voice from heaven saying, "Seal up what the seven thunders have said, and do not write it down." 5 And the angel whom I saw standing on sea and land lifted up his right hand to heaven 6 and swore by him who lives for ever and ever, who created heaven and what is in it, the earth and what is in it, and the sea and what is in it, that there should be no more delay, 7 but that in the days of the trumpet

call to be sounded by the seventh angel, the mystery of God, as he announced to his servants the prophets, should be fulfilled.

8 Then the voice which I had heard from heaven spoke to me again, saying, "Go, take the scroll which is open in the hand of the angel who is standing on the sea and on the land." 9 So I went to the angel and told him to give me the little scroll; and he said to me, "Take it and eat; it will be bitter to your stomach, but sweet as honey in your mouth." 10 And I took the little scroll from the hand of the angel and ate it; it was sweet as honey in my mouth, but when I had eaten it my stomach was made bitter. 11 And I was told, "You must again prophesy about many peoples and nations and tongues and kings."

Here again we see the working of an architectonic law in the structure of the Apocalypse, which we have already noted. Before the last, seventh trumpet sounds, these two chapters (10 and 11) are again inserted, as for instance, in an oratorio, when the chorus sings together again before the climax of the whole. At first sight we may be inclined to think that various literary features common to the apocalyptic tradition predominate in this passage to such an extent, indeed, that they almost swamp the seer's own vision, making his message almost unintelligible. But when we examine the text more carefully, and the aim of these two chapters becomes clear, we lose the feeling that the figure of the angel, who now appears, is an artificial literary composition. A comparison with the wonderful description of the angel in Dante's *Divine Comedy* (*Purgatorio* II,16ff) shows that in great art such descriptions arise naturally, and there is no need to inquire into the question of literary "sources."

The vision of this tenth chapter is delineated in broad outline. The setting of the vision is no longer the threshold of the heavenly palace where the seer had hitherto been standing. Now he is standing on the seashore, just as he must have stood countless times on the shore of his place of exile, Patmos, gazing over the waters of the Aegean Sea to the mainland and his home. This time, as he gazes at the dim line of coast on the horizon, suddenly he sees the vision of an angel, descending to the earth, surrounded by clouds of glory. Everything about this princely angel is radiant and powerful: the bright cloud which envelops him, the shimmering radiance which surrounds his head like a rainbow, and his face which glows like the light of the sun. His legs move with great power, like pillars of fire, over land and sea; this simply means that his step embraces heaven and earth. His voice is one of equal majesty, like the roaring of the lion in the desert. It was thus that the prophets of old described the voice of God (Amos 3:8). This voice, like the voice of God, when he speaks in the storm, awakens an echo—the echo of sevenfold thunder.

While the echo was still resounding, the seer was preparing to write down what he had heard (verse 4); but a voice from heaven—possibly that of the Lord Himself—forbade him to do it. These words that he heard remain "unspeakable words which it is not lawful for a man to utter" (II Cor. 12:4).

And yet the meaning of the vision is clear. The angel, whom the seer beheld standing on sea and land, answers the unspoken question of the waiting church. The impressiveness of his message is heightened by the vigorous gesture of his uplifted hand, as he swears, in resounding liturgical phrases, that God is "faithful, who has promised." Now, he says, the great promises of God will be fulfilled (e.g., Ps. 40:7; Heb. 10:7). Now the consolation which had been promised in Rev. 6:11 is realized. Primarily this verse only contains a very simple comforting statement: God will not delay much longer. This does not mean a profound speculation about the cessation of time. But we must always remember that God's time spans all earthly time, transcends it, transforms it, and finally does away with it. Here then we are reminded that to the extent in which God's time is realized and fulfilled, the transitory and changeable character of earthly time disappears.[4]

The comfort of this interlude consists precisely in this assurance; it breaks in suddenly, in the midst of the increasing horror of the visions. While the scenes of incredible plagues and miseries continually increase in intensity, and the heart of the church may tremble at the vision of the future judgment of the wrath of God, and particularly when the last and greatest plagues are imminent—at this very moment the faith of those in the church is strengthened once again by a profound and clear message in which they are called to look behind the scenes at the background of all history. There too, behind all things, the mystery of God prevails. Our human minds in their present condition cannot see this, it all looks confusing and hopeless. But those who look up to heaven in faith see that God gathers up all things in his holy will.

It is by no means accidental that the very words recall John 19:28-30.

Hence too this great consolation, "Only a little while longer! Wait until everyone will see why these things happen!"

This whole comforting assurance is not given in bare ordinary language, but in this magnificent scene, which comforts so many people all the more effectively because it is so fluid. Like a prologue in heaven it prepares for the new and decisive series of plagues, but the church is reminded that the greater the distress of the last days, the nearer comes the day when God will finally unveil his mystery.

The little scene which follows seems like a powerful confirmation of the seer's prophetic commission—it even has a touch of the Reformation spirit about it! The command to

[4] Lohmeyer, *op. cit.*, notes here the profound and beautiful words in Bede's commentary: "*Mutabilis saecularium temporum varietas . . . cessabit.*"

eat the little scroll, which the mighty angel holds in his hand as he appears upon the scene, is not so remarkable as it might seem at first sight. Even if we were unaware that here there is an echo of an Old Testament example—Ezekiel had to consume a letter from God, and in so doing he was greatly strengthened in his prophetic mission (Ezek. 3)—we could understand the picture as it stands. We too say sometimes, "I swallowed the book at a gulp." Here the servant of God is bidden to absorb God's prophesying Word as a whole. "He who has not received and eaten any little book cannot prophesy; he who has done so can very well do it." [5]

Actually, the point of this detail is that it is a repetition of the prophetic commission to John. Even when, in the midst of the distresses of the last days, he proclaims the divine consolation to his people, he is acting under a commission from God; for he has become one with the will of God. Of him too it is true that "he who heareth you hears me." The eleventh verse which carries this commission still further, and describes it more clearly, contains a significant statement: John is here placed directly alongside the prophets of the Old Testament. Hence it is said, "You must again prophesy" —like the prophets under the old dispensation.

One small feature in this whole scene is indeed a visible continuation of the Old Testament example. The document which Ezekiel received tasted sweet; this little book tastes both sweet and bitter at the same time. This probably means that the prophetic commission of the seer includes both the announcement of the future judgment of wrath, and the promise of divine succor.

This scene has been well represented by Dürer in a fine series of woodcuts on the Apocalypse. The picture, in which the seer begins to consume the book, in a spirit of devotion, represents this prophetic unity with the Word of God, which

[5] Bengel, *op. cit.*

also reflects the profound spiritual experience of the Reformation: "The Word must do it."

NOTES

The "seven thunders" (verse 3) reminds us of the Twenty-ninth Psalm, the storm psalm, in which the "Voice of the Lord" (Hebrew: *Qol Jahwe*) resounds seven times like thunder. According to an ancient view, the atmospheric heaven consisted of seven planetary spheres. Thus in the present passage it is said: the mighty thunder resounded throughout the whole of heaven—itself a messenger of God like the angels.

The "marks of the angel" (verses 1-2) suggest an angel of such dignity that he seems to be almost divine. The word "mighty" is perhaps a play on words, and a reminder of the fundamental Hebrew form of the name Gabriel. In any case this must be an archangel.

The "little scroll" (verses 2 and 8) is of course not the same as the sealed book in Chapter 4, which contains all the mysteries of the divine purpose for the world. This little scroll is opened, and it probably refers only to the next prophecy in the following chapter (Rev. 11:1-12).

Verse 6 is one of the starting points for Bengel's calculations on the Apocalypse. He understands the angel's statement to mean a *"Nichtseit"* (non-time) which he estimates as a thousand years. The second woe, he calculated for the years 725-836; reckoning from thence for this passage he reached the year 1836.[6]

Two Witnesses

(*Rev. 11:1-14*)

1 Then I was given a measuring rod like a staff, and I was told: "Rise and measure the temple of God and the altar and those who worship there, 2 but do not measure the court outside the temple; leave that out, for it is given over to the nations, and they will trample over the holy city for forty-two months. 3 And I will grant my two witnesses power to prophesy for one thousand two hundred and sixty days, clothed in sackcloth."

4 These are the two olive trees and the two lampstands which stand before the Lord of the earth. 5 And if any one would harm them, fire pours from their mouth and consumes their foes; if any one would harm them, thus he is doomed to be killed. 6 They have power to

[6] Bengel, *op. cit.*

shut the sky, that no rain may fall during the days of their prophesying, and they have power over the waters to turn them into blood, and to smite the earth with every plague, as often as they desire. 7 And when they have finished their testimony, the beast that ascends from the bottomless pit will make war upon them and conquer them and kill them, 8 and their dead bodies will lie in the street of the great city which is allegorically called Sodom and Egypt, where their Lord was crucified. 9 For three days and a half men from the peoples and tribes and tongues and nations gaze at their dead bodies and refuse to let them be placed in a tomb, 10 and those who dwell on the earth will rejoice over them and make merry and exchange presents, because these two prophets had been a torment to those who dwell on the earth. 11 But after the three and a half days a breath of life from God entered them, and they stood up on their feet, and great fear fell on those who saw them. 12 Then they heard a loud voice from heaven saying to them, "Come up hither!" And in the sight of their foes they went up to heaven in a cloud. 13 And at that hour there was a great earthquake, and a tenth of the city fell; seven thousand people were killed in the earthquake, and the rest were terrified and gave glory to the God of heaven.

14 The second woe has passed; behold, the third woe is soon to come.

This section is one of the most difficult to interpret in the whole of the Apocalypse because it contains so much that is dark and unintelligible. Doubtless behind it there is traditional material from Jewish apocalypses. It is scarcely a vision; it is rather a narrative or a record; nowhere does the expression, "I beheld," or "I saw" occur. In spite of this, however, it contains some important ideas, which are also significant for the understanding of the Apocalypse as a whole.

A short prelude (verses 1 and 2) opens the chapter. Like Ezekiel long ago (Ezek. 40:5; 42:15) so now the New Testament seer receives the command to measure the temple. But the symbolic significance of this process goes deeper; here the "measuring" means the same as the "sealing" in the seventh chapter. This is confirmed by the fact that the seer receives the commission to include not only the temple, but also those who are worshiping therein. Further, the whole incident is placed at a similarly important point, namely, before the sounding of the last trumpet, just as the "sealing" preceded the breaking of the seventh seal.

Once again we are assured, in an impressive way, that by the grace of God the church itself will be preserved. The coming distresses and plagues will come ever nearer to this church—as far as the "outer court." That is, the church, like the temple at Jerusalem, has an outer court (a fringe) which stretches far out into the world, and is also accessible to many in the world.

But the nearer the end comes, and the more acute the tension, the less will it be possible to preserve this "outer court." When it comes to this everyone will have to decide either to belong to the church of Jesus Christ, wholly, or to remain outside. "Uncompromising religion alone will count in the last struggle." [7] The last days will admit no compromise, no halfway position. There will come a moment in the life of the church when the link which connects it with the world and its institutions will have become wholly meaningless. When the time of the final sifting and decision arrives, this link will vanish into thin air. In the last days the church will be a "little flock."

But the main emphasis is upon the measuring of the temple. However difficult the time of sifting will be for those on the fringe of the church, the church itself will not be harmed. The altar of God, and all who worship before it (verse 1)

[7] Oman.

have their fixed place in God's plan; they will be preserved. It is the same consolation as in the case of the "sealing"; those whom God has included in his church will be preserved.

Thus the "temple of God" is a picture of the church; it is not necessary to apply this term to the temple at Jerusalem; still less is it a prophecy of the destruction of Jerusalem, a so-called *vaticinium ex eventu.* When these lines were being written, the temple was already in ruins. Thus there was no occasion to introduce, retrospectively, a prophecy about something everyone knew already, since everyone could prove that the city of Jerusalem was not devastated merely for forty-two months. Contemporary recollections may have helped to shape the picture, but from the very outset the aim of this section was quite different.

It is the general conviction of the Apocalypse that the nation of Israel has forfeited its privileges. Jerusalem, since it was the place where the Lord was crucified, is no longer the place of actual saving significance. But in spite of this, the allusion to the earthly Jerusalem is not to be understood purely symbolically, so that another image could have been used equally well. Biblical thought is realistic, not abstract like the Greek. Every picture is not only the expression of an idea, but has an actual foundation in fact.

Thus here Jerusalem is not mentioned merely as an empty theoretical metaphor. In some way or another the earthly, geo-historical Jerusalem will have its place in the history of the last days, just as the Old Testament prophesy is not simply forgotten, but will be fulfilled. This is already suggested in the words of Jesus about Jerusalem (Matt. 24; Luke 13:34ff); there is an echo of this in the eighth verse. This verse says more plainly than anywhere else that the political and religious history of Israel has come to an end; so far as earthly history is concerned, it has been rejected. The enigma of Israel can neither be understood nor solved from presuppositions within history; it remains a "mystery" (Rom. 11:25) which the end alone will solve. But that which God once willed for historical Israel and for Jerusalem will be fulfilled.

This observation is important, if we are to understand the following difficult section about the two witnesses (verses 3ff).

Who are these two witnesses?

The description of them is so clear that there can be no doubt about their earthly historical prototype; they are Moses and Elijah (Mark 9:4). We recognize them by the hairy garments of repentance, typical of the Old Testament prophets, as well as by the miracles which they perform, the plagues of Egypt which Moses conjured up, and the prayer that it "should not rain upon the earth" (Jas. 5:17) with which Elijah caused the heavens to be as brass. But they have developed into supernatural figures, far beyond anything known upon this earth, and within history. The magnificent night vision of Zechariah (Zech. 4) of the two olive trees and the two lampstands are mentioned in a general way, without attention to small points of detail. This shows clearly that the writer is here thinking of prophetic figures who will appear in the decisive period of the end—Moses and Elijah, prophets and men of God of the church of the old dispensation.

Before history comes to an end, within its course once again the prophetic witness of the prophets must reach its full development. Although earthly history often seems to be going on its way without God, yet these two figures of the end testify that God's Word will not return unto him void, but that it will "accomplish that which I please, and it shall prosper in the things whereto I sent it" (Isa. 55:11). The full glory of the prophetic office is summed up in the figures of the two witnesses who will appear visibly, together, during the last days, in the sight of the whole world.

The idea which they incorporate is possibly one of the most important in the whole of the Apocalypse. It is more important than all the detailed elements in the history of the last days. It is this: it is more important to be a witness to Christ, as he himself was "*the* witness," absolutely, than to penetrate into the mysteries of the last days. But for the witness to Christ there is no other way to bear this witness, and to stand up for Christ before the world, than to bear it "openly," that is, by suffering. The believing Christian is never more like his Lord than in the "fellowship of his sufferings" (Phil. 3:10). The true follower of Christ cannot evade the way of suffering.

This reminder of the way of the cross in this passage is emphasized by the fact that both the witnesses of the last days die a martyr's death in Jerusalem, the city in which the Lord was crucified (verse 8). This allusion to Jerusalem has a double meaning. Firstly, Jerusalem was the actual historical place where the representatives of the highest form of human religion rejected the testimony of Jesus Christ with such vigor that they killed "*the* witness" himself. But, secondly, what was once achieved in this historical situation will be repeated at the end of history, on a higher plane and on a wider scale. The hardest conflicts will take place in the last days, and perhaps at the very place where the earthly revelation of God in Jesus Christ reached its climax. The historico-political destiny of Jerusalem, like the historico-political destiny of Israel, is bathed in mystery. This city, which has been besieged and conquered nearly forty times, this bridge between Asia and Africa, has always played a special and unique part in history.

At this point in the Apocalypse there is the clearest reference in the whole book to the historical life of Jesus.

Now, however, it is clear that no one believes that because the Lamb has "conquered," Christian believers will be exempt from suffering, defeat, and martyrdom. We must not misunderstand the meaning of the "victory" of the Lamb. On the contrary, to bear a faithful Christian witness must lead to conflict with the world. This passage describes this conflict with the world very clearly.

Here for the first time the figure of "the beast" appears which later on incorporates the figure of the Antichrist, and whose activity will be described in so many terrible scenes or pictures. It is probably derived from Dan. 7:21. In the Book of Daniel it was the symbol of the King Antiochus Epiphanes who devastated the temple and the holy city, and thus committed sacrilege. After that, however, it became the symbol of the Antichrist. In the Apocalypse it signifies the incarnation of all those forces, at the height of their power, which are actively hostile to God. Worldly power, if it is hostile to God, is one of the concrete forms which it assumes. That is why the beast is described in political colors; for this symbol has been moulded by recollections of certain kings and emperors.

As the inevitable conflict now takes place, in the course of which the two prophetic figures of the last days are soon defeated, once more a twofold predestinarian element is emphasized, which has a consoling ring. This comes out in the significance of numbers (in verses 3, 9, and 11). "When they have finished[8] their testimony" (verse 7), the martyrs are killed, but not before. The service of both these last prophetic witnesses of God upon earth shows more clearly than ever, in the sight of the whole world, the working of an unalterable divine law which controls the lives of all Christ's witnesses, even the least: this mission of "witness bearing" will not end a day sooner than God wills. So long as their mission lasts they are inviolable. No earthly power can shorten their mission, just as no earthly power or art could lengthen it. God's plan is not altered for a single day. Like the underlying melody of a *basso sostenuto,* this conviction resounds through all the indications of number in the Apocalypse.

Further, all these indications of number in this chapter

[8] The same word as in John 19:30.

have eschatological significance: the forty-two months, during which the heathen will trample the outer court of the temple, like the twelve hundred and sixty days of prophetic service, and the three and a half days in which the corpses of the martyrs will lie unburied in the streets of Jerusalem. From the Eastern point of view such treatment is the greatest indignity which can be offered to any human being. Finally, the number seven thousand is a summary apocalyptic indication: it means that a whole generation is liquidated.

The jubilation of the nations over the death of the two prophets is realistically described (verse 10). This little touch shows that the seer is no facile optimist; he has not fallen into the idealistic error of believing that truth rules the life of nations. He is well aware that where the instinct which is hostile to God is aroused, it is expressed in a brutal lust of power, against which truth is powerless. Christians would do well to take this thought to heart.

The final element in the vision of the two witnesses again refers to the traditional example. As in Ezekiel 37, the Spirit of God suddenly descends upon them and the bodies of the prophets return to life; a voice sounds from heaven and summons them to come up into heaven; and amidst the amazed astonishment of men they ascend into heaven—a feature which is derived wholly from Jewish apocalyptic. There is a great earthquake, and a large number of people perish. Then even the most stubborn human resistance breaks down; men fall down and give God glory. There is no suggestion that this change may be due to fear and may not last—such ideas do not interest the writer. It is enough that God's power finally triumphs over resistance.

This interim scene signifies that the final victory of God is sure. That is the note of victory which is immediately taken up by the last trumpet and resounds in the following verses (15ff). This section is an essential contribution to the understanding of what witness bearing means.

Chapter 10

The Seventh Trumpet: The Seven Dragon Visions
(Rev. 11:15—13:18)

HEAVENLY SONG OF VICTORY
(*Rev. 11:15-19*)

15 Then the seventh angel blew his trumpet, and there were loud voices in heaven, saying, "The kingdom of the world has become the kingdom of our Lord and of his Christ, and he shall reign for ever and ever." 16 And the twenty-four elders who sit on their thrones before God fell on their faces and worshiped God, 17 saying,

"We give thanks to thee, Lord God almighty, who art and who wast,
that thou hast taken thy great power and begun to reign.
18 The nations raged, but thy wrath came,
and the time for the dead to be judged,
for rewarding thy servants, the prophets and saints,
and those who fear thy name, both small and great,
and for destroying the destroyers of the earth."

19 Then God's temple in heaven was opened, and the ark of his covenant was seen within his temple; and there were flashes of lightning, loud noises, peals of thunder, an earthquake, and heavy hail.

Once more we see the development of the artistic and literary structure of the Apocalypse; it is beautifully done. The seventh trumpet vision is like a flower whose calyx opens out into a corolla with seven petals. The echo of the seventh trumpet is only the introduction to the series of the next seven visions. But before this series begins to develop—which will itself heighten the impressiveness of the visions—the praises of the heavenly host re-echo through the wide spaces of heaven, transcending the final epoch of history, with its sorrow and pain and defeat, in glowing anticipation of the end itself. Henceforward, the history of the cosmos will only be regarded in the light of its end, the day of Jesus Christ. The heavenly choirs do not sing that God *will* conquer, but—in the prophetic perfect—that he *has* conquered. Even the terrible visions of "things to come" do not shake their perfect confidence in God.

These few verses are moving and impressive.

As the seventh angel blows his trumpet, the song of adoration of the heavenly hosts bursts forth into praise, in anticipation of that moment, when, in the sight of the whole universe, God will manifest his absolute sovereignty. We have already seen how frequently the Apocalypse emphasizes the fact that God's power and kingship will be made plain to the whole world, openly. There is an echo here of the ancient messianic psalms, especially of the messianic royal psalm (Ps. 2)—and here it is fulfilled.

In a dignified antiphonal rhythm the elders take up the response as they fall down and worship. The rhythm of this second choir is still more living, more fully developed, and more moving. Since then all the great prayers of the early church begin like this, since the victory of God has become visible.[1] The indignation of the peoples (the "raging of the heathen" in Psalm 2) is met by the holy wrath of God the judge—a majestic antithesis! The threefold work of God in judgment is dimly envisaged: the dead will be judged, the saints will receive—visibly and publicly, that is decisive—the reward of the victor. The enemies of God, those who destroy, will be annihilated.

What now follows we might describe as a third celestial choir composed of supernatural forces. The signs and voices

[1] Cf. pp. 79, 85.

of the last days join in the supernatural jubilation. Lightning and peals of thunder, majestic tokens of God's power, earthquakes and storms of hail, once terrifying signs of a world freed from God's rule and control—all are now controlled and changed into mighty voices of adoration, which the creation, with all its power and all its voices, must also offer. There will come a time when this world will be wholly God's world, and no terror of destruction will be allowed to break out in it. All that used to terrify men will be merely "signs" of the inexhaustible, mighty power of God the creator. At the end of history even the Twenty-ninth Psalm will be fulfilled.

There is one more important feature to be noted in this song of praise. While this mighty choir sings of the end of history, the portal of the heavenly temple is opened "and the ark of his covenant was seen within his temple" (verse 19). Here too, at first, it seems as though the writer were simply using an ancient Jewish expectation. It was believed that the ark of the covenant was not destroyed but only lost, and that at the end of time God himself would have it restored. But this expectation, like the preceding elements of ancient messianic expectation, transcends its particular origin. Here the seer is not thinking of the Jewish hope at all. The world is the scene and the place of divine victory, and all the barriers of a previous age have disappeared. Christendom is the saved "nation" of the last days, and the heavenly ark of the covenant is only the sign of the saving presence of God.

NOTES

The expression (in verse 15), "the kingdom of the world" (Luther: "the kingdoms of the world") is used in its plural form in Matt. 4:8.

In the phrase, "who art and who wast" (verse 17), the words "and art to come," are missing. This can scarcely be an accident. The final act of the period of the last days has begun, when God himself steps in; he is no longer "coming"; he is here.

The expectation that in the last days the hitherto hidden ark of the covenant will be seen again (verse 19) is also mentioned briefly in II Macc. 2:4-8.

In the Apocalypse the prophets almost take the place of the apostles (Rev. 10:7; 16:6; 18:20, 24; 22:6). This shows how highly prophecy is valued in this book.

BIRTH OF THE CHILD

(*Rev. 12:1-6*)

1 And a great portent appeared in heaven, a woman clothed with the sun, with the moon under her feet, and on her head a crown of twelve stars; 2 she was with child and she cried out in her pangs of birth, in anguish for delivery. 3 And another portent appeared in heaven; behold a great red dragon, with seven heads and ten horns, and seven diadems upon his heads. 4 His tail swept down a third of the stars of heaven, and cast them to the earth. And the dragon stood before the woman who was about to bear a child, that he might devour her child when she brought it forth; 5 she brought forth a male child, one who is to rule all the nations with a rod of iron, but her child was caught up to God and to his throne, 6 and the woman fled into the wilderness, where she has a place prepared by God, in which to be nourished for one thousand two hundred and sixty days.

The following sections may be compared with a high mountain range with some outstanding peaks. With a firm swinging step the description moves forward toward the summit, which is reached in the fourteenth chapter. At the same time, we now come to those chapters, which, along with the twenty-first chapter, have had most influence on the thought and life of Christendom. How often the twelfth chapter alone has been illustrated by the hand of the artist—the picture of the heavenly woman in the light of the sun, with the crown of stars and the silver sickle of the moon at her feet!

More and more we realize that we cannot understand the images or scenes in this section until we see that they spring from a mighty dynamic movement.

The gaze of the seer was still on the heavens where he had seen the portal of the heavenly temple open, and whence he had heard the sound of the heavenly song of praise and adoration.

As he was looking up at the movement of the clouds and the shining of the stars in the night sky, suddenly out of the blending of clouds and stars there appeared a ring of light, followed by the tranquil light of the moon, while the heaven above became lighter and lighter and more glorious, like the radiance of the sun, and finally, out of the radiance, there appeared the figure of a woman. As all the light of heaven seems to be concentrated in this figure, so also all the feeling and thought of the seer is concentrated upon her. At first she is only the radiant center of his prophetic vision: glittering in the sunshine, clad in the shimmering reflection of a shining cloud, the silver beam of the sickle moon at her feet, and a radiant crown of twelve stars upon her head. That is the picture of the "Queen of Heaven," as it is called in the history of art. It is a very "philistine" question to ask: how can a figure be clothed in light? Psalm 104 uses the same magnificent imagery. The details of the picture do not at present concern us; they disappear in the sublimity of the vision, which is meant to be seen as a whole.

The second impression, that is, the pangs of travail of the woman seen in the heavens, goes deeper, and surpasses the beauty of the first. The picture of the birth pangs which seize upon the woman, gives this vision something mysterious, which is both painful and joyful. The woman's cry echoes through the heavens with the unrestrained force of the Eastern woman—but it is mingled with expectation and joyful anticipation: something new is about to be born!

Then the scene changes; a fiery red lights up the sky; the dragon appears! As we follow the scene we can see the vision of light which envelops the woman suddenly shot through with fiery gleams of light, and all in terrifying motion. The glowing red tail of the dragon sweeps over the heaven and sweeps away a third of the stars (that is, simply, a large number), so that they fall upon the earth. It is possible that the seer may have actually seen something like this. The other details—seven heads, ten horns, the diadems, the tail—are only hints which succeed each other rapidly as the drama is played out; it is simply puerile to try to count and explain them. These images are simply used to impress upon our minds the terrible majesty of this monster who is so bitterly hostile to God. That is the point.

The scene and its reflection heighten the dramatic tension. Now the monster stands threateningly over the woman (whose cry of pain resounds through the heavens) in order to swallow up the child which she is about to bear. The emotion increases. Out of the quiet majesty and the impressive blend of pain and joyful expectation the scene has assumed an intensity which makes us hold our breath. Will the new life just born be cruelly killed at birth?

The dramatic tempo increases. As the child, a boy, is born, about whom all the messianic promises gather in fulfilment (a Christmas scene, but raised to an unusual height of intensity), it is caught away to the throne of God, and the mother is hidden in the infinite wastes of the wilderness, where God had been so close to his people in the Old Testament (cf. Hosea 2).

MICHAEL'S FIGHT WITH THE DRAGON

(*Rev. 12:7-9*)

7 Now war arose in heaven, Michael and his angels fighting against the dragon; and the dragon and his angels fought, 8 but they were defeated and there was no longer any place for them in heaven. 9 And the great dragon was thrown down, that ancient serpent, who is called the Devil and Satan, the deceiver of the whole world—he was thrown down to the earth, and his angels were thrown down with him.

At the height of this tension a mighty battle breaks out which affects the whole heavenly world: the archangel Michael, with the heavenly hosts, fights against the dragon who is now no longer alone, but is surrounded by his "angels," the hosts from the abyss. This is most impressive, but the actual conflict is described very simply: "but they were defeated" (verse 8). As the dragon with his whole host is thrown down from heaven, with sharp pain and anguish, the triumphant joy of the seer breaks out. The very names which are piled up in the ninth verse are like jubilant cries of victory shouted after the defeated enemy. What Jesus saw ahead in a vision—"I saw Satan fall like lightning from heaven!" (Luke 10:18)—is fulfilled in these mighty conflicts at the end of history.

HYMN OF VICTORY

(*Rev. 12:10-12*)

> 10 And I heard a loud voice in heaven, saying, "Now the salvation and the power and the kingdom of our God and the authority of his Christ have come, for the accuser of our brethren has been thrown down, who accuses them day and night before our God. 11 And they have conquered him by the blood of the Lamb and by the word of their testimony, for they loved not their lives even unto death. 12 Rejoice then, O heaven and you that dwell therein! But woe to you, O earth and sea, for the devil has come down to you in great wrath, because he knows that his time is short!"

The song of praise resounds through the empty spaces of heaven where the battle had been fought and won, from which the dragon with his hosts had been thrown down on to the earth. The seer does not say whose are these lovely voices of the heavenly choirs. Probably they are the voices of the martyrs at the foot of the altar (Rev. 6:9), the "spirits of just men made perfect," who now see that the hour of their deliverance has dawned.

STRUGGLE OF THE DRAGON UPON EARTH
(*Rev. 12:13-17*)

13 And when the dragon saw that he had been thrown down to the earth, he pursued the woman who had borne the male child. 14 But the woman was given the two wings of the great eagle that she might fly from the serpent into the wilderness, to the place where she is to be nourished for a time, and times, and half a time. 15 The serpent poured water like a river out of his mouth after the woman, to sweep her away with the flood. 16 But the earth came to the help of the woman, and the earth opened its mouth and swallowed the river which the dragon had poured from his mouth. 17 Then the dragon was angry with the woman, and went off to make war on the rest of her offspring, on those who keep the commandments of God and bear testimony to Jesus. And he stood on the sand of the sea.

The heavenly song of praise is followed by a fresh outbreak of demonic resistance, for the dragon is furiously angry. Thrown down to earth—a real devil—he has not by any means lost his game, so he chases after the woman. The scenes become more and more intense. The woman, given the eagle's power of flight (the ancient world had continually dreamed of the god-like power of flight) is hidden in the wilderness and cared for. The dragon spurts great masses of water at her out of his mouth, but God meets this increased assault of demonic force with still greater wonders of his power. Nature must help; a rent in the earth immediately swallows up the flood of water. With great daring the gaze of the seer pierces ever further into that play of divine and demonic forces which transcends all human experience.

The dragon then vents his anger on those who by faith and life belong to the woman. The menacing conclusion overflows into the next chapter. The satanic power is not yet exhausted; nor has the cup of suffering—caused by this final conflict at the end of history—yet been drunk to the dregs by Christian believers.

What do these three scenes mean which follow so hard on each others' heels?

If we keep close to the essence of the vision as John tells it, and do not let ourselves be confused by details, the three main figures in these scenes stand out clearly: the child, the woman, and the dragon.

For clarity of exposition we must first of all be quite clear that the main point in this passage is the birth of the messianic child.[2]

The messianic significance of this child comes out quite plainly in the language of the whole section. Once more we hear the language of the messianic royal psalm (Psalm 2) which has already occurred so often in the preceding pages of the Apocalypse. The most royal verse in this psalm (2:9) echoes very clearly here in the fifth verse: "One who is to rule all nations with a rod of iron." Here, as in the whole of this book, the subject is the final victory of Christ. Here too the enemy of God is well aware that the divine world ruler confronts him; the political metaphysic of the closing period of history reappears. Hence the birth of this child lets loose the fight of Michael and the dragon, a struggle which affects both heaven and earth, in the course of which Satan is hurled down to earth. Even if we do not immediately connect this event with the Lord's words about Satan falling from heaven (Luke 10:18) it would be evident that the messianic manifestation of Jesus is in the background.

This reminiscence is, however, lifted into the timeless sphere, or rather into the period of the last days. This event is a "sign." The real content of this sign is the *public character* of this birth of the Messiah. The first Christmas was

[2] Bousset, *op. cit.* "It is true that this realistic interpretation of the birth and ascension of Jesus has often been questioned, from Methodius to Kliefoth; the allegorical interpretation of Chapter 12 . . . is in any case, more impossible than the realistic one."

an event which took place in the greatest secrecy, humility, and concealment; "most secretly He wields His power" (Luther). What once happened at Bethlehem, is now re-enacted before the whole world, so that everyone can see it. Of course from the very outset we must be quite clear that this birth of the messianic child is a "vision" or a symbol. The birth of Jesus within time and space at Bethlehem stands behind it, and is not repeated on the human plane. The text makes it plain enough—and not only in this chapter—that the historical manifestation of Jesus is presupposed; without his epiphany, his first "coming," there will be no *parousia*, no "Second Coming."

But here the writer asserts that at the end of time the fact of the birth of Jesus—the world Savior and the world's King—will be made so public and universal that no one henceforward can miss it through ignorance or secrecy. The fact that he is the Messiah will be manifested to the whole world. In this sense the church (the saving community) will bear the Messiah afresh. Previously he was not known to the world, but only to his church; now he is visibly present to everyone. The time of living by "faith" and not by "sight" is over; through the public birth of the Messiah a new period has begun.

Then there is another feature in the earthly history of Jesus which is heightened in the Apocalypse. As the child Jesus, on the advice of the angel, was taken secretly into Egypt, and His life was saved, now the whole world will know that God preserves his Anointed, and that in the last days also his work will not be allowed to fail.

Both the other figures in this section must be understood in the light of this eschatological context. There is also another element in this imagery which excludes any literalist interpretation. These images are, as the psychologist would say, "supradetermined." This means that so many different ideas and emotions are blended and gathered up in them that it would be impossible to explain them in the light of one point alone.

The "woman," too, does not represent the historical mother of Jesus. The heavenly female figure is not the "Queen of Heaven." The marvelous representations of Mary from Dürer down to popular carols and ballads[3] are based upon a pleasant error, although it has been very fruitful in the history of art. For this is not a repetition of the historical birth of Jesus, even in a mythical way. Nor does this represent an historical Christian recollection in pictorial form. The stress on the public character of the birth of the Messiah, which emphasizes his claim, before all the world, to be the messianic King and Governor, shows that here the writer means us to understand that the Messiah, the Savior of the world, is made known to the world through his church, which proclaims him. In so doing the seer takes up the world-wide expectation of the divine child.

Thus the interpretation of this chapter depends far more on the labor pains of the woman than on the majestic figure at the beginning of the chapter.[4]

Originally, it is true, the woman was thought of as a real figure, like the child. This comes out in countless myths of the heavenly virgin and the heavenly child. Further, there can be no doubt that the "form elements" of this picture are derived from a very primitive myth of the birth of the world-

[3] Cf. the beautiful Paderborn song, "Wonderful and Glorious," whose second verse runs like this:

"The Sun accompanies thee,
the silver moon
falls at thy feet.
No imperfection
can dim thy glory;
Around thy head
the stars form a crown."

Actually Luther's "Hymn of the Holy Christian Church," which is based on this passage, is far more apt.

[4] Bengel, *op. cit.* "Such 'woes' . . . were the painful longing for the Kingdom of God, expressed in the sighs and prayers and fruitful 'waiting' of the saints."

deliverer which, in many forms, and often embroidered with astrological elements, was widespread in the ancient world. But although the seer uses these ancient literary traditional forms, he knows and testifies that the Redeemer of the world has appeared in the historical figure of Jesus Christ. So there can be no doubt that the figure of the woman, as a myth, does not fit in here; as a mythological figure this woman is a "foreign body." It is only if she means something else that we can understand why her figure is introduced at all.

It is true, of course, that in a very definite way the elements of a mythological tradition have influenced the style and treatment of the subject. But the decisive point lies elsewhere, which, even under the pressure and constriction of foreign traditional elements can be seen still more plainly: this woman is not an empty "form element," but a symbol of the church of Jesus Christ. The continuation of the description shows that here too in the whole scene of the woman in travail it is the church which is meant. She bears the messianic child, she is preserved by God's guidance, and hidden in the wilderness. During later persecutions by the dragon she is wonderfully preserved. Her figure is not limited in an Old Testament way, but she is the spiritual heiress and fulfiller of the task which once belonged to the people of God in the Old Testament.

Even in the later features in the vision of the woman and her destiny, we must always remember that they do not directly reflect historical events.[5] It has constantly been affirmed, for instance, that the woman's flight into the wilderness means the flight of the early Christian community at Jerusalem to Pella in the year A.D. 70. Apart from the fact that this interpretation is very limited, confining the meaning of the woman to the Jewish-Christian church at Jerusalem,

[5] Such attempts at "historizing" this passage could easily lead to the argument that these particular features were *vaticinia ex eventu,* that is, a later "working up" into literary form of historical events which had been known for a long time, and only apparently clothed in prophetic form.

its main defect is that such a pedestrian interpretation inevitably depreciates the significance of this passage.

Every educated reader of the Old Testament knew what the "wilderness" meant: it was the place where religion was at its purest. So long as the people of God wandered in the the wilderness they were preserved from the errors of nature religion, the cults of Baal and Astarte. So, in the last days, the church will be delivered from the dragon's wiles, and will escape into this world of true and pure religion, into that "wilderness" which saw the light of the first love of the people to its God, and the radiance of their first experience of the love of God: "When Israel was a child, then I loved him, and called my son out of Egypt" (Hosea 11:1).[6]

There should be less difficulty about the meaning of the dragon. The full description in verse nine is sufficient. The great enemy of God in the world, of which the Bible is well aware from the outset, and who here bears the same name as in the earliest biblical narratives (Gen. 3:1ff) is here fighting against God. The divine struggle to win his world will only come to an end when this enemy has been annihilated (Isa. 27:1; 51:9). The ten horns, symbols of universal political power, are taken from the symbolism of the Old Testament (Dan. 7:24).

It is significant that it is precisely at this point that the dragon appears. At the very moment when the divine claim to absolute sovereignty is made plain to the whole world, through the public birth of the Messiah, the demonic power which rebels against God, also becomes public and visible. To the extent in which the divine plan for the world becomes visible—and that always means "realized"—the enemy of God gathers all his forces and thus helps to disclose the true

[6] A beautiful modern example of the attraction of the desert as a place of "pure religion" is the book by the French author, Ernest Pschari, *Le Voyage du Centurion* (Paris, 1931). The author, a grandson of E. Renan, after years of agnosticism, found his way back to real religion through his experience of the desert.

meaning of history. When men begin to see Christ clearly, they also see Antichrist clearly.

This determines the conflict. Through this chapter we begin to see why, in the deepest and most divine sense, conflict is of the essence of history. Up to this point the writer has been speaking of the trials and troubles which will assail the church during the last days. Now, for the first time, there is a hint of the meaning of history as a whole. Hence this conflict, as the essence of history, must be explained in more detail.

The most difficult question for modern man (due to his preconceived ideas) is not even mentioned: "Why is this conflict necessary?" This chapter does not even consider such a question; it only speaks of events. These events prove that the conflict *is* necessary. This chapter, like the Bible as a whole, is opposed to the modern idea of Progress. To man's natural way of thinking it will of course be a constant temptation to assume that in spite of constant "set-backs," by dint of human effort, history can achieve a higher development.

Biblical thought, however, moves on other lines. If it is not a merely empty phrase to say that God is the Lord of history, this implies two things: first, that the forces which make for an upward development do not lie within history itself; and, secondly, that we must adore God's will in and above history, even when we can neither see nor recognize it. Since however the world, as it is, cannot of itself be God's world, and since, on the other hand, God has redeemed this world, and is carrying through his plan of world redemption, then conflict in history is inevitable. For God's world redemption can only be carried through against Satan, the great enemy of God.

The meaning of the apocalyptic disclosures about the final conflict is clear. When the final conflict begins, then the real theme of world history will become clear to all. Within the Christian church it is the task of prophecy to draw our attention to this background of history. Of himself man cannot know what the course of history will be. On his own presuppositions he must always seek for "interpretations," which will always prove illusory. Hence as a rule man oscillates between an overestimation and an underestimation of history, between an historical optimism or an historical pessimism. Prophecy prepares the way for the removal of this obscurity, because it teaches the church about the course and the secret of history.

The outline of this early Christian prophetic interpretation of history reflects the three stages of the conflict which this chapter describes.

First of all (verses 4-6), the dragon awaits the apparently certain final victory. In the figure of the dragon which stands ready to swallow up the child of the heavenly woman the moment it is born, the church shows that she is aware of the threats which the enemy of God is always preparing within history. The child is saved—God's plan for the world is at work. We must note that the deliverance of the heavenly woman is only mentioned casually; it is included in the fact that God's messianic work is being fulfilled.

In the second great scene, which has often been pictorially represented, Michael fights the dragon (verses 7-9). The calm and almost casual way in which the actual conflict is mentioned shows the certainty of victory in the early church. For the whole point of this scene is the victory, not the conflict itself. The victory consists in the fall of Satan. The phrase in the ninth verse, in which the seer's triumphant joy of victory, and that of the primitive church, sounds so loudly, sums up the work of Jesus Christ in a very characteristic way. Its result, which becomes visible in the last days, does not consist in an inward process, such as peace of soul, but in an actual event in the cosmic order; the enemy of God in the world is annihilated. That too is what the whole testimony of the early church meant, including that of Paul: Jesus Christ has appeared in order that he may destroy the works of the devil (Acts 10:38; II Tim. 1:10; I John 3:8). It was thus that Jesus described his work (Luke 10:18). The prince of this world has been judged (John 12:31).

So Michael's fight against Satan, and Satan's fall from heaven, have a double meaning.

The fact that Michael and the heavenly host must fight against Satan and that the seer sees this conflict achieved "in heaven," means that the decision about the power of the Evil One in the world is not made within history. Like the origin of evil, the victory over evil takes place in a sphere far beyond the framework of history. At the same time, we are assured that Satan is already disarmed. This will be explained more fully in the following verses.

This truth is proclaimed in the third scene (verses 10-12) of the conflict, in the scene of the heavenly song of praise. The church must know what Satan also knows: his time is short (verse 12).

It is no accident that here, for the first time, the seer speaks of himself ("I heard," verse 10). For in this truth the concrete and the personal are closely connected. What has happened already in principle, is also intended for the consolation of the individual Christian. The accuser, who night and day accuses the Christians before God, will not be allowed to terrify their consciences any longer. In the certainty of the victory of Christ, they pass through this world, in which for the moment Satan still has power, but over which, in spite of death and terror, there shines the radiance of the coming victory of Christ.

This consolation is important, because the final conflict of the last days is still going on. Even though the messianic child has been saved, yet all who belong to the family of the woman must still experience the wrath of the dragon. This expresses the Pauline idea that the church has to fill up the sufferings of Christ (Col. 1:24). This must actually happen at the end of history. But now, in face of the manifestation of the Evil One in the world, all the miracles by which God preserved his people in the past come out into the open, and are re-experienced in her midst. Just as once the earth opened and swallowed up the enemies of God in the days of the old covenant (Num. 16:31ff), and just as long ago the wild animals served Jesus in the wilderness (Mark 1:13), so also now God's people will receive fresh strength, so that they will mount up with wings as eagles (Isa. 40:31).

We may sum up the meaning of this great chapter, which contains the heart of the message of the Apocalypse, thus:

When the public assumption of power by Christ takes place, the crisis of history has begun. The meaning of that event we call the Incarnation, is now fully revealed to the whole world.

From the satanic resistance aroused by Christ's assumption of power, the church—where history is concerned—must learn that conflict is inevitable. There must be a real struggle, and real suffering; not merely an heroic temper, but a real victory.

Finally, the length of the conflict is already predetermined. In this chapter, even the precise numbers given show their full meaning. Originally derived from apocalyptic tradition, here they acquire a deeper significance. Time as a whole belongs to God; this will never be clearer than during these last days.

The eleventh verse of the song of praise contains an urgent personal appeal: like those who "loved not their lives even unto death," so also Christians must not cling to life, but must be prepared to give their lives for him, who as the Lamb of God, gave his life for them. It is only as Christians are thus prepared to suffer, that history loses its terrors.

NOTES

Michael is only mentioned here in verse 7, and in Jude 9 in the New Testament, and on both occasions as the most warlike of the angels. He is also thus described in Dan. 10:13 and 12:1. In the Greek translation of Dan. 8:11, he is called the *archistrategos,* the head of the army. Similar expressions occur in the Apocrypha, which has a special affection for this angelic figure. After the struggle on the eastern frontier of the empire was over, Constantine ordered a church to be erected and dedicated to Michael on the ridge of Haestiae on the Bosphorus. As he was once regarded as the champion of the chosen people, so, later on, he became the patron saint of the Germans. His picture figured in the banners of the German armies after the victory of Heinrich I at Riade on the Unstrut in March 933, and again after the Battle of the Lechfeld on August 10, 955, in which the German army saved the West from the assaults from the East.

The "twelve stars" (verse 1) are symbols of the complete number, like the twelve tribes of Israel or the twelve animals in the signs of the zodiac.

"Diadems" (verse 3) are symbols of political power, like precious stones.

There may be a political allusion in the Greek name, *diabolos,* for the devil (verse 9). The word originally meant one who denounced people; here it may be a recollection of trials from the time of Domitian. The "slanderer-in-chief," and all lesser "informers" will lose all their power to injure mankind.

FIRST BEAST: ANTICHRIST

(*Rev. 13:1-10*)

1 And I saw a beast rising out of the sea, with ten horns and seven heads, with ten diadems upon its horns and a blasphemous name upon its heads. 2 And the beast that I saw was like a leopard, its feet like a bear's, and its mouth was like a lion's mouth. And to it the dragon gave his power and his throne and great authority. 3 One of its heads seemed to have a mortal wound, but its mortal wound was healed, and the whole earth followed the beast with wonder. 4 Men worshiped the dragon, for he had given his authority to the beast, and they worshiped the beast, saying, "Who is like the beast, and who can fight against it?"

5 And the beast was given a mouth uttering haughty and blasphemous words, and it was allowed to exercise authority for forty-two months; 6 it opened its mouth to utter blasphemies against God, blaspheming his name and his dwelling, that is, those who dwell in heaven. 7 Also it was allowed to make war on the saints and to conquer them. And authority was given it over every

tribe and people and tongue and nation, 8 and all who dwell on earth will worship it, every one whose name has not been written before the foundation of the world in the book of life of the Lamb that was slain. 9 If any one has an ear, let him hear:

10 If any one is to be taken captive,
to captivity he goes;
if any one slays with the sword,
with the sword must he be slain.

Here is a call for the endurance and faith of the saints.

If the twelfth chapter has done more than any other in this book to fire the imagination of the artist, no other has occupied the thought of whole Christian generations more than the thirteenth chapter. Almost every century has brought a fresh attempt at interpretation; above all this is true of those periods in history which were turning points in human affairs. There are countless illustrations of this statement, from the Fathers down to Dostoevsky.

During the Middle Ages in Germany, one of the most profound poems on this theme was produced under the title, *Ludus de Antichristo,* the "Drama of the Antichrist." Probably it was a highly-placed ecclesiastic in the immediate entourage of the Emperor Frederick II who wrote this play. It serves to show how deeply the problem of a government which makes itself into an absolute dictatorship—and in so doing takes the place of Christ—must have been felt in the presence of that great Emperor who was such an enigma to his contemporaries. Much later, Jung-Stilling, basing his argument on this chapter, twice over dealt with the problem of the absolute ruler during the period of the Napoleonic wars. Finally the Russian philosopher, Soloviev, with his "legend of Antichrist," is another member of this band of prophetic souls who derived their prophetic view of history from the spiritual world revealed in this chapter.

Scarcely any other chapter in this book, however, has been

treated as violently, in order to gain a forced interpretation, as this one. This is due to the fact that people have been in too great a hurry to apply it to their own times and circumstances. Since the thought behind this chapter is so profound and so complex, it has often served as a springboard for speculations on the philosophy of history which drifted further and further away from any connection with Scripture at all, the more daring these philosophers became in spinning their own webs of speculation.

These various attempts to clarify the subject remind us once more of a rule which should always be observed in dealing with this chapter: before we can ask what it *means,* we must first of all find out what it actually *says.*

The setting (Rev. 12:17b) is quite clear. The seer is again standing on the seashore,[7] where once before in the midst of the roar of the waves and the motion of the clouds he had received a vision (Rev. 10:1). Still under the impression of the preceding vision, he gazes across the ocean, and while he is gazing a new vision appears.

The sea is not attractive. From the point of view of antiquity, below its waters lay the foundations of the earth, which was supported by the mountains which were like great pillars. It was also the abyss out of which the forces and spirits of the underworld rose to the surface. When the seer looked across the sea, he looked, in all probability, towards the west, for from time immemorial, to the people of the Old Testament, the frontier on this side was "the Great Sea toward the going down of the sun" (Josh. 1:4). This comes out in several other passages. In the west, however, lay the seat of the imperial power, the city of Rome. Whatever came from Rome was certainly significant.

Thus out of the western sea came the beast—that beast

[7] Many expositors prefer the better attested reading "he (the dragon) stood (*estathē*) on the sand of the sea." But if we read "I stood" (*estathēn*) the sense is better, and the evidence for this reading is almost as good as the other. In the Greek text a single letter makes the difference.

from the abyss, which has already been mentioned in anticipation (Rev. 11:7). As the monster slowly and terrifyingly emerges out of the swelling waters, the details gradually become clear, all of which are to be understood as parts of the vision as a whole. These must not be explained away in hasty attempts at interpretation. Ten horns and seven heads first become visible, symbols of power, as with the dragon (Rev. 12:3). As the beast emerges further from the waters it reminds the seer of Daniel's vision of the four beasts (Dan. 7:4-6)—those four beasts which represented the succession of the four great Eastern dynasties. But Daniel's vision here assumes the form of a terrible monster—summed up in one creature—a form which has the features of a leopard, a bear, and a lion—every detail is intensified into a cruel monstrosity because everything appears at once in the one single beast. The heads are adorned with symbols of power, and with blasphemous honorific titles.

Suddenly, the seer sees the meaning of this terrifying power. The menacing conclusion of the previous vision is still in his mind—the terrible outbreak of the dragon's wrath against the woman's offspring, to which he reacts with a kind of "metaphysical inherited hostility" [8] (Rev. 12:17). Now he has handed over his full authority to this beast; hence this monster has arisen out of the abyss as Satan's representative, in order to fulfil his work on earth. That is why he was received from the dragon "his power and his throne and great authority" (verse 2).

The seer has seen one particular feature of the picture very clearly. One of the seven heads shows traces of a severe wound in the throat. But although it looked like a mortal wound, it had healed up; the hope that the beast would die of this wound proved illusory. The presence of the power is never lost; the beast is not a transitory phenomenon of some particular period in history, but one which reappears

[8] Schlier.

continually at new periods of historical crisis.

Hence also the transference of the satanic power to the beast is not an illusion. It is at once evident that he must be taken seriously. The gigantic mouth opens in blasphemous speech; blasphemies and insults against heaven, and all that belongs to it, are hurled into the air. In grim contrast to the apostolic words, "God is not mocked," the beast makes it plain to all that "there are no flies on *him*"; he wages war on all with whom the dragon was wroth—and conquers.

This vast display of power seems a miracle to the people of that day. This vast extension of power seems to them to be absolutely supernatural. It never seems to enter into their minds to rise and combine to resist this usurper. On the contrary, they break out into paeans of praise; to the ears of the seer it is uncanny to hear this demonic transformation of the great biblical song of praise with which once upon a time the people of God had praised the Lord of history: "Who is like the beast? and who can fight against it?" (Cf. Exod. 15:11).

When we reflect on this vision for a second time, and try to fathom its meaning—that is, to discover what it was that flashed across the seer's mind all at once—we see that in this combination of mysterious forces it is the idolatrous elements in this scene which stand out most vividly. This shows that they are the main point of the vision. In every respect the beast seems to be a caricature of the Messiah, as a caricature of Christ he is Antichrist. The confused mass of heads is adorned with arrogant names—a blasphemous anticipation of the moment when the name of the true Christ will be made known (Rev. 19:13). It bears an apparently mortal wound in the throat, but this is merely in appearance. Actually, it has not given its life, like the Lamb who has been slain. The beast is the anti-Christian parody of the crucified and risen Lord (Rev. 5:6). It has hastily assumed that world dominion which the Son of God had once refused (Luke 4:6ff). It accepts adoration and deference which belong to the heavenly Lord alone; and indeed it demands it.

Finally, quite deliberately, the beast extends its dominion over the whole world; absolute world dominion is its goal, geographically and concretely, although the ancient prophets had proclaimed God as the only Lord of the world of nations, and although the many songs of praise in this book (not only those of the eleventh chapter) which ushered in this series of visions had praised Christ as the Anointed One of God, the World Ruler.

In conclusion, against this background we must now inquire into the significance of the beast.

In order to understand this, it is essential to perceive the first fundamental truth: that the beast represents a phenomenon of the last days—or, to put it more precisely—a phenomenon within this final period controlled by Christ. It is true, as we shall see in a moment, that the whole picture of the beast teems with important references to contemporary history, but these are only the material out of which the whole picture is composed. The actual picture includes a great deal more. It means more than an isolated historical phenomenon; it is "fulfilled" again and again in the course of history. Historical phenomena constantly occur which are completely symbolized by the picture of the beast; thus historical phenomena and facts are continually fulfilled in them. To this extent, the picture of the beast has actual significance for every Christian generation. For every generation Antichrist is contemporary.

First of all, it is true, there are plain indications of the contemporary scene which come out clearly in the figure of the beast. Almost every feature bears traces of emperor worship and of the political religion. Since the beast—which represents, as a whole, the anti-Christian elements of the time of Daniel—rises out of the sea on the west, a great Jewish apocalyptic tradition is united with a very fitting theme from the seer's own lifetime. But when we try to trace these contemporary allusions in detail, we are constantly reminded that the figure of the beast is not simply a contemporary interpretation clothed in the garment of prophecy, but that these contemporary allusions are to be understood merely as hints, pointing to the events of the last days, when all that these contemporary elements suggest will be fulfilled.

Thus the beast does not represent the imperial power as such. It is not the political order as such, which the Antichrist is meant to represent; that would be a false interpretation of the New Testament. Rather, it means the imperial world power as a perverted political institution, the cunning ruthless greed of the empire, which absorbs everything that it meets. The "perversion" consists in the fact that the imperial power adorns itself with a religious halo, and in so doing claims an absoluteness to which it has no right. This is the decisive feature which makes the seer so agitated that he cannot even describe it objectively.

The titles which the beast wears are blasphemies.[9] It is true of course that Augustus, in the year A.D. 3, in connection with the stabilization of the *Pax Romana,* or Roman world peace, refused the title *dominus.* He did, however, allow religious homage to be paid to his name first of all in Asia Minor, in the east of the Empire, and out of this very soon the real emperor worship developed—this "masterpiece of a *theologia civilis*" which henceforth accompanied the political reality of the empire like the radiance of the sun.

Historians are agreed that this religious intensification of the political achievement of Rome was a stroke of genius. Through this religion a spiritual unity and compactness was given to the vast empire which, with its very varied geographical and

[9] Paulus Orosius gives another parallel at the beginning of the fifth century. Augustus is said to have entered Rome in triumph on the very day of the Feast of the Epiphany; and for the first time he closed the doors of the Temple of Janus. If he had known of the truth of Jesus Christ, he would not have ventured, as a human being, to assume a title which was only fitting for the Lord of the Universe. Hönn, *Augustus* (1938).

ethnological composition, it would never have otherwise attained. The brilliant figure of the great Emperor Augustus stands at the beginning of this religious and visible unity of the empire as the symbol of a political monotheism. This was bound to lead to sharp conflict. The Christians could have coexisted on excellent terms with the Roman Empire itself. Its state was an example of strong political order, justice and tolerance, and the world-wide political system of Rome had everywhere cleared paths which made the swift expansion of Christianity possible. But the praises of the Roman Empire for its undoubted political achievement are only sounded in the Christian church (by the fathers of the church) suspiciously late, that is, during the reign of Constantine. A long trail led up to that point, marked by an increasingly acute and bloody conflict. For since the church was faced by a political religion, a political monotheism supported by the earthly symbol of the ruler, conflict was inevitable.

The opposition to the ritual language of this political religion gives the whole picture its character. It reminds us of the King Antiochus Epiphanes (in the Book of Daniel), that King whom no Jew could ever forget, because he desecrated the Temple and—as was then the custom in Hellenistic-Oriental court ceremonial—claimed divine honors for himself.

The outstanding example from a later date stems from the seer's own lifetime. According to Suetonius, Domitian (51-96) was the first Emperor to introduce into the official circulars of his procurators the formula, "Our Lord and God commands." From that time it was customary to address him as *Deus ac dominus noster*—"our Lord and God." [10] Other signs of this tendency had preceded it. Augustus had allowed people to call him, in his lifetime, *Divus* (one like the gods), and some towns in Asia Minor applied to him the deifying cult

[10] Discoveries made during excavations at Ephesus have brought to light ritual figures and imperial inscriptions which designate Domitian with the same official title. Stauffer, *op. cit.*)

of the Hellenistic ruling dynasty, and worshiped him as "world savior," and even as the Son of God. Thus there was a concrete image behind the seer's statement that the beast bore names which blasphemed God.

The whole atmosphere created by a political cult of this kind was still more dangerous. The development of this power was not repellent; on the contrary, it had a mysterious fascination. Power has its own fascination; it exercises a mysterious power of attraction. Just as there is a fantasy of power, so also there is a worship of power. For great, truly great power, always goes beyond the normal human level; even arrogant and misused power reminds us that all earthly power is derived from God's almighty power.

Here this origin is either forgotten or denied. The mass of mankind, which does not trouble to think, and usually has no principles, prostrates itself in worshiping amazement before such a manifestation of earthly power. Nothing is so convincing as success. Thus, as if what he has to say is incredible, the seer says explicitly, three times over, (verses 4 and 8) that "the whole world" worships the beast. This worship is expressed in a most tasteless and terrible fashion in the parody of the great song of victory in Exodus 15; (in the sphere of religion all imitation is tasteless). A cult which has to use borrowed material is only an imitation; it is not genuine religion.

The blasphemies of men are only exceeded by the blasphemous speeches of the beast itself. It has no message of its own; it can only curse. Nor has it any positive historical mission; it can only destroy. Hence to it war is as necessary a method of activity as blasphemy. Since, however, the "saints" are not defeated by blasphemy, there is nothing for it but war. This war is the historical heritage which the beast has received from the dragon; it is the extension of its great "wrath" (Rev. 12:17). Thus the "saints" must be under no illusion about the beast's attitude toward them; the verses which contain the first part of this vision, the picture of the Antichrist, leave them in no doubt on this point! In *this* war the only possibility for Christians is defeat. There is no human historical possibility of any successful resistance to the beast. It is obvious that it is precisely these last observations which cannot be understood as the seer's interpretation of contemporary history. They point to a region far beyond our present world. What really happened was this: as the seer looked at the background of contemporary history, and pondered over the truths of biblical apocalyptic, he gradually gained an insight into the working of the historical forces which were hostile to God, and of their fundamental principles which can be traced through the whole course of history.

The beast from the abyss, the symbol of Antichrist, is the most pictorial expression of the truth that the course of history is handed over to this power which fights against God, and that this anti-Christian power will not be overcome within the course of history, but that it will continue to grow, till at the very end of history it will be defeated, and completely annihilated by Christ, to whom all power alone belongs. The supreme expression and the most vigorous development of earthly power is here being exercised against God, not for him.

The growth of this final anti-Christian power does not in any way occur only in the sphere of political order. The church, too, can be its sphere as, for instance, when it becomes worldly and secularized, and falls a prey to the lust for power. This has been very clearly and sharply expressed by Dostoevsky is his legend of the Grand Inquisitor.[11]

At the climax of this chapter, which is also its turning-point (verse 10), there is the great grim clear-sighted warning about the need for patience and faith, for fidelity, and the power to resist. This is also the meaning of the previous lines

[11] At the same time, this interpretation should be accepted in the light of Newman's warning: "It is almost one of the marks of the True Church, to be decried as 'Antichrist.'" *Apologia pro vita sua* (Everyman ed.), p. 125.

in the tenth verse. If we follow the difficult rendering it must be translated in some such way: "to whom prison is appointed, to prison he must go. To whom it is appointed to die by the sword,[12] must perish by the sword." This passage reminds us of Jer. 15:2, and reiterates the truth which dawned upon the prophet in those difficult times of testing and tribulation. In the period of total judgment there is nothing to be done but to bow in absolute submission before the holy and unchangeable will of God. The great, beautiful saying which occurs in the very middle of the Apocalypse—"Here is the endurance and the faith of the saints"—extols the power of resistance and the firmness of faith of the community of believers, which is maintained by the fact that it accepts what God has ordained.

Thus Christ's disciples are called to tread the path before them with complete surrender to his will, with their eyes open, trusting wholly in his merits and without fear, to the bitter end of history itself, with all its blood and tears.

SECOND BEAST: PROPHET OF THE ANTICHRIST

(*Rev. 13:11-18*)

11 Then I saw another beast which rose out of the earth; it had two horns like a lamb and it spoke like a dragon. 12 It exercises all the authority of the first beast in its presence, and makes the earth and its inhabitants worship the first beast, whose mortal wound was healed. 13 It works great signs, even making fire come down from heaven to earth in the sight of men; 14 and by the signs which it is allowed to work in the presence of the beast, it deceives those who dwell on earth, bidding them make an image for the beast which was wounded by the sword and yet lived; 15 and it was allowed to give breath to the image of the beast so that

[12] In this rendering, like Lohmeyer, we follow the more difficult reading of the text (Rev. 13:10).

> the image of the beast should even speak, and to cause those who will not worship the image of the beast to be slain. 16 Also it causes all, both small and great, both rich and poor, both free and slave, to be marked on the right hand or the forehead, 17 so that no one can buy or sell unless he has the mark, that is, the name of the beast or the number of its name. 18 This calls for wisdom: let him who has understanding reckon the number of the beast, for it is a human number, its number is six hundred and sixty-six.

The beast whose portrait is drawn in the following verses (verses 11-18) expresses what Jung-Stilling used to call "the satanic trinity." Just as the first beast was the "ape" of Christ (Augustine), so this second beast, in every feature, is a caricature of prophecy. Antichrist too has his prophet, even a false prophet. What Satan was in the metaphysical order, that Antichrist is in the political order, and the prophet of the Antichrist in the intellectual order. He is instinct rather than spirit. Since this second beast, in contrast to the first, comes from the mainland (that is, from Asia Minor) he comes from the sphere of emperor worship and of the apotheosis of Caesar.

When this second beast appears the possibility of heresy begins in the church, for the beast is, so to speak, the theologian of Antichrist. It speaks, teaches, and confirms this proclamation by "signs" (verse 13), and indeed by no less a miracle than that which had once been worked by Elijah (I Kings 18). Its main task consists in winning adherents to the cult of the beast. It carries out this commission with wonderful astuteness. It creates the mobile ritual picture of the beast, just as the cult of emperor worship had mobile pictures. Above all it achieves a process which always emerges in the sphere of a political cult: the political symbol becomes the object of ritual homage. The beast understands how to provide the cult with a menacing claim to totality, to which all, great and small, have to bow. He who does not submit is "liquidated." He is either killed outright, or he is subject to an economic boycott. In order to carry through this rigorous claim a "token" is introduced which all followers of the beast have to wear in a conspicuous place.

It is significant that the expression here used is the same as that used to describe the imperial seals. This was, so to speak, the sacrament of the cult of emperor worship, the parody of baptism. To the members of the early church, baptism signified that they were sealed with Christ's token, making known to all men that they belong to Christ.

At the same time, this ritual picture is also the symbol of the omnipresence of the divine emperor, which cannot be separated, even in thought, from sacrifice and worship. Anyone who refuses to make the act of homage before this political symbol, virtually declares that he is against the government. Once again, very clearly, we are told what the "unveiling" of the last days will mean. Then it will be impossible to hide one's colors: each person will either bear the sign of Christ (Rev. 7) or the mark of the Antichrist; neutrality will be impossible.

This section is more prophetic than the preceding one. The contemporary touches are merely allusive; the symbolism of the priesthood of emperor worship which played an important part in Asia Minor is in the background. It is out of these echoes of the terrible demonic power and idolatry of the cult of emperor worship which the early Christians found so difficult, that the picture of the great trial of faith which will take place in the last days arises.

Then it will no longer be a question of faith or unbelief; but faith will confront faith, religion will fight against religion, the worship of the earthly lord against the worship of the heavenly Lord. The conflict of the last days will be a religious decision. At the end of history there will not be various anti-Christian views or opinions, but a real religion against Christ, distinguished from faith in Christ by the fact that it will impose its faith by the exercise of brutal force.

Thus although the final meaning of this chapter is only intelligible in the light of prophecy, at two points the contemporary scene comes through. The first is the mention of the "mortal wound" in the beast's throat, which had been healed (verse 3). This feature stands out so plainly in the whole description of the beast that we feel it must have been inserted for some purpose. But we are no longer in a position to guess to what it alludes. We have no clue to it. It is often thought that it refers to the supposed return of Nero; there were people who thought that this cruel emperor had not really died, but that he was living somewhere in obscurity, whence one day he would suddenly reappear. But whether the seer is really referring to this legend is uncertain. However, the permanent meaning of this feature is plain. Just as the annihilation of the beast proved to be an illusion, so also all hasty anticipations of the death of this enemy of God will prove to be unjustified optimism. He has his "time"; as long as it lasts, no one and nothing can harm him.

The other allusion to contemporary history, still more obscure than the other one, is the famous number at the end of the chapter: 666. The ancient world loved these complicated riddles, of which there are many examples. This tendency was increased by the fact that the numbers were written with the letters of the alphabet. Everything from the most sublime to the most ordinary was described in this way. A scribble on the wall in Pompeii has been discovered in which a soldier wrote on the wall: "I love thee, whose number is . . ." No one could decipher this save the one who was in the secret. That is why numbers were used on serious occasions, as in this instance. Possibly the number arose because someone was speculating with the Greek word for "beast"; if this were written with Hebrew letters it gave the number 666. What this number actually means has been lost to us for ever; even Irenaeus did not know it. Many attempts have been made to solve it. The most illuminating is that of Adolf Deissmann: "Caesar God." [13]

NOTE

The idea of the ritual picture has had a widespread effect. According to Eastern thought the ruler himself was present in his picture. Hence the absolutist Eastern emperors hated Christian ikons.

[13] *Light from the Ancient East* (New York: George H. Doran Co., 1927), p. 344.

Chapter 11

The Seven Visions of the Son of Man

(Rev. 14:1-20)

THE LAMB UPON MOUNT ZION

(*Rev. 14:1-5*)

14 Then I looked, and lo, on Mount Zion stood the Lamb, and with him a hundred and forty-four thousand who had his name and his Father's name written on their foreheads. 2 And I heard a voice from heaven like the sound of many waters and like the sound of loud thunder; the voice I heard was like the sound of harpers playing on their harps, 3 and they sing a new song before the throne and before the four living creatures and before the elders. No one could learn that song except the hundred and forty-four thousand who had been redeemed from the earth. 4 It is these who have not defiled themselves with women, for they are chaste; it is these who follow the Lamb wherever he goes; these have been redeemed from mankind as first fruits for God and the Lamb, 5 and in their mouth no lie was found, for they are spotless.

When the impressive series of visions of the period of the last days begins afresh, a totally different picture emerges. It is as though, after the terrible glimpses of the twelfth and thirteenth chapters, the seer pauses for a moment, and the scene changes. In the new vision, which is impregnated with the awe of worship and celestial jubilation, the actual goal of history again stands out clearly, that is, the final victory of Christ. The obscure and difficult prospects of the thirteenth chapter had to be faced in order that there should be no illusion about the seriousness of this final period. But from the bright vision which now begins we can look back on those obscure and difficult chapters and see that everyone of us may know that no suffering has been borne in vain, and that at the end of every dark path is the victory of Christ.

The implied pause emphasizes the fact that the "time" of the beast (the forty-two months of Rev. 13:5) is over. The watershed of this final period has been crossed. The clouds begin to part; once more the summit of divine history reappears.

In the following vision the seer takes in the whole scene in one comprehensive glance. The Mountain of Zion soars into the heavens, and only a very literal mind will want to know whether this is the actual historic Mount Zion or its heavenly counterpart. Above all, dominating the picture and the whole universe, stands the Lamb, surrounded by the countless hosts of the elect. But before the seer is quite conscious that in spite of all the preceding terrible trials this scene of victory is possible—that the Lamb is unconquered, and that the number of the elect is undiminished—a mighty sound like thunder and like the beauty of many waters rushing down the hillside breaks upon his ears in supernatural power and beauty. And as he listens, the thunder of the waterfalls changes into the sweetest music from countless harps. Then, suddenly, it is no longer the sound of harps, but the music of a great choir, whose songs of praise echo and re-echo through the wide spaces of heaven. This vision cannot be described in human words: the melody is both too mighty and too sweet. The cosmic hymn of the Nineteenth Psalm becomes reality, the song of the ages resounds! In modern language we would say: "The wholly Other" makes his voice heard. But the seer says it more simply—"they sing a new song"—which goes far beyond any praise which could be offered upon earth.

This scene which opens with such a majestic song of praise

is not, however, a mere repetition of the seventh chapter[1]—not even in the formal sense of the word. We should rather regard it as the repetition of the introit or of antiphons in the liturgy. Just as these significant phrases embrace the whole service with prayer, praise, and reading of the word, and constitute its framework and thus its meaning, so also here. Chapter seven was the anticipation or foretelling of the glory of martyrdom. After the great main section, which emphasizes the necessity for martyrdom in the plainest possible terms, there now follows in conclusion the same significant word: it looks toward martyrdom! Even from the point of view of content, this scene is not a mere repetition, for here, from the very outset, the Lamb himself is visible.

Further, here a twofold promise is fulfilled. The Lord himself has already said (Mark 13:27) that at the end of the days he would gather his own together, and an ancient prophecy (Joel 2:32) is here recalled that the Messiah would appear upon Mount Zion. These promises will be realized when the time of fulfilment comes. When the heaviest trial of all, caused by the Antichrist, is over, then men will see that the Lord preserves his church, those whom he has chosen and "gathered" together. Then the historical laws of this world will cease, and the "wholly Other" will begin. It is the new world of God.

But those who wish to see it must be free from the earth (verse 3). The Greek word in the text signifies a sharp and resolute decision. Those who want to share in the glory of Christ's final victory must incorporate the new way of God in themselves. They must be "pure" and "chaste," as the prophets have already foretold, free from the stain of idolatry, free from all foreign religions, pure as the sacrifice which is offered upon the heavenly altar has to be pure. It is of course quite possible that the expressions "chaste" and "spotless" are

[1] Bousset, *op. cit.*, says: "The fantasies [!] of Rev. 7:1-8 and 14:1-5 do not come from the same mind."

intended in the literal and not in the metaphorical sense. If that is the case, then we are here confronted by the same view which is now and again expressed by Paul that, for Christians, in view of the imminent end of the world, it is better to remain unmarried. If this is so, it would prove that ascetic tendencies developed very early in Christianity. In any case, these Christians are described in three ways: they are ascetics; they are martyrs who have followed the Lamb to a violent death; and they are true witnesses, for "in their mouth no lie was found"; that is, they were free from the taint of heresy.

So these few verses contain a great consolation. The two previous chapters have prepared Christians for the fact that during the last days they may be harassed beyond measure, and sacrificed like sheep. Now they are assured, that although they will be defenseless, their sacrifice will not be in vain. God has accepted it, and borne it up to his altar; their obedience is not in vain. Fidelity to the Lamb "makes sense of life."

The thought expressed in the words: "they follow the Lamb wherever he goes" (verse 4) is an impressive reformulation of the words of the Lord in Matt. 10:38: "He who does not take his cross and follow me is not worthy of me." The early church preserved this thought of the *imitatio agni* with great care.

When we look back at the seventh chapter we see that the note of consolation is stronger. The hundred and forty-four thousand which were sealed there are here already delivered. Thus not a thread which God has woven in his plan is broken! It *seemed* as though the floods of persecution, with their trail of suffering and death, had blotted out the church; but they could not throw God's plans into disorder. No single one of the elect will be lost; he who is sealed will be preserved. When the floods have passed, Mount Zion appears high above the waters; the Lamb is on the throne of glory, surrounded by the triumphant songs of his own; the gracious presence of God fills the universe.

NOTE

In later Greek the word for "understand" may also mean to "hear": "No one could hear the song of praise. . . ." If we keep this translation in mind, we find the original transformation of an ancient image by the apocalyptic writer. As Pythagoras used to speak of the "music of the spheres," which earthly ears could not hear, so the apocalyptic writer speaks now of the heavenly song of praise which only the elect can hear.

FIRST ANGEL: THE ETERNAL GOSPEL
(*Rev. 14:6-7*)

6 Then I saw another angel flying in midheaven, with an eternal gospel to proclaim to those who dwell on earth, to every nation and tribe and tongue and people; 7 and he said with a loud voice, "Fear God and give him glory, for the hour of his judgment has come; and worship him who made heaven and earth, the sea and the fountains of water."

In the second half of the Apocalypse the emphasis on final and complete victory increases in volume. It is as though the watershed of time had been crossed and the forces which hinder victory are becoming fewer and weaker. Time itself seems to be ever hastening toward the final victory. The more brightly the day of victory of Jesus Christ begins to light up the horizon of the universe, the more does that tense "anxiety" which afflicts the world begin to disappear.

Here indeed the task of the expositor is not easy. At essential points, the judgment which is now proclaimed remains obscure. We are not told exactly on whom, and where the judgment is to take place. But at least it is plain that the restoration of the divine order begins with judgment. The Judge himself does not yet appear. In his unearthly majesty he tarries until judgment has been executed upon the earth. But already angel messengers announce the divine restoration of order in the world. This message is proclaimed in a mighty threefold utterance.

The first angel appears, high in mid-heaven, visible to the whole world, and proclaims an eternal gospel to all nations, that is, an unchanging message of great joy. The word of promise is proclaimed from the same point at which the eagle cried "woe" (Rev. 8:13) to all the dwellers upon the earth. For when this angel appears, the promise is fulfilled that at the end of the days the mission of the Son of God to the whole world will become so evident that it will be like the lightning which flashes from one end of the world to the other (Matt. 24:27). The mission of the church is achieved (Matt. 24:14). The Lord calls the wandering sheep back to the divine fold. Once more all our ideas of time are thrown into the melting pot: "the hour of his judgment has come." The end is here.

NOTE

The phrase, "the eternal gospel" (verse 6), has often been regarded as something very mysterious, and has served as the starting point for many a strange doctrine, as for instance in the medieval chiliastic movement of Joachim of Flora (d. 1202), who already regarded the Papacy as Antichrist, and announced the coming of the "third kingdom," the kingdom of the Holy Spirit, for the year 1260.

SECOND ANGEL: JUDGMENT ON BABYLON
(*Rev. 14:8*)

8 Another angel, a second, followed, saying, "Fallen, fallen is Babylon the great, she who made all nations drink the wine of her impure passion."

It is the task of the second angel to anticipate with prophetic authority the fall of the world power. However powerful its anti-Christian proceedings may be, in the end its defeat is certain and final.

NOTE

Babylon (verse 8) is the name used in apocalyptic writings for the world power, and the early Christians applied it to Rome (I Peter 5:13). Here it simply means the anti-Christian world power as a whole.

THIRD ANGEL: PROCLAMATION OF JUDGMENT ON FOLLOWERS OF THE BEAST

(*Rev. 14:9-11*)

9 And another angel, a third, followed, saying with a loud voice, "If any one worships the beast and its image, and receives a mark on his forehead or on his hand, 10 he also shall drink the wine of God's wrath, poured unmixed into the cup of his anger, and he shall be tormented with fire and brimstone in the presence of the holy angels and in the presence of the Lamb. 11 And the smoke of their torment goes up for ever and ever; and they have no rest, day or night, these worshipers of the beast and its image, and whoever receives the mark of its name."

Finally, the terrible spirit of the previous chapter returns. The third angel brings the most grim warning. The beast would not tolerate any resistance; it was in the habit of forcing its totalitarian claim on all with bloodthirsty and ruthless power. But still less is God mocked; those who venture to resist him must drink the cup of his wrath to the very dregs, for the wine is the wine of the anger of God. The nations who have yielded to the pressure of the world-power have incurred the doom of the wrath of God, and this wrath cannot be evaded. All who have once accepted the mark of the beast, because it ensured them a share in world dominion, now see that it is this mark which singles out all who have rebelled against God.

BLESSEDNESS OF THE SAINTS

(*Rev. 14:12-13*)

12 Here is a call for the endurance of the saints, those who keep the commandments of God and the faith of Jesus.

13 And I heard a voice from heaven saying, "Write this: Blessed are the dead who die in the Lord hence-

forth." "Blessed indeed," says the Spirit, "that they may rest from their labors, for their deeds follow them!"

Nothing that God has promised is lost. Even the Word which once seemed like an empty promise against a dark horizon returns once more: "Here is the endurance of the saints" (Rev. 13:10). We can well imagine what these words must have meant to the Christians of that day, as they gathered together to worship God in face of the threatening storm of persecution. This patience was not exercised in vain. The turning point is already in sight, and the seer proclaims with glowing confidence: "Blessed are the dead who die in the Lord henceforth." The Spirit of God himself assures them that the "works of faith and patience" will accompany the disciples who suffer martyrdom. The call to martyrdom is here proclaimed in a very strong and confident way.

In these majestic words the book has reached its summit. Outwardly and concretely we stand at the highest point of the Apocalypse. This summit has been reached through the great and terrible visions which have preceded it.

SON OF MAN WITH THE SICKLE
(*Rev. 14:14-16*)

14 Then I looked, and lo, a white cloud, and seated on the cloud one like a son of man, with a golden crown on his head, and a sharp sickle in his hand. 15 And another angel came out of the temple, calling with a loud voice to him who sat upon the cloud, "Put in your sickle, and reap, for the hour to reap has come, for the harvest of the earth is fully ripe." 16 So he who sat upon the cloud swung his sickle on the earth, and the earth was reaped.

This section is illuminated with light from the summit already attained. The victory of Christ is proclaimed. The fulfilment of time is no empty process. In the vivid symbol of the harvest, which from the days of the prophets has always been used to describe the end of history, the verdict that the World King, Jesus Christ, will pronounce upon world history is announced.

The vision begins in majestic radiance. A beam of silvery light streams out from a shimmering cloud upon which the Son of Man and the world's Judge sits enthroned. A light from below shows up the shining glory of the golden crown which adorns the head of the Son of Man: for the first time the figure of Christ himself appears! In the Old Testament the cloud denoted a "God who hid himself"; here it is changed into dazzling light, and has become the scene of a new epiphany.

Something like a great shaft of lightning shoots across the sky and down onto the earth. This is the sickle, which denotes the harvest of judgment. It has a sharp, metallic radiance which causes the seer to start back in astonishment. Then, as behind the figure of the Son of Man on the shimmering white cloud, behind the gleaming gold of the crown and the flaming light of the sickle, the radiant outline of the heavenly temple appears, and the mighty figure of an angel emerges from the midst of the radiance. In a dignified liturgical manner he speaks to the Son of Man, who is enthroned upon the white cloud, in a word which sets the process of judgment in motion.

Once more the lightning seems to flash across the sky and down on to the earth. Once more he raises the sickle, in a silence in which everyone seems to be holding their breath, and as it is hurled on to the earth, the judgment begins. The call and gesture of the angel are not only a solemn liturgical action, but they mean something deeper: the hour has come; God's command now ushers in the actual final judgment. There is a predestinarian wealth of meaning about this sense of the irresistible forward movement of an order established by God.

NOTE

The "white cloud" (verse 14), also in Dan. 7:13, is the throne of the Son of Man, the symbol of the presence of God.

ANGEL WITH THE SICKLE

(*Rev. 14:17-20*)

17 And another angel came out of the temple in heaven, and he too had a sharp sickle. 18 Then another angel came out from the altar, the angel who has power over fire, and he called with a loud voice to him who had the sharp sickle, "Put in your sickle, and gather the clusters of the vine of the earth, for its grapes are ripe." 19 So the angel swung his sickle on the earth and gathered the vintage of the earth, and threw it into the great wine press of the wrath of God; 20 and the wine press was trodden outside the city, and blood flowed from the wine press, as high as a horse's bridle, for one thousand six hundred stadia.

Once more in the flickering gleam of the lightning the sickle shines brightly, this time in the hand of a second angel. And behold, a third angel steps out of the rose-red light around the heavenly altar of sacrifice. The picture of the harvest of judgment has become still more impressive, clothed in the familiar imagery of the grape harvest. Once more the horror mounts, red flames shoot up into the sky—like blood! As the juice of the grapes flows into the wine press, so the blood flows from the wine press and mounts "as high as a horse's bridle" (verse 20).

The double character of the vision, the twofold picture of judgment and harvest, is not only meant to describe the terror of the final judgment, but primarily to show very clearly the character of the will of God, which proceeds on its way almost with the precision of law. Impressive as the description of this judgment is, with its reflection of fire, the gleaming metal of the sickle, and the overwhelming radiance from the figure of the Son of Man—stronger than all these impressions is the certainty: Jesus is victor. The radiant dawn of the day of Jesus Christ begins to shed its light more and more brightly over the terrible colors of the final judgment.

It is a strong, clear light. Above the confusion of the world, and of world history, God's justice reigns. The most terrible anti-Christian distortion of history cannot in the end escape from God's dominion, just as little, as on the other hand, the fidelity, patience, and obedience of faith of Christians can be lost. The Spirit testifies that those who die in the Lord are "blessed," however little the world of their day knew them. The same Spirit testifies that God's judgments cannot be evaded, even if they are only the dark foil for the unchangeable purpose of grace, which is God's final will for the world.

Once again, this chapter only strikes the first note of the theme of the following chapters which describe the completion of the final judgment. A new septenary begins; this series is called the visions of the seven bowls.

NOTES

The "vine" (verse 18) is always the picture of the last days. Usually it signifies the fulness of grace of the last days, when the creation will again fulfil its God-given destiny. Here it is a phenomenon which accompanies the picture of the final judgment. The fact that the corn harvest and the grape harvest are placed alongside of one another corresponds exactly to Joel 1:10ff.

"Outside the city" (verse 20) the judgment on those who had been cast outside the community is carried out. This means: the separation has been completed—first of all by men, and now in judgment, by God himself.

The remarkable note of numbers at the close (one thousand six hundred stadia—300 kilometers) possibly merely means "the whole round earth." For sixteen hundred stadia are four times four hundred or forty times forty; and in this we may see perhaps, as the ancient commentator Victorinus (fourth century) thought, an allusion to the four ends of the earth (*per omnes mundi quattuor partes*).

It is interesting that this numerical note corresponds almost exactly with the length of Palestine from Tyre to the frontier of Egypt: sixteen hundred and forty-four stadia.

Chapter 12

The Seven Bowls of the Wrath of God

(Rev. 15:1—16:21)

CELESTIAL OVERTURE

(*Rev. 15:1-8*)

1 Then I saw another portent in heaven, great and wonderful, seven angels with seven plagues, which are the last, for with them the wrath of God is ended.

2 And I saw what appeared to be a sea of glass mingled with fire, and those who had conquered the beast and its image and the number of its name, standing beside the sea of glass with harps of God in their hands. 3 And they sing the song of Moses, the servant of God, and the song of the Lamb, saying,

"Great and wonderful are thy deeds,
O Lord God the Almighty!
Just and true are thy ways,
O King of the ages!
4 Who shall not fear and glorify thy name, O Lord?
For thou alone art holy.
All nations shall come and worship thee,
for thy judgments have been revealed."

5 After this I looked, and the temple of the tent of witness in heaven was opened, 6 and out of the temple came the seven angels with the seven plagues, robed in pure bright linen, and their breasts girded with golden girdles. 7 And one of the four living creatures gave the seven angels seven golden bowls full of the wrath of God who lives for ever and ever; 8 and the temple was filled with smoke from the glory of God and from his power, and

no one could enter the temple until the seven plagues of the seven angels were ended.

The following section again contains a kind of celestial interlude, before the act of punitive judgment begins and is completed. Once more the solemn way in which these short scenes are described makes it clear that even the judgment which is about to fall on mankind is not the outbreak of blind natural forces, but the fulfilment of a divine plan.

The first verse is simply a superscription. But even here the light of divine order shines through, as the concluding formula shows: "for with them the wrath of God is ended."

The actual vision again reveals part of the celestial liturgy. It is remarkable that all these terrors of the last days are announced in the form of a celestial act of worship. It is as though the seer were standing by the sea, on the lonely shore of Patmos, and the light of the setting sun were coloring the waves. Then in spirit he sees the sea of glass, crystal clear, shot through and through with gold and gleams of fire. Again suddenly, in the midst of this symphony of color, comes the sound of harps and singing, which re-echoes through the celestial spaces. It is not a blasphemous parody, like the song of the choir in honor of the beast (Rev. 13:4), but here there breaks out the most beautiful song of faith of the ancient dispensation, the song of Moses, the song of victory (Exodus 15) (which the followers of the beast have desecrated) in honor of the heavenly Lord.

It is prophecy in song; what the singers of the old covenant had sung in anticipation is now achieved. For the singers are the spirits of just men made perfect. They are the martyrs, those who have come out of great tribulation, out of the period when the dragon and the Antichrist seemed to rule the world. They are not lost, but united in the song of praise and victory. In the restored earth the nations are alive, not as before in apostasy, but in praise of the living God. This song of praise is also in three stages. Even if Satan were let loose in the cosmos, no word is uttered against God's creation. "The great works of God are glorious, as on the first Day of Creation." [1]

Even though the way of suffering with Christ was bitter, and although the abyss which is revealed in the Apocalypse is terrible, yet God's ways are true and righteous. Further, the righteous working of God is revealed in the sufferings of Christ, and in the sufferings of the church, which suffers with Christ. This consolation should not be forgotten, when the final series of plagues is about to begin.

A second scene of still greater impressiveness follows. The doors of the heavenly temple reopen. The seer sees the seven angels coming forth, who, as they march in the celestial procession, prepare to do their service. A shimmer of white and gold, a solemn and dignified symbol, surrounds them, a sign that they are not executioners of judgment, but servants of God, serving him in their order and office. Yes, it is a significant rite, for they themselves bear the tokens of honor which in the first chapter were borne by the Son of Man. In a dignified way, one of the living creatures now steps forth, and gives a bowl to each of the seven angels, filled with the wine of the wrath of God, a small yet significant symbol. The judgments of God are concealed in the solemn ritual of the heavenly worship. Again and again, and ever more urgently we are shown the vast difference between them and the arbitrary acts of a human tyrant.

The "smoke from the glory of God" rises from the altar and again completely conceals the doors of the heavenly temple. From this time forth they are hidden from the sight of the seer until the last series of the plagues has been completed.

This is the meaning of the vision: the more impressively the end of history approaches, the more profound becomes

[1] Cf. Rev. 15:1-4 (Peterson).

the conviction that God does not divulge his purpose to any earthly being. Even when the Apocalypse does reveal something, the mystery of the divine majesty remains unapproachable. Twice in this chapter we are assured that the judgment of the wrath of God must be completed (Rev. 1:8). It is the same holy majesty which already brooded over the earthly life of Jesus (John 19:28, 30)—the same in mercy and in judgment.

This chapter, with its two impressive scenes, is closely linked with the following chapter, in which the last series of plagues is described in a very orderly and compact manner.

NOTES

The "sea of glass" was already mentioned in Rev. 4:6. Probably behind this symbol there lies a hint or a reminiscence of the "heavenly ocean" of the Greeks, connected with Helios, the sun god, who drove across that ocean in a fiery chariot. This would also explain the phrase, "mingled with fire." It seemed to the ancients wonderful that the fire of lightning could flash in the ocean of the clouds.

The Milky Way seemed to the ancients to be the path along which the souls of the departed flew out of Hades into heaven. Again the Seer as it were brushes ancient pagan ideas aside—those whom the living God has chosen now stand at the gate of heaven and sing his praises.

The song in verses 3 and 4 is not really a song of victory, but a hymn of adoration. It is the third song of this kind which the purified souls sing (in addition to this passage see Rev. 7:9ff. and 12:10ff). This song is the one which bears most traces of the influence of the Old Testament. Moreover, it represents the highest degree of fulfilment.

OUTPOURING OF THE SEVEN BOWLS OF WRATH
(Rev. 16:1-21)

(Rev. 16:1)

1 Then I heard a loud voice from the temple telling the seven angels, "Go and pour out on the earth the seven bowls of the wrath of God."

The fundamental architectonic law on which the Apocalypse is constructed—which we have often noted—now goes further, and a new septenary begins. The seven trumpet visions lead to the fall of the dragon, the seven visions of the seven bowls now lead to the fall of the world-power. This repetition is not merely for the sake of literary effect; it is due to the fact that the nearer the time of fulfilment the heavier and more severe is the judgment.

The description of the plagues is more compact and solid than in the previous section; one follows another with the regularity of the strokes of a hammer. A loud command issues from the sanctuary. We are not told who is giving the order, but in the light of Rev. 15:8 there can be no doubt that God himself is calling, summoning his angels to do their duty. And then the uncanny gesture is repeated—seven times —with which the angels carry out the command and empty their bowls.

There are two reminiscences behind these visions: the Egyptian plagues (Exodus 7-10), and the trumpet visions of Revelation 8. But everything has become much sharper and more terrible.[2] The nearer the end approaches the more sharply is the picture outlined. There are no longer any exceptions. The whole cosmos comes under the same judgment; the mysterious connection which links the whole creation with the destiny of man reappears.

First Bowl

(*Rev. 16:2*)

> 2 So the first angel went and poured his bowl on the earth, and foul and evil sores came upon the men who bore the mark of the beast and worshiped its image.

The meaning of the plagues is quite clear.

The first plague is stronger than its archetype, the sixth

[2] Bengel, *op. cit.* "In the trumpet visions much is figurative, for the length of the periods does not spoil the actual meaning of the words; but wherever bowls are concerned, everything happens very clearly and swiftly."

Moreover, a comparison with the trumpet visions (Rev. 8-11) shows the similarity in both series of plagues, and thus the well-thought-out systematic structure of the book.

Egyptian plague (Exod. 9:10ff), for it affects the whole of mankind. All who once bore the mark of the beast are visited by the "marks" of God, which raise painful and ugly swellings. God does not leave unmarked those who have allowed themselves to accept a symbol of resistance and rebellion against God, whether they did this out of deliberate enmity or merely out of thoughtlessness.

Second Bowl

(Rev. 16:3)

> 3 The second angel poured his bowl into the sea, and it became like the blood of a dead man, and every living thing died that was in the sea.

The second plague too, which turns all the water into blood, is stronger than the second trumpet vision, because it affects the whole world.

Third Bowl and Song of Angel of the Water

(Rev. 16:4-7)

> 4 The third angel poured his bowl into the rivers and the fountains of water, and they became blood. 5 And I heard the angel of water say,
> "Just art thou in these thy judgments,
> thou who art and wast, O Holy One.
> 6 For men have shed the blood of saints and prophets,
> and thou hast given them blood to drink.
> It is their due!"
> 7 And I heard the altar cry,
> "Yea, Lord God the Almighty,
> true and just are thy judgments!"

In the third plague the same fate affects all the rivers and springs, and the "angel of water" (verse 5) has to explain the doom: the persecutors who shed streams of blood when they killed the martyrs must be visited with a similar judgment. "To men it is terrible to be punished in such a way that God is explicitly praised for it." [3] From the foot of the heavenly altar, however, where the souls of the first martyrs are kept, comes the response which praises God's righteous judgment.

Fourth Bowl

(Rev. 16:8-9)

> 8 The fourth angel poured his bowl on the sun, and it was allowed to scorch men with fire; 9 men were scorched by the fierce heat, and they cursed the name of God who had power over these plagues, and they did not repent and give him glory.

The fourth plague affects the sun, whose scorching heat hurts men so much that at last the pain causes them to cry out in blasphemy against God. The difference between this vision and that of the fourth trumpet vision consists in the fact that there the judgment of God only darkens the seer's light. Here it causes terrible torment.

Fifth Bowl

(Rev. 16:10-11)

> 10 The fifth angel poured his bowl on the throne of the beast, and its kingdom was in darkness; men gnawed their tongues in anguish 11 and cursed the God of heaven for their pains and sores, and did not repent of their deeds.

The fifth angel has to pour out his bowl with its plague upon the "throne of the beast," that is, upon the seat of world dominion, which is at enmity with God. With an uncanny precision, here as in the preceding judgments, the seer re-emphasizes the fact that God has not overlooked the blasphemies of the hostile world ruler: everything will be dealt with, and avenged. If we ask: Is Rome meant? or an absolute

[3] Bengel, *op. cit.*

world-dominion as a whole? we can only say that it must be the latter, for the sphere of earthly history has been left behind long ago. Those who once could not do enough to blaspheme God and his claim to sovereignty (verse 10), now cry out and gnaw their tongues in anguish.

Sixth Bowl

(*Rev. 16:12-16*)

12 The sixth angel poured his bowl on the great river Euphrates, and its water was dried up, to prepare the way for the kings from the east. 13 And I saw, issuing from the mouth of the dragon and from the mouth of the beast and from the mouth of the false prophet, three foul spirits like frogs; 14 for they are demonic spirits, performing signs, who go abroad to the kings of the whole world, to assemble them for battle on the great day of God the Almighty. 15 ("Lo, I am coming like a thief! Blessed is he who is awake, keeping his garments that he may not go naked and be seen exposed!") 16 And they assembled them at the place which is called in Hebrew Armageddon.

With the sixth plague the tension is greatly increased; the same thing occurred with the similar sixth trumpet vision (Rev. 9:13). Here, certainly, historical events *are* in the background of the writer's thought. The Euphrates was the great river frontier in the East. When it dried up, it was a terrible event, for the way was then open for the "kings from the East" to enter. This allusion suggests the Parthian invasions. This picture of great historical horrors is used to illustrate one of the plagues of the last days.

The forces of the deep come to the surface. The dragon, the beast, and the false prophet reappear, and also their messengers. The frogs appear which, from the time of the Egyptian plagues, were regarded as signs of sinister forces from the dark underworld. With their demonic capacity for working miracles they once again succeed in restoring the earthly political united front against God. These terrible hosts of darkness gather themselves together in a united army to the place where the final decisive battle will be fought: Armageddon. This is a word of Hebrew origin, and it means the mountain of Megiddo, that is, Carmel.

This place was deeply engraved on the memory of the Israelites, because it was connected with terrible events. At Megiddo one of the best Kings of Israel, Josiah, fell in battle against Pharaoh Necho, and some of the greatest political hopes of his people were buried in his grave with him (II Kings 23:29). Upon Carmel too, the "mountain of Megiddo," Elijah ended the conflict with heathenism against the cult of Baal with a terrible judgment on the priests of Baal (I Kings 18). In a place like this the final decisive battles of history will be fought, no longer against the armies of Egypt or of foreign cults, but against the hosts of darkness.

NOTES

The number "three" for the frog figures (verse 13) which come out of the mouth of the dragon, the beast, and the false prophet, should not lead us into futile speculation. They are simply the counterpart, as representatives of the sinful world, of the three angels in Rev. 14:6-9.

Luther, who unfortunately sometimes dabbled in apocalyptic speculations, regarded the three frogs as his opponents Faber, Eck, and Emser. Needless to say, we cannot follow him in this exposition.

On verse 15, cf. Rev. 3:3 (p. 88).

Seventh Bowl

(Rev. 16:17-21)

17 The seventh angel poured his bowl into the air, and a great voice came out of the temple, from the throne, saying, "It is done!" 18 And there were flashes of lightning, loud noises, peals of thunder, and a great earthquake such as had never been since men were on the earth, so great was that earthquake. 19 The great city was split into three parts, and the cities of the nations fell, and God remembered great Babylon, to make

> her drain the cup of the fury of his wrath. 20 And every island fled away, and no mountains were to be found; 21 and great hailstones, heavy as a hundredweight, dropped on men from heaven, till men cursed God for the plague of the hail, so fearful was that plague.

The seventh plague belongs to the series of impressive descriptions of the fall of the world-power. It is of course only an anticipation of what is to come, and should therefore only be understood as an introduction to the judgment on the world-power, which is grandly described in Revelation 17 to 19. Still, in this connection the seventh plague ushers in the mighty dramatic conclusion. As the angel—with a final menacing gesture—empties the contents of the bowl into the air, it is as though all the elements of stability disintegrate. In earthquakes and world-wide shattering natural events, everything breaks down. The destruction is fearful and universal. The "great city" (Jerusalem? Babylon? Rome?) breaks into three parts. Mountains and hills—the pillars upon which the earth is established—fall in, and bury humanity below, still crying out against God. The end of the earth is here.

In this chapter the description of the horror of the last days seems to grow in breathtaking intensity, but this gives the impression that a holy plan of God is being carried out without let or hindrance from any quarter. "Be not deceived, God is not mocked!" In point of fact the idea of vengeance must find some expression in the last days, not in the sense of petty revenge, but in order to protect the holiness of God, who, while he forgives the repentant sinner a hundredfold, still makes it clear, at the end of history, that his honor has not been left at the mercy of the ungodly hostile forces, however often in the course of history this may have seemed to be the case.

This confirms the majestic words which God himself pronounces: "It is done" (verse 17). One alone, at the turning point of history, was able to exclaim, "It is finished!" [4] Here again this recurs as the majestic Word which will end all earthly life forever. When this final series of judgments has been completed, the end of time will come. The wheel of history and of all earthly events will have run down. Although at present, after great historical upheavals, there is always the possibility that the course of history will be renewed from within, at the end of time this will not be so. At that moment there will no longer be any possibility of deliverance within history.

This chapter closes with this impressive contrast: God's majestic announcement that the course of earthly history is finished awakens the anxious cry of humanity which no longer possesses any other possibility of existence. All provisional earthly authority has disappeared. Once more God himself takes the reins of events into his own hands.

[4] John 19:30.

Chapter 13

The Seven Visions of the Fall of Babylon

(Rev. 17:1—19:10)

THE GREAT HARLOT

(*Rev. 17:1-6a*)

1 Then one of the seven angels who had the seven bowls came and said to me, "Come, I will show you the judgment of the great harlot who is seated upon many waters, 2 with whom the kings of the earth have committed fornication, and with the wine of whose fornication the dwellers on earth have become drunk." 3 And he carried me away in the Spirit into a wilderness, and I saw a woman sitting on a scarlet beast which was full of blasphemous names, and it had seven heads and ten horns. 4 The woman was arrayed in purple and scarlet, and bedecked with gold and jewels and pearls, holding in her hand a golden cup full of abominations and the impurities of her fornication; 5 and on her forehead was written a name of mystery: "Babylon the great, mother of harlots and of earth's abominations." 6 And I saw the woman, drunk with the blood of the saints and the blood of the martyrs of Jesus.

The final judgment is approaching its climax. The judgment on the earth has been completed. So much devastation and destruction has passed over it that there is no longer any resistance to God within history. All that remains is the final decisive act, by which God's enemies on earth, Satan and his instruments, will be annihilated. This last act contains the judgment on the world-power whose fall is now recorded, which bears the mysterious name of "Babylon." Here of course we are not dealing with a process within history, but with the decisive events at the end of history. But the original image[1] is even more remote than is usual in the Apocalypse. At the time when the seer was writing Babylon was in ruins. Even the allusion to the fact that "Babylon is on the edge of many waters" cannot be applied geographically to the historical Babylon. All that this phrase means is that the "great city" feels "utterly secure." [2] Here it is significant that we are not dealing with a process within history, but with decisions which are part of the end of history, which extend far beyond the sphere of history as we know it.

The first verse is a kind of superscription. But as so often in this book, which is full of drama and movement, it is not expressed in a theoretical formula, but through a figure which acts. An angel interpreter, one of the angels of the seven bowls, steps forward, and announces the next vision, in which the judgment on Babylon begins. With a decided gesture he lays hold of the seer and carries him off into the wilderness, that place of terror and awe, whence the judgment on Babylon was once announced (Isa. 21:1) and in which it is now being completed.

With the vividness peculiar to the seer's vision, and to his manner of presenting his subject, he now beholds a scene which is in active motion: the figure of a woman, sitting on a horse. While the vision of the woman, shimmering in purple and gold, passes swiftly over the stage, one detail after another reveals the religious quality of the vision.

The fact that the woman is riding upon a horse is in itself a recollection of an oriental picture of the gods. This vague reminiscence, however, is brought in here for a very definite purpose. The woman is riding upon the animal which was mentioned in the thirteenth chapter, the description of which, in spite of some differences, is here repeated. The seer is now

[1] German: *Urbild.* (Translator's note.)

[2] Lohmeyer, *op. cit.*

gazing at the beast from the abyss, the world of the Antichrist. The woman who is riding on the beast controls the empire.

This world is shimmering with purple and gold, the insignia of the Roman rulers, generals, and conquerors. The saddle cloth of the beast is scarlet, the garment of the great harlot is purple, glittering with gold and jewels—all marks of imperial dignity. They are symbols of political existence, surrounded by a halo of religion which controls the whole. The figure of the woman, according to widespread examples in the ancient world, is the symbol of the *Polis,* of the *Tyche,*[3] symbol and center of the ancient city-republic.

But everything the woman does suggests the sharp contrast which colors the whole description. Her whole attitude is that of a harlot. The fact that this woman is represented as a courtesan is not accidental. Of course here, as so often in the Bible, the expression "adultery" is used in a metaphorical sense, and is a symbol of the undisciplined character of the world-power. At the same time, a symbol of this kind is not chosen at random. The immorality of the harlot is only the outward sign of a deeper lack of discipline. Her "adultery" is of the kind so often described by the prophets: not "bound" to God, the Lord of all historical and political order, she gives herself to all, loses all sense of direction, and thus destroys all genuine order, since she also leads others astray (verse 2). This symbol of indiscipline also contains the suggestion that the political element is at home in the world of pluralism. At the end, when the majesty of Christ is revealed, it will become increasingly clear that a false political order, with no real foundation, has lost all sense of direction.

As the courtesan rides along on her horse she swings in her hand a golden cup, which is full to overflowing with "abominations and impurities." From the writings of Seneca and Juvenal we know that it was the custom for Roman prostitutes to wear their names in the fillet which encircled

[3] *Tyche,* the goddess of fortune. (Translator's note.)

their brows, so this woman wears her name distinctly upon her forehead, showing that, in spite of all this royal glamor, she is nothing but a prostitute. The "mystery" of this name (verse 5) is doubtless contained in the word "mother." In the religion of the ancient world the word "mother" often had a religious connotation. Here too, in this figure which sums up man's enmity toward God, it is an expression derived from the semiobscurity of feminine cults. This religious sphere, which was nourished by the dark forces of the subconscious and by erotic influences, explains too why this woman is "drunk," drunk with that passion which clouds the mind, and throws a cloak over lies and deceit (verse 6).

The last feature in this scene is clearest of all: the woman bears traces of the blood of the disciples of Jesus. This one detail must be an allusion to some persecution on a large scale, possibly to that under Nero. In any case, the coming judgment will fall on that power, because it has so often shed the blood of the church.

NOTE

In the fifth verse most Greek texts read "mother of harlots. . . ." The most ancient Latin manuscripts, however, read "mother of adultery. . . ." This reading seems to give a more exact counterpart to the "abominations." Possibly it reflects the original sense of the words.

INTERPRETATION BY THE ANGEL

(*Rev. 17:6b-18*)

6b When I saw her I marveled greatly. 7 But the angel said to me, "Why marvel? I will tell you the mystery of the woman, and of the beast with seven heads and ten horns that carries her. 8 The beast that you saw was, and is not, and is to ascend from the bottomless pit and go to perdition; and the dwellers on earth whose names have not been written in the book of life from the foundation of the world, will marvel to behold the beast, because it was and is not and is to come. 9 This calls for a mind with wisdom: the seven heads are seven hills

> on which the woman is seated; 10 they are also seven kings, five of whom have fallen, one is, the other has not yet come, and when he comes he must remain only a little while. 11 As for the beast that was and is not, it is an eighth but it belongs to the seven, and it goes to perdition. 12 And the ten horns that you saw are ten kings who have not yet received royal power, but they are to receive authority as kings for one hour, together with the beast. 13 These are of one mind and give over their power and authority to the beast; 14 they will make war on the Lamb, and the Lamb will conquer them, for he is Lord of lords and King of kings, and those with him are called and chosen and faithful."
>
> 15 And he said to me, "The waters that you saw, where the harlot is seated, are peoples and multitudes and nations and tongues. 16 And the ten horns that you saw, they and the beast will hate the harlot; they will make her desolate and naked, and devour her flesh and burn her up with fire, 17 for God has put it into their hearts to carry out his purpose by being of one mind and giving over their royal power to the beast, until the words of God shall be fulfilled. 18 And the woman that you saw is the great city which has dominion over the kings of the earth."

Apart from chapter seven, this is the first time in the Apocalypse that an angel appears with an interpretation, and a detailed one at that. The brief verse (seven) which introduces it is significant. Confronted by this phenomenon the seer is "amazed." This amazement is not an expression of curiosity, but it is akin to that amazement which was felt by men who saw the beast rising out of the abyss (Rev. 13:1), that dangerous preliminary stage which led to honoring and worshiping the beast. But before this temptation (which merely flashed through the seer's mind) could reach his heart, the heavenly messenger himself warned him against this emotion.

The way in which he does this is significant: he reveals the mystery of the beast. The godless character of the woman—this symbol of the imperial power—only needs to be shown in its true colors, and she immediately loses her power. The moment has come when all the forces working against God will be unmasked. The time is fulfilled; all that is provisional is over. Hence the authority of this figure, which was only an arrogant assumption of power and not a genuine authority, crumbles into dust. In the person of the seer, the whole of Christendom is reminded of the First Commandment—those who believe in God will not even wonder at the growth of a human power which arrogantly claims the right to meet God on a level of equality. God alone is LORD.

The actual interpretation is full of echoes of contemporary events, but it is not in the least confined to them.

The beast which "was and is not and is to ascend" out of the abyss (verse 8) is the satanic counterpart of him "who is and was and is to come." This world-power, represented by the beast, is most closely related to that great incarnation of imperial power which the seer knew in the form of Rome. We can only understand the ninth verse if we regard it as an allusion to the City of the Seven Hills, Rome.[4] The seer uses this city, center of the greatest form of world-power of that day, as a symbol of that secular power which is hostile to God, and the twice repeated expression "abominations," (verses 4 and 5), probably refers to cults which sprang up as satellites of the self-deifying power. This power, and the exuberant cult of the senses which the woman upon the beast represents, have a common root: visibility. Man sees what is before his eyes; that is what he most easily and most willingly worships. He understands success and enjoyment. Nothing convinces like success, and nothing is so attractive as the pleasures of the senses. How can faith meet such a mood, when its very essence consists in being "convinced of what we do not see?" (Heb. 11:1).

[4] Virgil, *Aen.* 6:782; Horace, *Carm. saec.* 7.

Originally too, the remarkable use of numbers in verses 9-12 may have contained allusions to contemporary events; but even if this were so it has no significance for us today. Any attempt to throw light on this group of numbers from the examination of contemporary historical events will be fruitless, because this passage is not intended to be connected with contemporary events. As the beginning of the ninth verse suggests, these numbers are not meant to be taken in a mathematical sense, but metaphorically.

Of course, this emphasis on numbers reminds us of their significance in some spheres of religious belief, seven is the perfect number, for instance, five denotes imperfection, while eight means that which is excessive. At the same time, it is possible that these numbers may be influenced by astrological ideas, for instance, the number of the planets and the signs of the zodiac. But for real interpretation all this means very little, just as it is pointless to try to calculate the five kings in terms of Roman emperors. Linguistically, this would be possible, because in the New Testament the Roman emperor is usually the "king." But in spite of this, it does not work out, for if we try to make this calculation we never find an emperor who fits into the scheme. The first five emperors were Augustus, Tiberius, Caligula, Claudius, and Nero; but if we leave out the "interim" ones, Galba, Otho, and Vitellius, who were regarded as "revolutionaries," then the sixth emperor would be Vespasian; the seventh, Titus. But this conclusion leads us nowhere, especially if we accept the view that the Apocalypse was not written during the reign of Vespasian, but some twenty-five years later, under Domitian. Thus the meaning of this passage must be sought upon another plane, where time is transcended. Probably, its meaning is as follows.

As the seer gazes into the world of his day, against the background of the end, he sees the many forms assumed by the imperial power, all of which were sharply opposed to God. The series is not yet completed; but the end is approaching.

The "eighth," the final, decisive, world-ruler is expected; he will be the beast from the abyss. As the eighth ruler he breaks through the fixed series of seven, and the new chapter, the end of history, begins. He himself does not belong to this series, and yet he "belongs to the seven" (verse 11), i.e., by his very nature he belongs to it. To this extent the allusion to Nero is not wholly out of place; at the end of history just as bloodthirsty a man will be in this position. But "it goes to perdition" (verse 11). World history has now reached the utmost limit of its possibilities. Antichrist is the final form in which all emnity to God will be expressed. It is its supreme expression—and the last.

The commission of the ten lesser kings (verse 12) is possibly an allusion to the Satraps of the Parthians. This is also seen in the light of the end, whose coming is sure. These kings represent a minor power, but they share in the world-power. Their task within the final act of history is limited—"for one hour"; for now everything is hastening towards the end. The vassal kings of the last days may think highly of their royal dignity themselves; but in reality it is but a fleeting moment in world history, nothing more, and they are only satellites in the time of decline.

They have a threefold mission.

At the beginning stands the world-embracing federation, an imposing sign of political uniformity. In reality of course it was only a vassal relationship; there was no freedom for political development. Here we may recall that the earlier fathers of the church always regarded the political universality of Rome with distrust. They regarded the unity of the Roman Empire, "the grave of nations," merely as an imitation of the unity created by the Gospel. For instance, one of the most fruitful writers after Origen, Hippolytus, who worked in the first half of the third century, wrote in his commentary on Daniel: "When, in the twelfth year, the Lord was born under Augustus, from whom onwards the empire developed, the Lord, however, through the apostles, sent out his message to all nations and tongues, and created the believing people of the Christians; then the empire, the kingdom of this world, which rules 'through the power of Satan,' on its part gathered out of all nations the noblest men it could find, preparing them for war, and calling them 'Romans.' Thus the first 'numbering' under Augustus took place when the Lord was born in Bethlehem, in order that the men of this world might be registered for the earthly king, and called 'Romans,' whereas those who chose to serve the heavenly King who were signed on the brow with the token of Christ's victory over death, were called 'Christians.' " [5] This passage, the "boldest expression of Christian self-consciousness" [6] suggests that the early Christians, and the seer also, did not regard the function of the vassal kings as accidental. This world-embracing organization expressed a will to unity which could not lead to the goal. True ecumenicity only comes through the gathering of all believers, "sealed" by baptism, into the divine community, the church.

The second task of these vassal kings is to wage war upon the Lamb. In so doing they betray their origin and the political purpose which they serve. For they are doing just what the dragon and the beast from the abyss had done (Rev. 12; 13:7). There is no foundation for an understanding between themselves and the Lamb. But they cannot remain neutral toward the Lamb, since they have become the servants of the satanic beast who imitates him. Hence, the only form of contact with the Lamb is war. Like a first flash of lightning the certainty of the final victory of the Lamb darts into the description; the Lamb will conquer them (verse 14). In the tense political atmosphere of decision of the last days it will also become clear in the challenging title now given to the Lamb: "Lord of lords and King of kings" (verse 14).

[5] Hippolytus IV:9.
[6] Adolf Harnack.

From the time of the great kings of Babylon this was the title of the supreme ruler, and remained so down to the days of the Roman emperors. This title is now given to the Lamb, and in this designation it is plain that all ideas of defenselessness and humiliation have disappeared. The "chosen" and "called"—so Paul had already said—are with him; they are the vassals of Christ, in true surrender, called to freedom, and bound to their Lord by fidelity.

With their third task these vassal kings fulfil once more—and for the last time—a terrible and mysterious law of political history, according to which every revolutionary power contains within itself the seed of self-destruction. The revolution is swallowed up by its own children. The war-like hatred of these vassals suddenly turns against their own Lord, the prostitute is destroyed by her own followers, just as cruelly as she herself tried to destroy the followers of the Lamb (verse 16). Thus the imperial world-power of the last days will be overthrown by other demonic forces; it will itself be "knocked out," and the church will not need to do anything about its destruction! The church does not need to use the political method of violence; God has instruments, who, even when they seem to be rebelling against him, are obliged to carry out his "decree"—to use the language of an oriental court.

In the accomplishment of the final judgment everything takes place on that high plane which is under the absolute control, at every point, of the holy will of God.

NOTE

Concerning the question of what significance there is in the mysterious play on numbers and the seventh king, Bousset insists upon the notion that here, at least as an underlying motive, we have the expectation of the return of Nero, which only arose at the end of the reign of Vespasian. The scholars who reject this theory arouse Bousset's anger, because he clings to this legend. Where it is obvious that no proof can be found, he would rather cling to a different version of this legend than give it up.

LAMENT OVER BABYLON

(*Rev. 18:1-3*)

1 After this I saw another angel coming down from heaven, having great authority; and the earth was made bright with his splendor. 2 And he called out with a mighty voice,

"Fallen, fallen is Babylon the great!
It has become a dwelling place of demons,
a haunt of every foul spirit,
a haunt of every foul and hateful bird;
3 for all nations have drunk the wine of her impure passion, and the kings of the earth have committed fornication with her,
and the merchants of the earth have grown rich with the wealth of her wantonness."

The course of events is moving steadily toward its climax and the climax of judgment is recorded as judgment on the "great city." It says a great deal for the genuineness of the seer's presentation that in what follows he does not say "I saw," but only "I heard." He cannot have seen Rome, and probably, with the exception of Ephesus, he had not seen any of the other great cities of the ancient world. But what the eye does not see the ear can hear still more plainly. Thus the actual accomplishment of the judgment is described in a special art form, like a mighty oratorio. In these one and a half chapters there is "the greatest and most shattering music of revelation," which combines "the song of triumph and the wailing strains of lamentation." [7]

The structure of this passage is clear and well arranged.

At first the verses strike up a kind of prelude in which the whole judgment is described in a comprehensive act of anticipation. In a ray of light which irradiates the whole round earth, once more an angelic form steps forth from heaven. Majestic radiance surrounds this herald of God who now,

[7] Lohmeyer, *op. cit.*

with supreme authority, must announce that God's judgment on Babylon has been carried out. The city lies in ruins, it is the dwelling place of demons, and all kinds of foul creatures who haunt the ruins. In its fall it has involved in a terrible solidarity of ruin all who were guilty of the same blasphemies which it had committed.

The grim announcement, in spite of its terrible character, is bathed in a consoling light; the heavenly messenger, with his calm radiance, conveys the certainty that here the holy will of God is being fulfilled. Now God has really begun to act, and the judgment which, from the human point of view, was always being postponed, is now hastening to its completion. This is a great consolation to the church which awaits her Lord.

Above all the *achievement* of judgment is recorded with the same majestic detachment. There is no effort to give a poetic and moving description of this accomplishment of doom, nor is God himself involved in the lower levels of such action. The only people here who speak are those who see or hear this judgment. It is the way in which they speak about it that conveys a sense of its power, just as those who hear the noise of the guns become aware of the heat of the battle—a magnificent biblical *teichoskopia*.[8]

CRY OF VENGEANCE OVER BABYLON, AND LAMENTATIONS OF KINGS, MERCHANTS, AND SEAFARING MEN

(*Rev. 18:4-19*)

4 Then I heard another voice from heaven saying,
"Come out of her, my people,
lest you take part in her sins,
lest you share in her plagues;
5 for her sins are heaped high as heaven,
and God has remembered her iniquities.

[8] Literally, "looking from the walls." The title of the third book of the *Iliad*. (Translator's note.)

6 Render to her as she herself has rendered,
and repay her double for her deeds;
mix a double draught for her in the cup she mixed.
7 As she glorified herself and played the wanton,
so give her a like measure of torment and mourning.
Since in her heart she says, 'A queen I sit,
I am no widow, mourning I shall never see,'
8 so shall her plagues come in a single day,
pestilence and mourning and famine,
and she shall be burned with fire;
for mighty is the Lord God who judges her."

9 And the kings of the earth, who committed fornication and were wanton with her, will weep and wail over her when they see the smoke of her burning; 10 they will stand far off, in fear of her torment, and say,

"Alas! alas! thou great city,
thou mighty city, Babylon!
In one hour has thy judgment come."

11 And the merchants of the earth weep and mourn for her, since no one buys their cargo any more, 12 cargo of gold, silver, jewels and pearls, fine linen, purple, silk and scarlet, all kinds of scented wood, all articles of ivory, all articles of costly wood, bronze, iron and marble, 13 cinnamon, spice, incense, myrrh, frankincense, wine, oil, fine flour and wheat, cattle and sheep, horses and chariots, and slaves, that is, human souls.

14 "The fruit for which thy soul longed has gone from thee,
and all thy dainties and thy splendor are lost to thee, never to be found again!"

15 The merchants of these wares, who gained wealth from her, will stand far off, in fear of her torment, weeping and mourning aloud,

16 "Alas, alas, for the great city
that was clothed in fine linen, in purple and scarlet,
bedecked with gold, with jewels, and with pearls!
17 In one hour all this wealth has been laid waste."

And all shipmasters and seafaring men, sailors and all whose trade is on the sea, stood far off 18 and cried out as they saw the smoke of her burning,

"What city was like the great city?"

19 And they threw dust on their heads, as they wept and mourned, crying out,

"Alas, alas, for the great city
where all who had ships at sea grew rich by her wealth!
In one hour she has been laid waste."

JUBILATION IN HEAVEN

(Rev. 18:20)

20 "Rejoice over her, O heaven,
O saints and apostles and prophets,
for God has given judgment for you against her!"

A second angel summons the people of God and tells them to leave the city. All the prophets knew that there comes a moment when any connection with the world, however tenuous and remote, is no longer possible, and that the only thing to be done in obedience to God's command is to sever all connection with the world. This "coming out" is the fundamental law of the church, both in the Old and in the New Testament (Isa. 52:11; II Cor. 6:17).

Just as there are precursors of the last judgment even within human history, and as all historical decisions of the church are, or should be, a preparation for the final decision of God upon history, so also this final separation from the world has its historical anticipation in the repeated separations from the world which have been forced upon the church in the course of her history. St. Augustine, who in his own way has given a spiritual interpretation of this chapter in the Apocalypse, says on this passage: "This prophetic command must be understood in a spiritual sense—that is, that we must renounce our rights as citizens of this world, and flee unto God on the wings of faith." [9] At the end of history the final separation will take place.

Because God executes judgment, the call for repayment must not be understood in the petty sense of human revenge.[10] *"Sancti sancto modo reddent"*—"the saints 'repay' in a holy manner" [11]—means that they are not animated by joy over destruction, but by the certainty that God achieves his purpose, in spite of the arrogance of this secular power.

Those who belong to the people of God cannot execute their own judgment; this is, and remains, in God's hands—"mighty is the Lord God who judges her" (verse 8). As in Roman legislation for the Jews—the emperor alone could order the death penalty to be carried out—so also here; it is not the "saints" but God who executes judgment: "vengeance is mine." But this judgment is a sign of the unchangeable majesty of God. In one day it breaks in upon the doomed city; it is destroyed at a blow, although it took its complete security for granted. All at once, a period full of persecution and sorrow seems to shrink into a passing moment!

And now the voice of the angel who explained the judgment to John, ceases, and is followed by the sound of the choirs which now begin to chant the great dirge for Babylon. This takes place in a spirit of poetic greatness; no word of this description has anything petty or mean about it. The choir now sings the threefold lament over Babylon, but this makes it all the more impressive.

First of all *the kings*. The world-power has had its vassals, eager satellites, who live on the love of show, the intoxication of power, and the desire for enjoyment and luxury. As the smoke rises from the ruins of the great city, the center of their existence expires and vanishes before their eyes; their existence

[9] *De Civitate Dei,* XVIII, 18 (Eng. tr., Everyman ed.), II, 191. (Translator's note.)

[10] D. H. Lawrence, *op. cit.* This is how Lawrence understood these words. He says, "How one hears the envy, the endless envy, the screeching envy through this song of triumph! It is the Christianity of the middling classes."

[11] Bengel, *op. cit.*

is defenseless and meaningless. So they can only stand at a distance, shaking with fear, giving vent to helpless cries of distress; there is no longer any question of fidelity. They represent the bankruptcy of an arrogant existence which believed that it was "secure" because it was living in a perverted political order. In an hour it is "finished"; it vanishes like a breath, as if it had never existed at all. So the proud claim of the empire to "last for ever" crumbles into dust.

Then *the merchants.* It is significant that their lament is the most detailed. When the glory of earthly power has gone they lose most. The fall of Babylon suddenly reveals the fact that the political brilliance of the international merchants was based only on their economic advantages. The long list of purely luxury articles sounds like bitter mockery, as the overflowing wealth of great oriental markets is displayed, a list which includes everything, from perfumes and jewels to chariots and domestic slaves—everything that the most refined love of luxury demands. Even human beings—"slaves, that is, human souls" (verse 13)—a shattering expression, which is true not only of slaves but of all those human beings who had been ruined, body and soul, by the arrogant behavior of the debased political power. It was all over in an hour. Wealth, luxury, overweening enjoyment of life—for pleasure is the most shortlived of all attempts to live without God.

And, finally, *the shipmasters,* with their army of seafaring men, who had also gained riches from the world-power, the content of whose lives has also been destroyed, because apart from this power they did not possess anything at all.

This threefold lament, in which each strophe ends with almost the same rhyme, is balanced by a heavenly song of jubilation. All who had suffered under the brutal rule of force of the imperial power rejoice at the approach of the day of deliverance—the saints, that is, the members of the church of Jesus Christ, the apostles who have suffered martyrdom, and the prophets (verse 20).

NOTES

"The widow" is the Biblical symbol of extreme outward desolation (verse 7). Here it is the symbol—very effectively expressed—of that arrogant pride which, at the next moment, will be in worse plight than all these who are desolate.

The merchants' list of wares (verses 12ff) is interesting from the point of view of civilization. The word for "silk" originally meant "Chinese." This list is less suitable for Rome than for Asia Minor.

There is a good deal to be said for the view that the allusion to the martyr apostles (verse 20) refers to the execution of SS. Peter and Paul in Rome, although neither this tradition, nor that of their common martyrdom, can be actually proved with any certainty.

DIRGE OVER BABYLON

(*Rev. 18:21-24*)

21 Then a mighty angel took up a stone like a great millstone and threw it into the sea, saying,
"So shall Babylon the great city be thrown down with violence,
and shall be found no more;
22 and the sound of harpers and minstrels, of flute players and trumpeters,
shall be heard in thee no more;
and a craftsman of any craft
shall be found in thee no more;
and the sound of the millstone
shall be heard in thee no more;
23 and the light of a lamp
shall shine in thee no more;
and the voice of bridegroom and bride
shall be heard in thee no more;
for thy merchants were the great men of the earth,
and all nations were deceived by thy sorcery.
24 And in her was found the blood of prophets and of saints,
and of all who have been slain on earth."

Poetically, the last part of this chapter is the most significant and impressive (verses 21-24).

Once more the seer's great power of imagery and expression rises to the height of another great picture. All we see is that tremendous gesture of the angel who takes up a "stone like a great millstone" and hurls it into the sea—one single gesture, which symbolizes the whole judgment on Babylon! (verse 21).

And now there follows, in wonderful lyrical language, which no translation can really render, the dirge sung by heavenly beings over the fall of Babylon, a dirge which is lyrical and almost tender. The melancholy recollection of the pulsing life which once filled this city with the joy of life trembles through these lines. The sorrowful recurring echoes in repeated phrases, which sound so much softer and fuller in the original, ". . . the sound . . . shall be heard in thee no more," sound like footsteps dying away in the distance, in a desolate city which lies in ruins.

NOTES

Those who can read Greek should read this dirge over Babylon (22ff) aloud in the original in order to hear the cadences of the poem. Here there can be no question of literary incapacity on the part of the seer, although obviously his Greek is defective. Perhaps J. Leipoldt is right in suggesting that possibly John wrote bad Greek on purpose, in order to remove his message out of the language of everyday life into the sphere of the dignified and the unusual.[12]

Theodor Mommsen suggests that the remark that the blood of the prophets and saints was found in the great city (verse 24) refers to the fact that sentence of death—especially death in the arena from wild beasts—was usually carried out at Rome.

CELESTIAL JUBILATION OVER FALL OF BABYLON

(*Rev. 19:1-8*)

1 After this I heard what seemed to be the mighty voice of a great multitude in heaven, crying,

"Hallelujah! Salvation and glory and power belong to our God,

[12] *Urchristentum und Gegenwart.*

2 for his judgments are true and just;
he has judged the great harlot who corrupted the earth with her fornication,
and he has avenged on her the blood of his servants."
3 Once more they cried,
"Hallelujah! The smoke from her goes up for ever and ever."
4 And the twenty-four elders and the four living creatures fell down and worshiped God who is seated on the throne, saying, "Amen. Hallelujah!" 5 And from the throne came a voice crying,
"Praise our God, all you his servants,
you who fear him, small and great."
6 Then I heard what seemed to be the voice of a great multitude, like the sound of many waters and like the sound of mighty thunderpeals, crying,
"Hallelujah! For the Lord our God the Almighty reigns.
7 Let us rejoice and exult and give him the glory,
for the marriage of the Lamb has come,
and his Bride has made herself ready;
8 it was granted her to be clothed with fine linen, bright and pure"—
for the fine linen is the righteous deeds of the saints.

In an almost incredible contrast to the dirge the song of heavenly jubilation now breaks out. Like the lament of the kings, merchants, and seafarers in Revelation 18, it is arranged in a threefold ascending scale.

The whole heavenly choir strikes up, once again confirming the judgment, which no bare record could describe. Now however, it is shown in the only right way, for neither the unrestrained lament of the kings, merchants, and seafarers could express it aright, nor the lament over the city. The celestial praises break forth; they are consecrated anew by adoration, and after all their misuse in the cults of imperial Rome they are once more offered at the throne of God, which is the only place of true worship.

The choir, which sings antiphonally, is answered by the response of the elders and the four living creatures.

Finally, the voice of a heavenly priest summons the worshiping church, composed of those who have fought the fight and finished their course, to break out into praise (verse 5); the final song of rejoicing in which all the psalms and praises of the church seem to be gathered up into one (verses 6-8) resounds with indescribable power and supernatural impressiveness.

NOTES

The fourfold "hallelujah" (verses 1, 3, 4, 6) only occurs here in the New Testament. It has been transferred unchanged from the worship of the Old Testament, and since then it has remained an integral part of Christian worship.

The close of verse 8, perhaps like that of verse 10, is a later addition. These somewhat pedestrian explanations do not seem to belong to the framework of the heavenly worship and praise, and they disturb the art form. The thought expressed at the close of verse 8 itself is properly biblical, as for instance Eph. 2:10 shows. But in the Apocalypse white garments are a sign of fulfilment, not of "good works" (Rev. 3:5; 6:11). Otherwise, according to the view of the New Testament, the works too are gifts of grace; here they may be meant to show the inner connection between grace and glory.

BEATITUDE

(*Rev. 19:9-10*)

> 9 And the angel said to me, "Write this: Blessed are those who are invited to the marriage supper of the Lamb." And he said to me, "These are true words of God." 10 Then I fell down at his feet to worship him, but he said to me, "You must not do that! I am a fellow servant with you and your brethren who hold the testimony of Jesus. Worship God." For the testimony of Jesus is the spirit of prophecy.

The song of the last choir was full of joy, because God had assumed his great power—openly—and was reigning; at the same time this song contained some echoes of rejoicing over things temporal. This image of the marriage gathers up everything that has been said in the Old Testament about the relation of God to his people. It is the final and decisive contrast with the unfaithfulness, lack of restraint, and immorality of an earthly world alienated from God, which was finally represented by the woman who rode upon the beast.

The picture of the marriage feast which is about to be celebrated is significant, because it is an image of that longing with which the church waits for the end of all history and the dawning of the age of fulfilment. Time, earthly time, is no longer only transparent, it has dissolved in fervent heat.

So the fourth beatitude in the Apocalypse (verse 9) closes with this significant picture of the scene of heavenly victory.

Under the shattering impression of this great final chorus, with which the actual conflict of history is concluded, John falls down at the feet of the messenger of God. But the angel rebukes him in words he could never forget—a proof of the purity of the divine vision which dominates the whole book; it is not to be obscured by the slightest breath of angel-worship. The words of the angel, in the allusion to those who hold the testimony of Jesus (verse 10), are particularly impressive.

So the greatest and most inspiring section of the Apocalypse ends on a note of sober restraint: the thing that matters most of all is—*witness*. The martyr, the "witness" in the fullest sense of the word, is the one who can really receive this revelation of the end; he is the legitimate reader of this book.

With these strains of organ music the great main section of the Apocalypse closes, with its description of the final conflict of history. All that now follows already points to the picture of glorious fulfilment.

NOTES

The way in which the seer records the rebuke he received from the angel—"You must not do that" (verse 10)—shows how conscientiously he observes the First Commandment. His ethical and religious judgment has not been swamped by any ecstatical experience. His obedience is alert.

In his commentary (1857) on this chapter as a whole, Karl August Auberlen regards the figure of the prostitute as the apostate, deformed, and secularized church. This view has found many followers, especially among the sects of the present day. Perhaps our present exposition has shown that the reference to the secularized church is too narrow and one-sided an interpretation.

Chapter 14

The Seven Visions of Fulfilment

(Rev. 19:11—21:5a)

CHRISTUS VICTOR

(*Rev. 19:11-16*)

11 Then I saw heaven opened, and behold, a white horse! He who sat upon it is called Faithful and True, and in righteousness he judges and makes war. 12 His eyes are like a flame of fire, and on his head are many diadems; and he has a name inscribed which no one knows but himself. 13 He is clad in a robe dipped in blood, and the name by which he is called is The Word of God. 14 And the armies of heaven, arrayed in fine linen, white and pure, followed him on white horses. 15 From his mouth issues a sharp sword with which to smite the nations, and he will rule them with a rod of iron; he will tread the wine press of the fury of the wrath of God the Almighty. 16 On his robe and on his thigh he has a name inscribed, King of kings and Lord of lords.

Two impressive scenes—all the more effective because they are so sharply contrasted—open the section on fulfilment.

The doors of heaven open and, as the overwhelming radiance streams out, a rider on a white horse appears. The light which surrounds him is so strong that the glance from his eyes is like a flame of fire, and his head is surrounded by a sparkling halo of light, streaming from many crowns—all of which are tokens of royal dignity.

Royal is the fulness of the titles: Faithful and True (verse 11), The Word of God (verse 13), King of kings and Lord of lords (verse 16). Royal also is the host which surrounds him riding on white horses and clothed in white garments, and royal, too, the flashing sword which seems to issue from his mouth—an apt symbol for the Word of God. Gathering up all the images which, from the days of the Old Testament, had been used to show the power of the Messiah, it bears witness to the greatness of his royal authority, the authority of the conqueror, who is Lord of all.

There is no need to ask: who is the rider upon the white horse? Christ himself comes for the final decisive judgment. As the seer, overwhelmed by the dazzling light, cannot at first decipher the name inscribed upon the rider's girdle, so also the unbelieving world does not at first know who He is. But the believers know him by his Name, the name by which he has already been acclaimed in the prologue to the Fourth Gospel: the "Word." This Word is both his whole being and his only weapon. Is there a better name for Jesus Christ than this, which was already ascribed to him in the prologue to the Gospel of John, and at the beginning of the first Epistle of John? But this Word has power (Heb. 4:12). He alone is worthy to receive the name above every name, the title of supreme authority, which had formerly been usurped by great earthly rulers (verse 16). His fame is no empty one, for his white mantle has been "dipped in blood," and around him is the heavenly host.

Here the return of Christ is revealed to faith. As the whole book of the Apocalypse does not develop a particular theory, nor even a doctrine, so also the vital truth proclaimed in these verses is not clothed in doctrinal forms. We *see* Christ coming again. We see also, and immediately, the essential marks of his return: he will be the conqueror. This is still more impressive and consoling than the picture given in the Gospels, which represents him mainly as the world's judge. Although the Apocalypse gives a different point of view, there is no doubt—not even a question—of the reality of Christ's return.

Those who believe in the reality of the resurrection of Jesus Christ must also look for his return. We then see clearly that whatever we may think of some of the details of the imagery used to convey its message, the Apocalypse—with its spacious outlook—is dealing with a reality which vitally concerns us, as Christians.

NOTES

Several details in the first verses of this vision are influenced by the Old Testament. Thus the name of Christ as "Faithful and True" (verse 11); he assumes the Hebrew name *Emeth* (faithfulness) and *Amen*. The first name is one of the most beautiful titles applied to God in the Old Testament. The rabbis called it the "Seal of God," because this word, consisting of three letters, comprised the first, the middle, and the last letters of the Hebrew alphabet. Thus Christ is the beginning and the end of the ways of God, or—as the Apocalypse expresses it elsewhere—Alpha and Omega.

The reddened garment in verse 13 and the image of the wine press (verse 15) are probably both drawn from Isa. 63:1-3.

The name inscribed upon the thigh (verse 16) cannot be read at first (verse 12). This little detail shows how exactly the seer has recorded his vision; out of the radiance of the vision, as it proceeds, the inscription gradually becomes legible.

Verse 15 echoes the messianic royal psalm (Psalm 2).

VICTORY OVER THE BEAST AND HIS VASSALS

(*Rev. 19:17-21*)

17 Then I saw an angel standing in the sun, and with a loud voice he called to all the birds that fly in mid-heaven, "Come, gather for the great supper of God, 18 to eat the flesh of kings, the flesh of captains, the flesh of mighty men, the flesh of horses and their riders, and the flesh of all men, both free and slave, both small and great." 19 And I saw the beast and the kings of the earth with their armies gathered to make war against him who sits upon the horse and against his army. 20 And the beast was captured, and with it the false prophet who in its presence had worked the signs by which he deceived those who had received the mark of the beast and those who worshiped its image. These two were thrown alive into the lake of fire that burns with

> brimstone. 21 And the rest were slain by the sword of him who sits upon the horse, the sword that issues from his mouth; and all the birds were gorged with their flesh.

Once again in highest heaven a ray of light flares out. An angel stands in the full light of the sun; this scene is introduced with radiant yet profound dignity. With a mighty voice the terrible judgment is pronounced and carried out. The angel, with an uncanny gesture, invites the birds of the air to a great feast on the battlefield of history—reminding us of all the cruelties which the church had suffered at the hands of God's enemies, whose insane defiance of God now makes it an obvious victim of judgment. God is not mocked.

For a moment the glow of a terrible hatred seems to breathe through these lines. But it is only a fleeting recollection of the arrogance and cruelty of that hostile power upon which, with relentless severity, God's judgment now falls, executed by Jesus Christ himself. The most important element in this vision is this: Jesus is the conqueror. For faith, all that this terrible vision reveals is the fact that "Christ is Victor." Revenge does not enter it; for faith all that matters is that in the last days God's all-conquering power should be seen and proved in sight of the whole world.

The terrible threat was carried out. Since the seer does not intend to describe scenes of horror, but the will of God at the end of history, the final conflict is not described. The gigantic hosts of the beast and of his false prophet once more gather themselves together. For a moment we see the same picture as in Revelation 16 (verses 14-16), where the anti-Christian armies gather at Armageddon, at the mount of Megiddo. Once more the vast hosts of the anti-Christian power take the field against the little flock of Christ. But all at once this power proves hollow; the gigantic numbers are simply ridiculous. The battle is won before it has begun. Not a breadth of battle and conflict may mar the majesty of Christ; there is no longer any question of a battle.

It is now evident that the earthly development of the power of the beast was not a real power, but only the working out of the mysterious divine purpose in history. The very moment when this purpose of God is fulfilled, the mighty power of the beast shrivels up like a collapsed balloon, as if it had never been. It has been unmasked, and its true character revealed: it was empty, futile presumption.

That is why no serious conflict is now possible. For there is no real enemy. How strong and defiant is the seer's faith! He seems to say: "Could the church *really* believe that Satan could seriously oppose the will of God? Could they *really* think that this was even possible?"

Before the fight breaks out, the beast and the false prophet, the Antichrist and the apostle of the anti-Christian cult, are annihilated; the terrible judgment which has been foretold comes upon their followers. Only a period of extreme distress and persecution would choose to paint the picture of the sovereignty of God and the unalterable character of his holy will in such harsh and cruel colors.

NOTES

With the angel's words to the birds, cf. the eschatological words of Jesus in Matt. 24:28: "Wherever the body is there the eagles (or vultures) will be gathered together."

On the "lake of fire," cf. Matt. 5:22; Mark 9:43; Jas. 3:6.

THE DRAGON IS CHAINED

(*Rev. 20:1-3*)

1 Then I saw an angel coming down from heaven, holding in his hand the key of the bottomless pit and a great chain. 2 And he seized the dragon, that ancient serpent, who is the Devil and Satan, and bound him for a thousand years, 3 and threw him into the pit, and shut it and sealed it over him, that he should deceive the nations no more, till the thousand years were ended. After that he must be loosed for a little while.

The seer is still dealing with the victory of Christ. But he is not merely repeating what he has said in the previous chapters.

The great enigmas of history which the seer's vision has been skirting throughout the preceding chapters cannot be solved within history. The enigmas of suffering, death, sin, and of the world's hostility toward God, point beyond the framework of history toward a suprahistorical solution. In spite of this, however, the thread of history is not simply broken off in an arbitrary manner.

If the course of events were broken off in a chaotic way, God's work of creation would have been destroyed by Satan, and deprived of its fruit. The real solution of that riddle can only be given by an act of God which at the same time brings all earthly events to an end. It is only natural that faith should not want to see the course of history simply ending in Satanic confusion. Faith longs to perceive God's answer to this riddle, at least in the form of a hint or an "earnest" of future solutions. This is where the explanation of this chapter arises.

It does this, it is true, in a language in which the longing for the fulfilment of history, as in most of the higher religions, is mingled with other forms of expression, which already formed part of the stereotyped material of Jewish apocalyptic. But in spite of this type of language, we must not overlook the fact that this section is part of the witness of the early church. For in the Gospels, as in the Pauline epistles—even if only in passing—the thought is suggested that the conclusion of earthly history will be a period of Christ's sovereignty, before his final Return. See what St. Paul says in the first epistle to the Corinthians (15:24ff). If we compare the seer's description here with the dim hints thrown out by the apostle, it is like the finished picture compared with the outline sketch.

Another angel steps forth. As soon as the seer, dazzled at first, can distinguish his form within this blaze of light, he sees that he is carrying a great shining key and a great iron chain. Silently and powerfully, without visible struggle, the angel seizes the dragon and fetters him "for a thousand years" in the bottomless pit. The door of the abyss is closed and sealed.

THE MILLENNIUM

(Rev. 20:4-6)

> 4 Then I saw thrones, and seated on them were those to whom judgment was committed. Also I saw the souls of those who had been beheaded for their testimony to Jesus and for the word of God, and who had not worshiped the beast or its image and had not received its mark on their foreheads or their hands. They came to life again, and reigned with Christ a thousand years. 5 The rest of the dead did not come to life again until the thousand years were ended. This is the first resurrection. 6 Blessed and holy is he who shares in the first resurrection! Over such the second death has no power, but they shall be priests of God and of Christ, and they shall reign with him a thousand years.

After Satan has been bound, a great period begins. The martyrs, all the witnesses from the time of the dominion of the beast, are brought to life again, but they alone. Together with Christ they exercise the power of judgment, and reign "for a thousand years."

This is the passage upon which the doctrine of the "thousand-year kingdom" has been founded.

When we remember that this passage has been treated in a very contradictory way in the doctrinal teaching of the church, we might think that the difficulties of conveying its meaning to the Christian church of our own day would be insuperable. For instance, two tendencies have existed side by side. The early church tended mainly in a chiliastic direction, therefore it supported the doctrine of a reign of a thousand years. On the other hand, the Augsburg Confession decisively rejected this view as "Jewish doctrine."

It is not the expositor's task to decide whether certain views propounded in the history of dogma are correct or not. His task is to try to determine what the text actually says—what is "there." Then, in the light of what is "there," he has to expound the passage in the light of Scripture as a whole.

The first question that arises is that of the actual numbers mentioned in this passage.

If we try to deal with these numbers in the mathematical sense we shall find, of course, that the whole passage, from the outset, is thrown out of gear.[1] It makes no difference whether we calculate exactly a thousand years forward or backward, that is, whether we look for the coming of a thousand-year dominion in the future, or whether we think that this period of a thousand years has already begun, in church history. From the time of Augustine, the latter was the usual view.[2]

Similarly, at the time of the Reformation the view was held that the great epoch of church history, from Constantine to the first appearance of the Turks, was the "thousand-year period"; individual calculations vary. But these "numbers" in the Apocalypse must not be treated mathematically at all. This is not a mathematical or chronological matter; in this sense, the "thousand years" are not a thousand years.

In spite of this, however, this numerical element contains an important clue for the understanding of this passage.

All historical thinking begins with the attempt to arrange history in periods. We try to bring some order into the mystery of historical impressions by dividing it into sections. People have often spoken of cosmic "days" or "weeks" sometimes in a quite artificial way, yet such language often represented a profound effort to master the differentiated course of history, and to impose some kind of order upon it.

[1] This is where Bengel went wrong in *Gnomon* (*op. cit.*). For him these were "a thousand ordinary years, and indeed, quite precisely so." Further, he seems to have assumed 2000 years were meant in verses two and four.

[2] *De Civitate Dei,* XX:7.9.

The Bible too has made such efforts, in the apocalyptic of the Old Testament, for instance, and there are several traces of these attempts in the Apocalypse itself.

Here it is only the last section of history which is important, the last period of the course of history. In connection with Psalm 90:4 and II Peter 3:8 we might also speak of the "last days" of history. The "six days" which preceded it are not relevant here; all that matters is the last day. Now the great Sabbath of history dawns on which the course of history is to come to an end, as the great work of creation once came to an end. We may also apply these words to this Sabbath of history: "and God blessed the seventh day."

God himself, in his work of creation within history, attains his goal. This last day of history is once more linked with the first day of creation; it is evident that Satan has not taken God's work of creation out of his hands. In this last period God's purpose for the earth, when the power of destruction and perversion no longer dominates it, will become clear. Then too, his own who have become his witnesses through their martyr deaths, will no longer be frustrated by any anti-Christian power; they will taste the full truth of the words "have dominion over the earth." They will have a direct share in Christ's work of judgment and dominion, not only as at present in faith and expectation.

This throws light on the difficult passage about the resurrection of believers, or the first resurrection. This idea is not peculiar to the Apocalypse. Paul also mentions it (I Cor. 15:23). The chief difference between Paul and the Apocalypse consists in the fact that in the Apocalypse the lines are drawn out clearly at which Paul only hints. Obviously, Paul also distinguishes between the resurrection of Christians and the actual "end," without saying how long the interim period will last. In addition, he speaks of "Christians" in a quite general way, while the Apocalypse speaks of the "martyrs" as those who share in the first resurrection. The Johannine distinction between the resurrection to life and the resurrection to judgment (John 5:29) also seems to be closely connected with this idea. This is the direction in which we must look for a clue to the understanding of this passage. For those martyrs who died in faith in Christ there comes the moment when they pass into life; death will have no power over them.

The whole section is treated in a very restrained manner. There are no colorful descriptions of a future golden age, usual even in the great non-Christian religions, nor of those glowing descriptions of the messianic era of late Jewish apocalyptic. In rejecting chiliasm as "Jewish doctrine" the Augsburg Confession rejects these nationalistic Jewish expectations. Here, on the contrary, with an almost matter-of-fact sobriety, the writer states that God's will in creation and redemption reaches its goal within history. Beyond that there is no room for any flights of imagination. The colorful expectations of the future in other apocalypses do not even come within the horizon of the seer. The threefold content of this time of blessing gives sufficient indication of its nature: deliverance from all Satanic perversion. The course of history will come to an end in accordance with the purpose of the original creation; believers will share in the life and reign of Christ in the world.

The mistakes of a perverted chiliasm have always consisted in going beyond the limits of this reserve. Either it has tried to calculate where, by its very nature, calculation is impossible and can only be accepted in the obedience of faith, or it has indulged in fantastic speculations by which obedience to the word of Scripture has been gravely injured.

A genuine chiliasm has been taught almost everywhere in the church, and has been held for centuries. In the early ages of the church, it was part of the true faith. So long as the church lived under the cross she held fast to this doctrine; the change took place when the church entered the sphere of public life under Constantine. "Later, when the church came under the protection of worldly potentates she looked at things differently, and relegated the chiliasts without distinction to a place among the heretics." [3]

From the time of Constantine, as Eusebius used to say, the "thousand-year kingdom" has become the present history of the church. Henceforward the church began to teach that the "thousand-year kingdom" was a period in church history. At the moment when Augustine took over this interpretation (of this chapter) from his predecessor Tyconius (d. *c*400) the power of chiliasm in the official church was broken. On this point too the Reformers only took over the general doctrine of the Catholic church. They too were influenced by their anxiety about the chiliasm of the sects, which proliferated all the more vigorously because there was no legitimate place for it in the church itself.

This also explains the rejection of the doctrine by the Augsburg Confession, in its seventeenth article, which says that it is a "Jewish opinion." So far as this simply meant the repudiation of a fanatical chiliasm, exclusively concerned with this world, this conclusion was justified. But it is not based on a sound biblical exegesis. When however, we reflect on the fact that the eschatological doctrine of the Augsburg Confession is incomplete, and that it is silent on many vital "signs of the end" taught in the Bible, it is only fair to say that the attitude of the Confession as a whole is not as much one of "rejection" as an *abbreviatur*. Therefore, we need not argue that there is an irreconcilable contradiction between the Augsburg Confession and the Bible.

The modern rejection of chiliasm is usually based on dogmatic considerations, not on biblical exegesis. Some hold the view that "the goal of humanity cannot be attained upon this earth as it is, unchanged, before sin has been extirpated." [4]

[3] Bengel, *op. cit.*

[4] Martin Kähler, *Wissenschaft der christlichen Lehre* (3d ed.). Some modern Lutherans, like V. Hoffmann, Löhe, and Frank, on the other hand, support a biblical chiliasm, though with many differences in detail. Frank,

By itself this fundamental consideration cannot be taken as the standard which determines the exposition of the present passage, for it is not absolutely opposed to it. Over against the view that the doctrine of a "prefulfilment" within history is theologically unnecessary and unfounded, this passage claims that, in principle, God's creative work must be fulfilled within history.

Of course it is not easy to say how the Bible student of the present day is to understand this biblical doctrine. If he wishes to remain within the sphere of biblical thinking he must beware of making "fancy pictures." Even the equation of the thousand-year kingdom with the visible church could be an untenable interpretation. It seems likely that this chapter is only speaking of a final spiritual possibility of the church on earth; there is no question here of an external world-power. The forces of the abyss are bound, and thus in principle powerless. Therefore, in spite of all threatening dangers it is still possible for the church to witness to Christ, and indeed it is her duty to proclaim the gospel throughout the world in the last great epoch of the missionary church.

NOTES

One of the most important earlier passages for the interpretation of the thousand years is that of Augustine, already mentioned, which he took over from Tyconius: the number "thousand" is not to be understood literally; it has been chosen *ut perfecto numero notaretur ipsa temporis plenitudo.*[5]

Verse 6 contains the fifth beatitude of the Apocalypse.

VICTORY OVER THE DRAGON

(Rev. 20:7-10)

7 And when the thousand years are ended, Satan will be loosed from his prison 8 and will come out to deceive

in his *System der christlichen Wahrheit,* explains in detail the relation between creed, confession and chiliasm. Hermann Bezzel, *op. cit.,* as his collection of Bible studies on the Book of Revelation shows, also held firmly to the idea of the "thousand-year kingdom."

[5] *De Civitate Dei,* XX:7.

the nations which are at the four corners of the earth, that is, Gog and Magog, to gather them for battle; their number is like the sand of the sea. 9 And they marched up over the broad earth and surrounded the camp of the saints and the beloved city; but fire came down from heaven and consumed them, 10 and the devil who had deceived them was thrown into the lake of fire and brimstone where the beast and the false prophet were, and they will be tormented day and night for ever and ever.

Once more the conflict begins, the final one. But the seer's vision suggests such haste to reach the real end, that the description is foreshortened. The record is brief. Once more Satan is set free, once more he is successful in gathering powerful forces together to fight against God in the world. We see the tumult of the countless hordes from many nations—the power of numbers is preparing to celebrate its last triumph upon earth. The vast hordes of the armies of the anti-Christian power encircle the camp of the saints, the undefended beloved city of Jerusalem. These are all vivid pictures, but there is no detail. Here again no real conflict takes place. Fire from heaven falls upon these hosts, and annihilates Satan and his armies. God's will has triumphed gloriously; the "lake of fire" means no more than this. Beyond this it has no meaning, no ground for speculations about purgatory.

NOTE

"Gog and Magog" (verse 8) were originally (in Ezekiel 38) the names of a prince and his land. The Greek translation of the Old Testament turned these words into names of nations. Here they are only typical names for the powers of the final resistance to God. Luther regarded this as a prophecy of the wars with the Turks, and from this point of view he reckoned the end of the danger from the Turks.

THE LAST JUDGMENT

(*Rev. 20:11-15*)

11 Then I saw a great white throne and him who sat upon it; from his presence earth and sky fled away, and

> no place was found for them. 12 And I saw the dead, great and small, standing before the throne, and books were opened. Also another book was opened, which is the book of life. And the dead were judged by what was written in the books, by what they had done. 13 And the sea gave up the dead in it, Death and Hades gave up the dead in them, and all were judged by what they had done. 14 Then Death and Hades were thrown into the lake of fire. This is the second death, the lake of fire; 15 and if any one's name was not found written in the book of life, he was thrown into the lake of fire.

The great description of the "last judgment" follows, which has been represented so often in art. The element which distinguishes it from the mass of pictorial representations, with their "fancy pictures" and vivid details, is its strange, unearthly character. The whole scene is bathed in a transparent light which is not of this world at all. For instance, if we compare Rubens' picture, *"The Last Judgment"*—with its exuberant vitality—with the description in this chapter, the difference is immense; for here everything that belongs to our earthly life fades out of sight. The name of God is not even mentioned. God's throne glows with a white radiance. As in late Judaism, as in the language of Jesus in the gospels, and as in chapter 4 of the Apocalypse, the presence of God is of such transcendent majesty that it can only be described indirectly. The fact that he himself is the judge is all the more impressive.

Heaven and earth "flee away"—a phrase one can never forget—and fade into the background. They disappear; they are no longer there. This void means that all that made human life on earth possible has vanished. All that is left is a vast open space of spiritual emptiness, in which no human being could breathe or stand—peopled only by the dead in countless numbers, undifferentiated, without any earthly and historical differences, bound together by one thing only: that they are "before the throne of God." This expression really means the "second resurrection." All that the preceding chapters of this book have constantly emphasized becomes clear: God has kept the last judgment in his own hands. It only *seemed* as though the course of history ran counter to his holy will. But no single day in earthly history has been able to detract for one moment from God's sovereignty.

One feature in this passage which suggests great tension is the moment when "the books were opened." It is an overwhelming thought that in God's sight nothing is forgotten. Forgetting, which is one of the most despicable ways in which man tries to deal with his past, his distress, and his guilt, has no place in the sight of God. All that has happened on earth, all that was said, done, omitted, or forgotten—all has been kept. Here again, however, the picture is not embroidered. The great thought of judgment stands alone, supported by the conviction that it is GOD who judges. If we compare this description with the great picture given by Jesus of the final judgment (Matt. 25:31ff), we note that the seer has not gone any further than the Lord himself. Indeed, not only has he not gone further than the gospels, but his words are not so vivid, since the whole scene is on a universal transcendent plane.

At the end comes God's most imposing act of judgment. He destroys death—a thought that transcends the bounds of human thought. Annihilation is itself annihilated. All that remains is the majesty of life, which is God himself. He will be all in all (I Cor. 15:23, 28).

NEW HEAVEN AND NEW EARTH

(*Rev. 21:1-5a*)

1 Then I saw a new heaven and a new earth; for the first heaven and the first earth had passed away, and the sea was no more. 2 And I saw the holy city, new Jerusalem, coming down out of heaven from God, prepared as

a bride adorned for her husband; 3 and I heard a great voice from the throne saying, "Behold, the dwelling of God is with men. He will dwell with them, and they shall be his people, and God himself will be with them; 4 he will wipe away every tear from their eyes, and death shall be no more, neither shall there be mourning nor crying nor pain any more, for the former things have passed away."

5 And he who sat upon the throne said, "Behold, I make all things new."

This scene is so full of meaning that it seems strange that it should be treated with such brevity. However, the following verses show why this is so: everything is hastening toward the end, the victory of Christ. Even the judgment is only a transition to the new world, to the new order of things. So the strong and consoling light of the new morning shines with a growing radiance. From the pastoral point of view it is significant that after the visions of judgment the book closes with one of the most solemn and beautiful pictures in the whole work. All the distress of the previous judgments is forgotten. The fact that God is "making all things *new*" blots out every other thought.

In spite of this, this chapter is not only a "beautiful framework" [6] for traditional material. The main point of this chapter is its message.

The theme of the Bible is "the new creation"; it is the real content of the Christian life, the description of God's purpose for the world and for men. It is the main theme to which, with an overwhelming unity of mind and heart, all bear witness: prophets and evangelists, apostles and apocalyptic writers, and Jesus himself. The seer gathers up this united witness to the divine new creation in this radiant scene. If we want to find a comprehensive summary of the whole

[6] Bousset, *op. cit.*

message of the Bible—of the "gospel" in the widest sense of the word—these words fill the bill.

It must have been a great consolation to the first readers of this book that it closes not with some pessimistic theory of the philosophy of history, but, after all its scenes of judgment and prophecies of ruin, with this testimony to God's new creation and his new order.

The greatness of this description consists in the fact that it gathers up and heightens all the hopes, promises, and assertions of "good things to come," to the highest degree, without a touch of exaggeration. The joy which it expresses is kept within bounds, with a severe economy of expression. So this scene proves to be the "opposite number" to all that was said about the great city, the harlot Babylon. The graceless prostitute is contrasted with the bride of Christ, who belongs to One alone. Here we have no drunken woman waving a golden goblet of godlessness. The wild pictures of those days are forgotten. Here is clarity itself, irradiated with the presence of the eternal Word.

For the first time in the whole of the Apocalypse, God himself now steps forward as the one who acts, even though he is still the one who silently executes judgment. Only at the end of all time will Christendom, which until then has walked by faith and not by sight, see God himself directly in action.

He, before whom the earthly world, heaven, and earth, flee away (Rev. 20:11), does not remain in an empty sphere. When all earthly possibilities have been destroyed, all men's former belief in human possibilities, in "progress," and in continual development, must die, for the "former things have passed away." But God himself does not die.

He creates a new order of things. Upon a new earth, spanned by a new heaven, he completes his work. In the image of the new holy city which is adorned like a bride prepared for her husband, the seer creates a dignified and tender picture of the new reality, equally removed from pale abstractions about the future life, as from a heaven of sense enjoyment.

A great deal is summed up in this phrase, which had already resounded in the chorus of the heavenly hosts in Rev. 19:7.

First of all, there is the contrast with the picture of the "great city." The incarnation of all godless apostasy, the "harlot," is contrasted with the bride, the symbol of God's presence and God's love (Rev. 21:2). Here is no unhealthy excitement, no glorification of man as such, but only the restrained reverence of genuine worship. Here is no picture of a "lost" world, with its kings and rulers either practicing the debased rites of pagan cults, or else living in complete ignorance of God. Here rather is the vision of the church, gathered out of all nations, which is the biblical counterpart of the political unity of the Roman Empire, the godless "international." No longer are we confronted by the bleak picture of human life without God, full of pride and arrogance; no, here we see life filled to the brim with God's presence.

The ancient promise of Isa. 7:14, "God with us," has been fulfilled (cf. end of verse 3). No longer do we see the gloomy vision of cosmic anxiety, which makes men helpless victims of all the problems which afflict humanity: sorrow, grief, guilt, and death. Here we see a world where there is no more pain, where all tears have been wiped away, where death no longer has any power over life, but all is joy, unspeakable, holy joy—a world in which God's original holy purpose is completely realized—for here is life itself, real life, God's sacred gift.

Verse 4 also is important.

"The former things have passed away." Some linguistic echoes remind us of the dirge over Babylon (Rev. 18:21-24) and show that this verse is like a little song which represents the contrast to that dirge. This verse has the same content as verse 1: the whole of the old familiar world, with its threefold order—heaven, and earth, and sea—has passed away. The end of the old world and the old order is proclaimed with great majesty. The most terrible feature of all human life—the fact that everything passes away—has disappeared, so that we can only say in the profound words of the fourth book of Ezra: "That which passes away will itself pass away."

Paul once summed up his message in the phrase: "The old has passed away, behold, the new has come" (II Cor. 5:17). Here the seer is saying the same thing, but in a greater and more majestic way. God himself speaks: "Behold, I make all things new." When he says this, all the great promises of the Old Testament are fulfilled.

NOTES

It is worth while reflecting for a moment that even the sea (verse 1) will cease to be. "For ages there was resentment against the sea: the bitter corrupt sea as Plato calls it." [7] In W. Bonsel's *Journey in India* we find a similar passage about the restlessness of the sea, and this verse is mentioned in it.

The Old Testament quotation in verse 3 has been significantly altered. The Greek text of Revelation does not say they will be "my people" as in Ezek. 37:27 but "my peoples"! This is the biblical counterpart of the political world-wide empire.

The image of the bride and the marriage (verse 2, cf. 9ff) is often used in the East without any embarrassment. When the seer uses it he is suggesting the fulness of communion with God. The perfected church will desire nothing more than to belong undividedly and wholly to her Lord. This fact is not suggested by the abstract word "love," but by the picture which expresses, for every Oriental, the most complete joy in life.

[7] D. H. Lawrence, *op. cit.*

Chaper 15

The Promise

(Rev. 21:5b—22:7)

THE DIVINE PROMISE
(Rev. 21:5b-8)

5b Also he said, "Write this, for these words are trustworthy and true." 6 And he said to me, "It is done! I am the Alpha and the Omega, the beginning and the end. To the thirsty I will give water without price from the fountain of the water of life. 7 He who conquers shall have this heritage, and I will be his God and he shall be my son. 8 But as for the cowardly, the faithless, the polluted, as for murderers, fornicators, sorcerers, idolaters, and all liars, their lot shall be in the lake that burns with fire and brimstone, which is the second death."

At the beginning of the Apocalypse (Rev. 1:19) the seer was told to write down what he had seen. Now for the last time, he is again told to do so by God himself: "These words are trustworthy and true" (verse 5). What Jesus revealed in his own nature (Rev. 19:11) is now a fact. God himself adds: "It is done!" This is the divine conclusion to this book —the divine FINIS to the book of visions. That is why (verse 6) God's solemn "Name" is repeated—Alpha and Omega, the Author and Finisher of our faith. When the seer began his book, he ended each exhortation to the seven churches with a promise of victory. All these promises of the second and the third chapters are now fulfilled: "they shall be the children of God" (verse 7). Here the thirst for God's presence, the great longing for himself, is forever fulfilled.

But the reference to "thirst" may mean something more

definite than the mere longing for God's presence; it may mean the longing of Christ's disciple for martyrdom. If that is the case here, then the promise in the following verse would seem still more apt; the "conqueror" would then be the disciple who by faith has achieved martyrdom. It is impossible to tell what this word means in this context. As a rule, the desire for martyrdom did not arise till a generation later. The time of Ignatius is full of it.

The fact that verse 8 contains a final word of warning shows very clearly that there is nothing superficial or sentimental about the joy of this final vision. The possibility of judgment remains the dark foil against which the glory of the new world stands out. It is also a serious possibility which confronts every reader of the book. But this last warning must have a special meaning. Everything has really come to an end; everything that had to be said about judgment *has* been said. Henceforth (except in Rev. 22:15), it will not be mentioned again.

THE ANGEL'S PROMISE
(Rev. 21:9—22:5)
(*Rev. 21:9-27*)

9 Then came one of the seven angels who had the seven bowls full of the seven last plagues, and spoke to me, saying, "Come, I will show you the Bride, the wife of the Lamb." 10 And in the Spirit he carried me away to a great, high mountain, and showed me the holy city Jerusalem coming down out of heaven from God, 11 having the glory of God, its radiance like a most rare jewel, like a jasper, clear as crystal. 12 It had a great, high wall, with twelve gates, and at the gates twelve angels, and on the gates the names of the twelve tribes of the sons of Israel were inscribed; 13 on the east three gates, on the north three gates, on the south three gates, and on the west three gates. 14 And the wall of the wall of the city had twelve foundations, and on them the twelve names of the twelve apostles of the Lamb.

15 And he who talked to me had a measuring rod of gold to measure the city and its gates and walls. 16 The city lies foursquare, its length the same as its breadth; and he measured the city with his rod, twelve thousand stadia; its length and breadth and height are equal. 17 He also measured its wall, a hundred and forty-four cubits by a man's measure, that is, an angel's. 18 The wall was built of jasper, while the city was pure gold, clear as glass. 19 The foundations of the wall of the city were adorned with every jewel; the first was jasper, the second sapphire, the third agate, the fourth emerald, 20 the fifth onyx, the sixth carnelian, the seventh chrysolite, the eighth beryl, the ninth topaz, the tenth chrysoprase, the eleventh jacinth, the twelfth amethyst. 21 And the twelve gates were twelve pearls, each of the gates made of a single pearl, and the street of the city was pure gold, transparent as glass.

22 And I saw no temple in the city, for its temple is the Lord God the Almighty and the Lamb. 23 And the city has no need of sun or moon to shine upon it, for the glory of God is its light, and its lamp is the Lamb. 24 By its light shall the nations walk; and the kings of the earth shall bring their glory into it, 25 and its gates shall never be shut by day—and there shall be no night there; 26 they shall bring into it the glory and the honor of the nations. 27 But nothing unclean shall enter it, nor any one who practices abomination or falsehood, but only those who are written in the Lamb's book of life.

(*Rev. 22:1-5*)

1 Then he showed me the river of the water of life, bright as crystal, flowing from the throne of God and of the Lamb 2 through the middle of the street of the city; also, on either side of the river, the tree of life with its twelve kinds of fruit, yielding its fruit each month; and the leaves of the tree were for the healing of the nations. 3 There shall no more be anything accursed, but the throne of God and of the Lamb shall be in it, and his

servants shall worship him; 4 they shall see his face, and his name shall be on their foreheads. 5 And night shall be no more; they need no light of lamp or sun, for the Lord God will be their light, and they shall reign for ever and ever.

At first sight the following description seems very different from those in the previous scenes. This chapter, with its description of the heavenly city stands by itself, just as at the beginning of the book we had the vision of the Lord of the church. Here it is quite clear that a new final section has begun.

The greatest, and probably quite deliberately the most spacious scene in the Apocalypse, the picture of the heavenly city and the glimpse of Paradise, is not recorded at the stormy pace of the previous visions. There, one scene succeeded another, often in a stormy dramatic fashion, here, there reigns a heavenly repose and dignity. The conflict is over; God's purpose has been fulfilled. As this closing vision passes before the eyes of the seer, it sounds like a mighty choir singing in a minor key; no longer agitated by the terror of the moving pictures of judgment, he gazes in quiet contentment at the new city of God. In this scene of solemn repose he once more uses some features from the wealth of Old Testament imagery; what the prophets had described in joyful anticipation, he now unites with the prophetic word which has been committed to him, his own message, and the joy of victory flows into the song of the mighty city with its supernatural and glorious beauty.

Further, this section contains another characteristic feature: the seer's desire to give comfort and strength to the church. Having trodden in spirit the whole way of the final conflict, once more his deep pastoral longing to give help and consolation comes to the fore. At the beginning of the book this desire was wonderfully expressed in the messages to the seven churches; since then, like an undercurrent, it has remained in the background of all his visions. Out of this deep desire to help and serve the souls of those to whom he is writing, and the church of his own day, his mind is filled with a mass of ideas and feelings, images and promises, memories of the past and hopes for the future, which he expresses in the form of purely pastoral exhortations. These come to a head in the great, grave closing sentences of the last chapter. This is what makes this chapter so different from the previous ones.

The opening words of this last great vision show that the seer himself has now awakened from his visionary ecstasies, and has begun to turn his attention, once more, to the immediate situation of the church. The language of the visions is no longer so direct; an angel appears, in order to give the message, and to show him what is to come. He is one of the angels of the seven bowls; John sees him still holding one of these vessels of wrath in his hand. Formerly, in the seventeenth chapter—the phrase used is the same—the angel came to proclaim judgment. Now follows the glorious and consoling counterpart. But this recollection is a fleeting one, passing swiftly, like a cloud across the sky on a sunny day, over the first lines of this final vision. Then the seer is carried up to a high mountain. As Moses, the friend of God, was once shown on a high mountain "the pattern . . . in the mount" for the tent of meeting, and later, from another high mountain, saw the promised land (Deut. 32:48ff), so now John beholds the heavenly city, in a vision of color and beauty.

The first impression of this majestic picture is of an indescribable wealth of light, radiance, and color. The imagery of the jewels in particular gives the whole description a glow of supernatural purity and radiance. The fact that he begins with this quite general comprehensive impression means that this is not only a picture of sublime grandeur, nor it it only a proof of the seer's artistic powers of description.

Here the jewels have a deeper significance; they are symbols of political dignity, clothed in religious form. As the seer gazes at this wealth of precious stones, in which the radiance of a dazzling whiteness predominates, his whole soul is filled with a great sense of certitude. All the political and religious forces which had previously tried to hinder the fulfilment of God's purpose—typified by the false glamour of the "great city"—are now outshone by the radiance of the heavenly city, to which alone such glory belongs. In this way, impressively and without further words, the seer concludes his polemic against the cult of emperor worship, and all that it implied and involved.

The most impressive symbol is all that makes the city a city: the walls, the gates of precious pearl, and their foundations. An ancient prophecy (from Ezek. 48:31ff.) is here fulfilled: the names of the twelve tribes are inscribed on the foundations of the holy city. But what the old dispensation could not do, since Israel had forsaken God's order, is fulfilled in the spirit of the New Testament; hence the foundation stones bear the names of the twelve apostles. For in the whole of the ancient world no one thought of engraving such names—merely for remembrance—as in modern memorials. They bear witness to a claim. They testify to the fact that, according to the accepted apostolic teaching—as we see also in Eph. 2:20—that the heavenly city, the pure, completed church, is founded upon the apostles and prophets. The picture of the heavenly city in its glory is therefore a great and consoling assurance to the struggling and suffering church. Nothing will be lost of all the missionary service and witness of the church; no moment of God's work through his messengers will be lost. At the moment of supreme fulfilment their service and their witness will be openly and splendidly acknowledged.

The measuring of the city like the similar vision in Ezek. 40:3ff is merely meant to show its perfection. The vast size which these numbers suggest is of course not to be taken literally; it simply means that the city is magnificent beyond all that the human mind can conceive. The stress on the fact that "the city lies foursquare" means the same thing; the square is a symbol of completeness.

Apart from this, a good deal of this description reminds us—whether this is intended or not—of the original picture of the great city of Babylon. Herodotus records that Babylon was laid out on a square pattern; also the remarkable order of the direction of the winds (east, north, then south and west) is most easily explained in the light of the geographical situation of ancient Babylon. It was divided by the Euphrates in such a way that there was no direct path from north to west; only in the east was there a bridge over the river.

One other feature, the one main street of pure gold, which leads through the city, which is surrounded by gates of pearl (verse 21), recalls ancient Babylon; it had only the one great street along the banks of the river, the "shore street."

Finally, the remarkable statement of verse 16, that the city is equally long, broad, and high, must be understood from this point of view, for it probably means that the writer is not thinking of cubic form, but of the pyramid. And the buildings of which he was thinking would be the "skyscrapers" of Babylon, the many towering buildings in pyramid form, which abounded in Babylon.

Although the seer himself can scarcely have known Babylon, it is not at all surprising that he uses so many details which remind us of this city. For from time immemorial Babylon was *the* "great city," *par excellence,* and the picture of this city, with its imposing central street down which marched great processions, and its great towering buildings, had engraved itself deeply on the memory of the ancient world.

There is another source too, from which the seer has drawn some of his imagery. So many details of this description remind us of astrological ideas that we cannot overlook them: the recurring number of twelve for instance, the jewels (verses

18ff), above all, the twelve gates, which remind us directly of the signs of the zodiac. Possibly too, behind the picture of the one golden main street there is an allusion to the Milky Way. If this were so, we would then be able to understand—and only then—the extraordinary misproportion between the great breadth of the city (1,500 miles) and the comparatively low wall (only 216 feet). According to the cosmic beliefs of Babylon, which helped to color those of the Bible, the mighty vault of heaven rested upon a very narrow rim, the horizon.

One feature of the seer's description is very characteristic of his work as a whole: he uses all this material derived from the ancient cosmogony in order to describe the final glory which transcends all that any human mind could ever conceive. In order to do this, he draws his illustrations from every possible human source; but when he uses these images they lose all their superstitious elements, which simply fall away.

And now we come to the climax. Illuminated by this overflowing radiance, the heavenly city no longer needs a temple. The temple, like all earthly worship, belongs to time, since here we must walk by faith and not by sight. The period of "religions" and cults is over. The age-long striving of humanity toward a supreme goal—leading it sometimes to real heights, and sometimes also to great depths—expressing in all these ways its profound longing for God, here reaches its goal. Even the history of religions, which reflects the deepest intuitions and most remarkable perversions of the human mind, comes to an end and is fulfilled.

Now faith receives the most complete fulfilment of all it has ever sought. The shimmer of pearls, the glow of gold, the sparkling beauty of precious stones, and the crystal clarity which impregnate the city with a transparent impalpable radiance, and surround it like an aureole, are irradiated with the light of the presence of God. Long ago there brooded over the tabernacle the reflection of the presence of God upon earth —the Shekinah. Here, transcending all earthly examples and standards, the light of the eternal presence of God dawns. This true "dawn of the day of eternity" makes the light of the stars and the planets, which used to illuminate the earth during night and day, superfluous. One single day of God sheds its unending radiance over the world—the presence of God in his eternal grace.

As the seer tries to describe this unspeakable glory in liturgical phrases, language fails him. Instead of using his own words, the most glorious words of the prophets of the Old Testament spring naturally to his lips. Now the longing for a kingdom of eternal peace is fulfilled; the gates of the city stand open night and day. Since, indeed, there is no night there, this means the whole day long. Processions of kings from all the world stream in to offer the praises and the choicest treasures of the nations to God. Here again is an allusion to the book of life, and to all whose names are written therein—but this time no longer in a judging and separating sense, but only as a confirmation of the fact that the purity of the presence of God may not be dimmed by such things any more. All that is sinful and mean is plunged into nothingness, as though it had never been.

"Paradise has returned" is what this last vision means, and expresses so beautifully. The water of the river of life streams past, springing sparkling and crystal clear from the throne of God; so life from God streams unceasingly through the renewed world, and the Lord's promise during his days on earth (John 7:37) is fulfilled beyond measure. Here, once more, is the tree of life; no more can the sacrilegious act of an apostate human being throw a dark shadow over the world; now all eat of its fruits and receive eternal healing. The time of refreshment (Acts 3:19) has dawned, in which the world which was once God's world is once again restored to its original purity and beauty.

Everything ends in a wonderful clarity. The fulness of light in which henceforth the nations walk, and the servants of God and Jesus Christ reign like kings, is the restoration of that which was impossible for man throughout the whole of time, the vision of the glory of God.

At the end there is a twofold fulfilment of two promises of Scripture. The ancient blessing of Moses is fulfilled: "The Lord make his face to shine upon thee!" and the great promise of Jesus has become reality: "They shall see God."

NOTES

For the image of the Bride, see p. 278.

The word for "glory" (verse 11) originally meant radiance.

The number of the twelve apostles (verse 14) is a formula; there is no thought here of Judas. If we feel a need for explanation, then we must either add Matthias (Acts 1), or Paul (I Cor. 15:9).

"A man's measure" (verse 17) here means: according to the measure usual among men.

The measures which are given for the city are twelve thousand stadia (about 2400km.). This indication presumably does not mean the whole circumference, but the distance from the center. The square as a symbol of completeness is mentioned in Plato and Aristotle (Plato, *Prot.* 344a; Aristotle, *Rhet.* III, II, 2). Ezek. 45:2 and 48:16 also mention it.

The precious stones (verses 19-20) are more familiar to the Eastern mind, and far more used, than in the West. Since their names changed in the ancient world we cannot be quite sure what color some of them represent. Possibly they are the following: Jasper—transparent and light; sapphire—dark blue; agate—probably a gleaming black; emerald—deep green; onyx—yellowish; carnelian—flesh-colored; chrysolite—golden yellow; beryl—green or golden brown; topaz—green or yellow; chrysoprase—pale yellow; jacinth—bluish-red or a fiery red; amethyst—rosy violet. The whole conveys the impression of magnificent dignity and quiet beauty. In the ancient world jewels were often used as symbols of the signs of the zodiac.

Pearls (verse 21) are something modern for the seer. They were not known in Old Testament times; hence they are not mentioned in the Old Testament.

On verse 25: The Old Testament prophecy said (Isa. 60:11), "Thy gates also shall be open continually; they shall not be shut day nor night." The seer alters this passage on his own responsibility because there will be no night there. This alteration shows the deep sense of prophetic authority which he felt he possessed alongside the prophets of the Old Testament.

"Glory and honor" (verse 26) really mean the precious possessions which the heathen kings no longer take to Babylon, the city of commerce, but which they bring to the throne of God as their offerings to him (cf. Isa. 60:3ff).

"His name shall be on their foreheads" (22:4) means upon the fillets which bound their brows; the name of God has been inscribed as a sign that they have again become the image of God.

THE PROMISE OF CHRIST

(*Rev. 22:6-7*)

6 And he said to me, "These words are trustworthy and true. And the Lord, the God of the spirits of the prophets, has sent his angel to show his servants what must soon take place. 7 And behold, I am coming soon."

Blessed is he who keeps the words of the prophecy of this book.

The concluding section of the book opens with dignity: the phrases sound like the opening sentences of a liturgical act of worship. It was a Sunday (Rev. 1:10), the "Lord's day" when these visions began to appear; now the "Lord's day" is drawing to a close. Whether all these things really happened on one particular Sunday, whether the visions succeeded one another with dramatic suddenness, although this is not impossible, is beside the point. Actually, in any case, it was a "Lord's day" which was now drawing to a close. Hence a liturgical close to this Lord's day and to the book as a whole is entirely fitting. No new vision appears; there are only voices. This is illuminating: the vision disappears, all that the seer can take in, and to which he can bear witness, is finished. But the voices carry a spirit of religious solemnity into the concluding section.

It is in accordance with liturgical practice that the last part of the book—as in an act of corporate worship—returns to the beginning. The great notes which were struck in the introit (Rev. 1:1-8) are repeated. This emphasizes the solid and compact character of the book, which from beginning to end deals with one theme. It also shows the writer's artistic ability and power of compression, which he never loses in the midst of the richness and variety of his imagery.

The voices which we hear in the concluding section are full of a seriousness which lifts this book high above the realm of divination and speculation. The visions cease, but once more, as at the beginning of the book, the writer exhorts his readers. No longer does it matter whether more or less insight into the spiritual meaning of these visions is given to one man or another. This distinction does matter where knowledge of the fundamental spiritual laws which govern the last days is concerned; but all that has to be said in conclusion is quite clear. The voices which we now hear, demand one thing only: obedience. We must not overlook the fact that this seriousness at the close also has a retrospective effect which ennobles the whole book. Anyone who uses this book in order to feed his imagination with wild speculations has misunderstood it completely. The only way to hear aright is through obedience. To read this book apart from obedience, will mean that we miss the point completely.

There is an overwhelming sense of prophetic authority behind this book. The whole point of these closing verses is that they confirm the prophetic authority of the book. The writer is either speaking with a sense of overweening self-assertion, or he is claiming an authority which is not his own, but is of divine origin. If the latter is the case, then it is unwise to refuse to give the obedience which this book demands. For it is claimed not for himself, or in his own name, but in the name and for the sake of Christ.

So first of all, we hear the voice of Christ (verses 6-7). This gives the book the highest possible authority. The words of this book are true, because they are simply the reflection of the eternal Word, who was in the beginning, who is himself called the "Word of God" (Rev. 19:13). Thus this book does not contain speculation but divine truth, for a prophet does not say what "comes into his head," but what he has to testify. What a sense of his own prophetic mission this verse contains! God, the Lord, himself, who gave the prophets his Spirit, has made John his messenger! (verse 6). The only eschatological doctrine which possesses authority and power is one which bears the stamp of prophetic truth.

Again, this book returns to its beginning in another way. Once more the peculiarly transparent feeling for time, characteristic of the Apocalypse, is apparent. The little word "soon"—"Behold! I am coming soon"—gathers up all the longing and passionate desire of the centuries. The course of history through time is foreshortened when our eyes are opened to see the end towards which it is hastening. This accounts for the stormy pace of the seer, who in spirit hastens over all the dark abysses of the course of history towards the great day of the Lord. "The Lord will come as a mighty one!" (Isa. 40:10). With what urgency therefore can he cry aloud in the sixth beatitude of the Apocalypse the summons to hold fast obediently to this prophecy.

Chapter 16

The Final Scene

(Rev. 22:8-19)

VOICE OF THE ANGEL

(*Rev. 22:8-9*)

8 I John am he who heard and saw these things. And when I heard and saw them, I fell down to worship at the feet of the angel who showed them to me; 9 but he said to me, "You must not do that! I am a fellow servant with you and your brethren the prophets, and with those who keep the words of this book. Worship God."

As if he were making a liturgical response, the seer himself answers what Christ has assured him, in his own words. Again we see—as in Rev. 19:10—how deeply he is moved by the fact that once more he falls down at the angel's feet, and tries to worship him. Once more the angel forbids him to do so. But this scene is more than a mere repetition of Rev. 19:10. When the angel raises him to his feet, he places John alongside himself, and in so doing confirms the incomparable dignity of his prophetic service. In view of all the visions and mysteries which John has communicated down to this point, it is now made clear that he has been performing the same service as the angel, who has communicated to him the truths of God's mighty acts and considers him a "fellow servant" and brother to the prophets. John is confirmed in his New Testament prophecy, but his high sense of a prophetic mission is held within sober bounds by the injunction to "keep the words of the prophecy of this book."

VOICE OF THE LORD

(*Rev. 22:10-16*)

10 And he said to me, "Do not seal up the words of the prophecy of this book, for the time is near. 11 Let the evildoer still do evil, and the filthy still be filthy, and the righteous still do right, and the holy still be holy."

12 "Behold, I am coming soon, bringing my recompense, to repay every one for what he has done. 13 I am the Alpha and the Omega, the first and the last, the beginning and the end."

14 Blessed are those who wash their robes, that they may have the right to the tree of life and that they may enter the city by the gates. 15 Outside are the dogs and sorcerers and fornicators and murderers and idolaters, and every one who loves and practices falsehood.

16 "I Jesus have sent my angel to you with this testimony for the churches. I am the root and the offspring of David, the bright morning star."

Once again the exalted Lord is speaking (verses 10-16). The command, not to seal up this book, that is, to make it accessible and to testify to it, is the clearest proof of the difference between it and all previous apocalyptic literature. The apocalyptic writers of the Old Testament and of late Judaism knew of a coming day of the Lord, but what was to them a dim awareness, or a secret knowledge, is here brought out into the light of day. Here the end is really known, for the writer knows that it is the day of Jesus Christ, and Christians know him because he has come in the flesh. The earthly manifestation of Jesus was already the first dawning of the sunrise of eternity. The time is really "short" (verse 10).

This truth cannot remain the secret possession of a select pious circle; like the whole gospel it must be proclaimed to the whole world (cf. Rev. 14:6). No other feature distinguishes the Apocalypse so sharply from all previous apocalyptic writings than this command to proclaim these truths openly and publicly. It was when the church claimed the greatest publicity that the sharpest conflict, with actual martyrdom, broke out (Rev. 12ff). Here this claim to come out into the open has a quite new, decisive significance: in principle it does away with apocalyptic altogether. This message becomes merged in the proclamation of the gospel itself.

The categorical warning of verse 11 is the motto of Christian martyrdom; the same phrases recur almost literally in the earliest letters of the Christian martyrs. The time of final separation and decision has begun.

A further sign of the coming fulfilment is that God will be all in all (I Cor. 15:28), that at the end the exalted Christ will bear the name which until then had been borne by God alone: the First and the Last, the Beginning and the End of all things.

The next two verses make the separation clear. While all who have not turned to God remain outside—outside the heavenly world and the presence of God—the martyrs who have served the Lamb and sealed their testimony with their blood receive the final, seventh, beatitude of the Apocalypse. This beatitude contains a promise in which three images are blended, which have already been mentioned in the preceding pages: white robes, signifying full possession of the salvation which Jesus has wrought; the right to the tree of life, signifying that they will no longer be tempted to self-glorification, as formerly, but that they now participate fully in eternal life; and the right to go through the gates into the city, signifying that they are no longer "strangers and foreigners," but full fellow citizens of the city of God.

The exalted Lord here makes it quite clear that he himself has granted these visions of the end to John, and has commissioned him to bear witness to this truth.

For the last time in the New Testament we hear the Lord's word "I am," which occurs so often in the Fourth Gospel, a phrase which covers all time in its span, from the very beginning unto the end. In any case, that is the deeper meaning of the following phrase, which, at first sight, seems rather difficult to understand: "I am the root and the offspring of David." This phrase not only contains an allusion to the "stem of Jesse" and the "branch" which will "grow out of his roots" (Isa. 11:1), but it also refers to the spiritual generation of David. "Root" and "offspring" mean the origin and the whole course of history, the beginning and the way, creation and fulfilment, all summed up in Jesus Christ, who is the content of all history. In passing, we may note how this phrase sums up and transcends all the preceding sacred history! As the pre-existent One, he was present at the beginning when the chosen people began its way through history. Through the preaching of the prophets, through God's "mighty acts" with his people, through psalms and prophecies, he led them towards their fulfilment. Spiritually, he has fulfilled his purpose; when Israel—the people of God, and of the covenant—failed to fulfil their vocation, he summed up all God's purpose in the Old Testament in himself.

He is the bright and morning star. This is a new and impressive expression for a turning point in history. It is Jesus Christ himself who announces the radiant beginning of the new day of God. The morning star was already mentioned in Rev. 2:28, as the symbol of world dominion. What all great imagery foreshadowed is expressed still more strongly in this closing formula: CHRISTUS IMPERATOR.

NOTES

"Every one who loves and practices falsehood" (verse 15) is a phrase quite peculiar in the New Testament. But in it we can see a Johannine origin; cf. John 3:21. There to "do the truth" means to believe in Jesus Christ. Thus to do the opposite is to "practice falsehood."

"The dogs" (verse 15) meant originally the male slaves dedicated to the service of a god, mentioned in Deut. 23:17ff. Later this term was sometimes applied to the unbaptized (Matt. 7:6. *Didache* IX:5).

VOICE OF THE SEER

(*Rev. 22:17-19*)

17 The Spirit and the Bride say, "Come." And let him who hears say, "Come." And let him who is thirsty come, let him who desires take the water of life without price.

18 I warn every one who hears the words of the prophecy of this book: if any one adds to them, God will add to him the plagues described in this book, 19 and if any one takes away from the words of the book of this prophecy, God will take away his share in the tree of life and in the holy city, which are described in this book.

Now the seer, in the heavenly worship, hears the voice of the Bride, that is, of the perfected church. The Spirit here represents the church since through his Spirit Christ always dwells in the church, and makes it his body. This worshiping church, which is not visible, but can only be perceived as it were from a distance by the sound of its praises, now on the threshold of fulfilment, sings the great concluding versicles. Here, at the close, there rises from the Christian church that ancient versicle, so full of longing: "Lord! Come!" In a consoling and invigorating versicle, it illuminates the final gospel promise, that here the water of life is to be had without money and without price. The church which is waiting for her Lord is the place where the longing for the presence of God can be answered. This prayer includes all the prophecies of the God who in his mercy stoops to the poor and needy, and the message of Jesus Christ, who delivers us from guilt and the fear of death, and brings us into God's new world.

In the address to the "hearers" (verse 18) in this invisible service of worship, the seer himself is speaking. At first sight it seems as though what he says is almost defiant. His words may be taken in two ways: either as an expression of a greatly exaggerated self-consciousness, or simply as an ancient concluding formula, by means of which the author wishes to protect his work from injury at the hands of strangers. We can only accept these words if we believe the assurances of the seer in the preceding verses (verses 6-8) that this book is not the fruit of his own imagination, but that in it he is communicating what God has "shown" him, through Christ. Also, he means us to realize that he is convinced that he has no right to alter anything that Christ has commissioned him to say. In dealing with this subject he has become, so to speak, "the founder of the New Testament canon." [1]

The last human word of this book shows the absolute seriousness which is involved in all prophecy given by God. Because it is derived from God, man may not alter or criticize it; the only possibility that remains is that of believing obedience. Nowhere is the temptation to human speculation more evident than in the sphere of prophecies about the end of the world; but each hearer has to submit his imagination obediently to the divine discipline, as John has done. This obedient disciplined temper alone preserves the church from the dangers which are involved in exaggerated preoccupation with this prophecy concerning the end of the world.

To go astray from lack of knowledge now and again will not matter very much. But when anyone makes God's prophetic message about the end of the world a subject of futile speculation, he will be punished by losing his way in the bypaths of his own imagination. Then it will be true, as the seer says: God's plagues will fall on those who are disobedient; and those who do not read this book in the spirit of obedience will imperil their hopes of eternal salvation. It is a good thing that this urgent exhortation to salutary discipline and sobriety forms the conclusion to the book.

Finally in this liturgical closing chapter we hear the concluding antiphon. The exalted Lord speaks, in words of warning and of promise—and through both he sums up the

[1] Hans Windisch.

whole book, and crowns it, in the words: "Behold, I am coming soon." The church responds with the ancient cry of longing which must have been chanted at the end of every service of worship, and has been handed down to us in other passages in the original language, Aramaic: *Marana tha*—"Our Lord, come!" [2] The very fact that this prayer found such fixed liturgical form in the early church shows that its whole life was tuned to the truth which sounds so clearly at the end of this New Testament book.

In the later history of the church this desire naturally altered. It could not always remain at the same pitch of glowing actuality. But it has not disappeared; it has only changed into what has been called a "theology of homesickness." The presence of this expectation is a sign of life in every church which has not become worldly and secularized. It is a fundamental presupposition of all ecclesiastical doctrine and preaching, which, at regular intervals, through difficult experiences, is kept alive in the church.

[2] I Cor. 16:22; *Didache* X:6. Bousset, *op. cit.*, rightly points out that this passage is decisive for the elucidation and exposition of I Cor. 16:22. From the linguistic point of view the indicative ("Our Lord comes") would be possible, but only the imperative ("Our Lord, come!") is significant.

Chapter 17

Conclusion and Blessing

(Rev. 22:20-21)

20 He who testifies to these things says, "Surely I am coming soon." Amen. Come, Lord Jesus!

21 The grace of the Lord Jesus be with all the saints. Amen.

In verse 20 the words "surely"[1] and "amen" both mean the same thing, the one in the Greek and the other in the Hebrew form. Verse 20 reminds us of the language problem of the early church: the bilingual or even trilingual character of its message. But as with real missionaries everywhere, this linguistic problem did not weigh very heavily upon them. Their one aim was to proclaim the message, sure that the form would find itself, for anyone who has something to say will find a way of expressing it. When God gives a commission to someone, he will also give him the power to carry it out. The whole missionary history of the early church proves this. This verse is also a contribution to the question of the language of the apocalyptic writer.

The Sunday on Patmos is drawing to a close; and with it the remarkable act of worship to which we owe this book. In any case that is the literary situation. It is pedantic to inquire whether this book could have been dictated in a single day—of course that was impossible—or whether such a condensed series of visions could have taken place on one day. Both these questions are beside the point. The liturgical

[1] Or "truly" (German: *wahrlich*). Cf. Rev. 3:14, where the "Amen" refers to the heavenly Christ, "the true and reliable one." (Translator's note.)

framework of the whole, however, also determines the conclusion.

The closing antiphon and the blessing bring the whole to a systematic conclusion. The apostolic blessing, again in an ancient form, literally transmitted through Paul (II Cor. 13:14), yet slightly and significantly altered, concludes the liturgical closing chapter exactly as the early Christian act of worship—often in distinction from the Jewish—must have ended. Once again we hear the ancient prayer: "Lord! Come!" And as we think of the great community of those who from the very earliest days of the church, down to the present day, have received this eschatological message, we are reminded afresh that the true church only exists where Christians await their Lord.

Chapter 18

The Message of the Apocalypse

Let us now cast one last glance at the solitary figure of the seer, still standing on the shore at Patmos, gazing into the distance, into the heart of that celestial glory which will surely come when the horrors of history have passed away. He stands there in the place of us all, on the very edge of all earthly existence, gazing at that which God has revealed to him about the end of history and the glory of the world to come.

Can we in spirit stand by his side?

The generation which still lived in the period of civilized security must have found it very difficult to understand this emphasis on the Lord's return. But the generation to which we belong, which has passed through two world wars, many grave spiritual crises, and great historical revolutions, possesses a promise which cannot be overlooked. By God's action, the eyes and ears of this generation have been opened to perceive that world history has mysteries which we cannot see with our eyes, nor touch with our hands.

But the question of understanding this book does not depend on historical and intellectual considerations; like the whole Word of God, it can only be understood by faith, through revelation. If this great book, the last in the Bible, has attracted and held our attention—with its wealth of imagery, with the dramatic force of its visions, with its colorful pictures of the future, with its poetic power of representation which covers the whole universe—we will try once more to sum up the religious message of the Apocalypse.

It is the Book of the End. Those who have no use for the

"historicity" of eschatology, and only regard the eschatological expectation of Christendom as a particular way of understanding existence, will not be able to understand this book. In its whole presentation there is no doubt that it speaks of a real end.

It is true of course that, like the whole of the New Testament, the Apocalypse does not speak of "history" in the modern sense; this conception is foreign to it. But it does speak of the conclusion of the work of Christ.

The world does not stand still. All that opposes Christianity and makes faith difficult is not conquered by moving into a new consciousness of existence. But, just as surely as death confronts man with a question which the Christian knows is answered by the resurrection from the dead, so surely also the world is not "altered" by the fact that man has learnt to look at it differently, or has found a different point of view from which to judge it. Something really happens: God attains his end.

In any case, that is the message of the Apocalypse, and in the impressive language of its imagery it is expressed in unmistakable terms. It cannot by any means be confused with a philosophy of existence.

It is not a change in human consciousness which sets in: but just as faith in God the creator means reality, and as the resurrection of Jesus also means reality—and not a change of outlook in the religious consciousness of the disciples—so also this primitive Christian book speaks of the end, of the victory of Christ. In it the faith of the church is fulfilled.

The seriousness of this message consists in the fact that the reality of the end of history is as serious for man as his own end.

When we become aware of the truth—which we can never achieve by ourselves, but must always be revealed to us by God—that the history of the world must have an end, we no longer dream of progress in the sense of a natural advance within history, but we understand that at the end of world history there will be an unparalleled conflict, which can only be endured by God's grace. How far this truth is from spiritualism, astrology, and other still more foolish things! These are only the substitutes at which men grasp when they have lost their living faith. The apocalyptic writer makes it very clear at the end of the book (Rev. 22:11) that these things matter more than anything else: "Let the evildoer still do evil, and the filthy still be filthy, and the righteous still do right, and the holy still be holy."

The visions in this book may often make us stand still and ask: "What does this mean?" But this question is not necessary at the end. This same man, a member of the early Christian church, who had seen and proclaimed a message of such indescribable glory, makes his meaning quite clear. He says, in effect, "you do not need to be caught up by the Spirit, before you know what God wants from you! We cannot all tread the path of prophetic ecstasy, but we can and must be obedient and watchful. The Lord is near! There is no Christian existence without being released from the things of this world and of time."

The seriousness of this message constitutes its consolation. This book, which is like no other in its description of the horrors of the last days, is also like no other in its power of consolation. But this consolation is strangely unemotional and direct; it offers no easy lyrical assurance, but the comfort which springs from facing the whole human situation in the sight of God: "*God* will conquer!" is the controlling, fundamental meaning of his visions. It may be that—to human eyes—this victory of God may involve a long time of waiting—but God *will* conquer! It is possible that the final conflict of history will call many disciples to bear witness by their own death as martyrs, sealed by their own blood—but God will conquer! It may be, that the final victory of Jesus Christ may be preceded by many individual victories of earthly forces—but, at the close, God will conquer!

Supported by this strong concrete consolation, the early church strode forward on its difficult path through history. During the first two Christian centuries the possibility of persecution faced every Christian. Not all had to bear it. Many Christians lived without actually having to undergo persecution. But it was always there in their minds and consciousness as a possibility. From the human point of view, it is evident that the Christians would not have held out so long against the competition of so many other popular religions of the ancient world if they had been made of softer material. This book presupposes "believing heroism," and the phrase is not too strong, since it implies a courage which includes an ardent readiness for martyrdom (Rev. 13:10; 14:12). In this respect it is far from being an average book. But the consolation which it proclaims is not based on the fact that it extols human heroism, but that it proclaims the future victory of God. God has fixed the times of this conflict and has counted all its days; it will not end a day earlier than God wills. This book reiterates the Pauline conviction—greatly enriched and enhanced by the glowing symbolism and dramatic force of its visions—"God will be all in all."

So at last we understand that the hope which this book proclaims is not a distant speculation, but a present force. In the periods when this hope languished, the church became dull and confused, and its witnessing power faded. The times of fruitfulness in the church were always those (often in opposition to the expectations of observers within history) when there was a living faith in the Lord's return. This was inevitable, for eschatology is the fulfilment of the Easter faith of the church. Faith in the returning Lord is only the fruit of faith in the risen Lord. The world cannot remain as it is because Christ did not remain in the grave.

Type used in this book
Body, 11 on 13, 10 on 12 and 9 on 10 Times Roman
Display, Radiant
Paper: "R" Standard White Antique